The Tarot Journey

Tarot study is a journey into a vast realm where you can explore possible futures, learn from the past, and gain invaluable insights into your thoughts, feelings, and motivations.

You are the master of your own destiny. Although Tarot is sometimes referred to as fortunetelling, the Tarot does not predict a single, unchangeable future outcome. To do so would deny the concept of free will, for the future is constantly in flux, awaiting our choices in the present.

What the Tarot can do is show you the most likely future outcome based on your current actions in any situation. If you like the outcome of your reading, continue along your current path. If you see trouble ahead, adjust your actions accordingly, and continue to consult the Tarot to monitor your progress.

In addition to teaching you how to read the Tarot for prediction and advice, *Tarot for a New Generation* shows you how to broaden your Tarot studies and deepen your connection to your deck by using the cards in different ways. Activate the power of the cards to create your own luck and pursue your dreams through visualization exercises, Tarot spells, and special techniques for gaining advice. Let the Tarot help you probe the meaning of your experiences and forge stronger connections with other people. For high school and college students, imaginative interactions with Tarot images can aid your studies and memory, and generate inspired ideas for art and writing projects. You can even use Tarot imagery techniques to help manage learning disabilities.

Tarot opens the door to endless possibilities. As you set out upon your Tarot journey, let this book be your guide to strange and wonderful places you might not otherwise discover.

About the Author

Janina Renée holds a B.A. degree in Anthropology, and is a scholar of such diverse subjects as material culture, folklore, mythology, ancient religion, psychology, medical anthropology, culture studies, history, and literature. Renée is currently a graduate student; her research interests include the use of ritualism in nature writing, the ways we ritually interact with material objects, and the role and subject position of high-functioning autistic people in history, literature, and culture. When she is able to take time away from work, school, writing, and family, Renée likes to take short road trips in search of the magic that awaits discovery in the American Heartland.

To Write to the Author

If you wish to contact the author or would like more information about this book, please write to the author in care of Llewellyn Worldwide and we will forward your request. Both the author and publisher appreciate hearing from you and learning of your enjoyment of this book and how it has helped you. Llewellyn Worldwide cannot guarantee that every letter written to the author can be answered, but all will be forwarded. Please write to:

Janina Renée
℅ Llewellyn Worldwide
P.O. Box 64383, Dept. 0-7387-0160-2
St. Paul, MN 55164-0383, U.S.A.

Please enclose a self-addressed stamped envelope for reply,
or $1.00 to cover costs. If outside U.S.A., enclose
international postal reply coupon.

Many of Llewellyn's authors have websites with additional information and sources. For more information, please visit our website at http://www.llewellyn.com. For Llewellyn's free full-color catalog, write to *New Worlds* at the above address, or telephone 1-800-THE MOON.

JANINA RENÉE

TAROT

♡ = cups
◇ = rods
♣ = swords
♦ pentacles

FOR A NEW GENERATION

2003
Llewellyn Publications
St. Paul, Minnesota 55164-0383, U.S.A.

FIRST EDITION
Third Printing, 2003

Cover art © 2001 by Jonathan Hunt
Cover design by Kevin R. Brown
Editing and book design by Karin Simoneau

Library of Congress Cataloging-in-Publication Data
Renee, Janina, 1956-
   Tarot for a new generation / Janina Renee.
     p. cm.
   Includes bibliographical references.
   ISBN 0-7387-0160-2
    1. Tarot. I. Title.

   BF1879.T2 R455 2001
   133.3'2424—dc21
                                         2001029466

Illustrations are from the following decks:
Legend: The Arthurian Tarot © Anna-Marie Ferguson
World Spirit Tarot © Lauren O'Leary
Universal Tarot © author/artist A. E. Waite and R. De Angelis. Used with permission by the Italian publisher Lo Scarabeo.

Llewellyn Worldwide does not participate in, endorse, or have any authority or responsibility concerning private business transactions between our authors and the public.

    All mail addressed to the author is forwarded but the publisher cannot, unless specifically instructed by the author, give out an address or phone number.

    Any Internet references contained in this work are current at publication time, but the publisher cannot guarantee that a specific location will continue to be maintained. Please refer to the publisher's website for links to authors' websites and other sources.

Llewellyn Publications
A Division of Llewellyn Worldwide, Ltd.
P.O. Box 64383, Dept. 0-7387-0160-2
St. Paul, MN 55164-0383, U.S.A.
www.llewellyn.com

 Printed in the United States of America on recycled paper

Also by Janina Renée

Tarot Spells
Playful Magic
Tarot: Your Everyday Guide

This book is dedicated to my mother,
whose love and support have made it possible.

Contents

INTRODUCTION

As the title makes obvious, the Tarot card interpretations and other information in this book are oriented toward questions that are on the minds of many young adults. Of course, there is also an abundance of new information that adults and beginners will find interesting.

As I wrote the chapters on card interpretation and was deciding which topics to include, I tried to keep the interests of young adults in mind. For example, in talking to young people, studying some popular magazines, and doing other research, I learned that many young men and women, some as young as thirteen or fourteen, are involved in romantic relationships, to different degrees, and are very preoccupied with the quality of these relationships. Also, although they don't always share their feelings with their parents, many young adults are deeply affected by the quality of life at home; they want to find better ways to communicate and connect, and they worry about their parents' problems. Other things that weigh heavily on many of their minds are a desire for social acceptance, fear of embarrassment and exclusion, and the desire to be taken seriously as intelligent people who care about making a difference. Because many young people are students, concerns about school projects, school life, and future educational and career choices are major concerns. Also, because a number of the young people in my social circle are artistic types, and many suffer from learning disabilities, I tend to look for ways in which the cards speak to the sort of frustrations and challenges that these students must contend with.

Although it is not possible to cover every important subject that is of concern to young adults, I have tried to provide enough information for people to use the Tarot as a guide for leading more examined lives—that is, to help them think about all of the forces at work in their lives, and to enable them to make better life choices. Because young adults may have less experience applying the cards' meanings to different life situations, the pages in this book dedicated to interpretation show how the cards can have different facets of meaning in relation to different areas of life (rather than just supplying a list of key words).

One of the challenges in writing for young adults is that there are a number of ways in which their concerns are not so different from those of older adults. For example, certain Tarot cards are relevant to different health issues; initially, I thought about not including items on health and healing, as these are often seen as older folks' concerns, then I remembered that I've known many young people whose health problems are major factors in their lives. I have also known young adults who hold down jobs, bear heavy responsibilities for their families, and may even have children of their own. Indeed, I was a teen Tarot reader who ran a household at age eighteen and became a mother at nineteen. (When I say I was a teen Tarot reader, I mean that I pursued Tarot as an interest and read cards for friends and family; I never actually "worked" as a card reader.) Because young adults also worry about the important people in their lives, they sometimes consult the Tarot when they have questions pertaining to their parents or other older people. However, some areas in which many young peoples' experiences differ from those of older adults are their personal mobility and ability to make certain choices. Those who are dependent upon parents or others cannot always go where they please, and their lives can be profoundly affected by other peoples' actions and decisions. On the other hand, many adults have settled down into their jobs (whether they enjoy them or not) and their ways of life, so they aren't looking forward to many changes or choices, while for many young people, the future is still a mystery—a largely unopened book that is full of possibility. Indeed, in the years to come, many young people will be able to follow paths that we can't even begin to imagine today. Therefore, the card interpretation chapters try to keep these kinds of issues and external circumstances in focus.

With these things in mind, I have tried to show how the interpretation of Tarot cards can apply to the special needs of young adults. For example, when I discuss Kings and Queens in chapter 7, I have written more than usual in order to detail what these cards may reveal about relationships with parents and authority figures, and what their motivations may be, so it will be easier for young people to get along with adults.

For this book to be user friendly and appeal to people of all ages and backgrounds, I have tried to avoid using language that is patronizing. While I realize that not all of my readers will be able to understand everything, I am confident that they are reasonably intelligent individuals who will be able to grasp the most important meanings, and will further build upon their understanding through practice. (The glossary in the back of the book may be helpful in providing a fuller explanation of some of the words I use.) Also, I maintain a positive and upbeat focus, showing how cards that seem negative can provide clues as to how we can manage the problems that may arise. However, I don't sugarcoat the cards' meanings, because most young adults already know that real life has its share of troubles.

Learning the Tarot

Reading the Tarot involves approaching the cards with a question in mind, spreading them out in certain patterns, and then interpreting their meanings in the context of your question and your personal circumstances.

Sometimes young adults and other beginners are afraid to study the Tarot because they worry that they'll never learn the meanings of all seventy-eight cards; therefore, they never pursue their desire. Well, of course, who does have the time to memorize all of the cards and their meanings? I suspect that most Tarot readers got their start by simply jumping into it, like I did. I got my first deck of cards when I was about fifteen or sixteen and, being impatient, I started right away by simply asking a question, laying out the cards, thinking about the pictures and what they might mean to me, and then looking up their meanings in my book.

Naturally, any beginner has to bear in mind that more study and experience are necessary to develop greater understanding and accuracy. Knowledge of the Tarot is cumulative: the more one works with the cards, the more their meanings become clear, and the individual cards become easier to remember. As time goes on, the reader will become more familiar with the standard card interpretations, and also discover ways the cards convey some highly personalized messages and information that goes beyond whatever she could get out of a Tarot manual. (In this way, the symbols in Tarot cards are similar to dream images.)

How the Tarot Works

The Tarot images are symbols that speak directly to your personal unconscious, because symbolism is the language of the unconscious—that larger realm of the mind that includes the subconscious. (See the glossary for a detailed explanation of "unconscious" and related terms.) Even if you don't understand all of the cards' symbols or likely interpretations, you will still have intuitive responses to them.

You may not always be able to sort all of your perceptions or explain them to other people, but have faith that you will get something out of the reading, that your *deep mind* is working with these symbols on other levels. This is because the Tarot images correspond to archetypes that already exist in your unconscious mind. Archetypes are symbols, experiences, social and biological roles, and major events that are so fundamental to human psychology and life experience that they recur in the dreams, stories, and artwork of individual people, as well as in the religious rituals, mythology, transition rituals, and other important institutions of many different societies. They are loaded with spiritual and psychological signifi-cance, though they can take on different shades of meaning in different cultures, and individuals experience them differently. We experience and sometimes act out certain archetypes at important stages in our lives. For example, most of us encounter the archetype of the Emperor (card number Four) when we have to deal with powerful authority figures; we act out the role of the Hermit (number Nine) when we become seekers of wisdom; and the archetype of the lightning-struck Tower (number Sixteen) is active when disruptive events force us to under-go major changes in our lives. Because they deal with archetypal images, Tarot cards provide a way for your unconscious to communicate its messages to you. In other words, your unconscious is able to lay out the ideas it wants to communi-cate in front of you by means of the Tarot cards that correspond to symbols that are already ingrained in you. The card images give your conscious mind some-thing to work over, too, while enabling your unconscious to reflect on its own issues (it becomes a matter of the unconscious reading the unconscious).

But by what mechanism do these cards come up in meaningful patterns? How are they able to get into the right positions?

In the old days, Tarot readers believed that spirits or spiritual forces arranged the cards. Later, people became interested in extrasensory perception and the spe-cial powers of the human mind, so they suggested that your own unconscious moves the cards through powers of telekinesis. Some people don't believe that anything supernatural is involved, but feel that the cards' images act like inkblot tests (Rorschach images), enabling people to examine subconscious issues through psychological association, and to confirm their personal observations—things they already know or suspect. However, although I don't deny the possibil-ity of spiritual forces, ESP, or the power of psychological projection, the explanation that I favor, and the one that is becoming the most popular, is that there is a seemingly magical reality behind the appearance of ordinary reality, in which everything in the universe is interconnected, and in which a person's outer, "real world" circumstances mirror the internal reality of his unconscious. For this reason, divinatory objects like Tarot cards, rune stones, or tea leaves can fall in patterns that reflect this underlying order. Indeed, with practice you can learn to read events in your life, such as peoples' comings and goings and other things that crop up, as you would read Tarot cards, examining the special symbolic roles they play in your life. (Limitations of time and space don't allow for a more thorough discussion of the interconnectedness of all things, but if you'd like to know more about this subject, Michael Talbot's book *The Holographic Universe*[1] provides some very interesting thoughts on how reality may be structured.) Spirit worlds and other alternate realities can also be part of this larger reality that responds to the Tarot's archetypal images.

Because of your mind's connection with physical and spiritual forces in the larger web of energies that connects everything within the universe, the Tarot's ability to present true and meaningful information is not dependent upon your knowledge, skill level, and psychic talent. The cards will usually come up in the right positions anyway. It is true that a certain amount of psychism can be helpful in understanding how the cards' generalized meanings apply to individuals' unique situations, but so can the cultivation of human experience and empathy. Also, practice with the cards will help you develop intuition and stimulate psychic senses that you didn't know you had—even if you're normally as psychic as a brick—because working with archetypal images brings you into rapport with the life energies of the universe.

Value of Tarot Reading

Aside from the obvious advantages of being able to get a glimpse of future events and gain a greater understanding of past and present events, there are many ways that the Tarot can benefit young adults, which is why many Tarot readers get their start at an early age.

In studying the Tarot's allegorical images, you are interacting with the philosophical traditions of the ancient world, and you are able to feel a part of something that is very old, mysterious, and powerful. By experimenting with the same archetypal images that have inspired artists, poets, mystics, magicians, and philosophers for hundreds of years, you can discover the role that these symbols play in your own psyche and life story, providing insights into your own personality, your life path, and your progress in striving to become a better human being. By observing how different archetypes express themselves in your life, you can decide which of them you want to be more or less active. The realization of shared archetypal personalities and experiences also connects you with other people: with your friends and family, as well as people across time and in other cultures. These images also connect you to metaphysical realities that enable you to appreciate your place in the web of energies and relationships that unite us with past, present, and future, and with all living beings. Because the philosophical and metaphysical aspects of the Tarot serve as positive tools for gaining an understanding of your life and studying the human condition, there is really nothing to fear from the Tarot if you are a sensible, positive person.

Working with the Tarot does increase your chances for rewarding interactions with other people. When your friends and acquaintances learn that you have skill with the Tarot, many of them will ask you to read their cards. (Of course, you should only read for intelligent, mature individuals; a thorough discussion of reading for other people is in chapter 3.) Even if you are normally rather shy, you will find that sitting down with another person to explore her hopes and dreams as you read the cards will create a special bond between you. As the cards present their often astonishing revelations, your rapport with the person for whom you are reading will increase, promoting a psychic link that will enable you to offer additional insights.

Working with the Tarot can also help you to envision—and, therefore, go on to create—a good future for yourself. In recent years, I have been very concerned about the growing number of young people who do not seem to have a sense of what they want to do with their lives. There are many who aren't seriously devoting themselves to study or planning for careers, and they have only a vague idea of what sort of life path they'd like to follow. While it is true that there have always been a certain number of people who don't know what they want and can't plan for the future, I would think that in this media age, more young adults would be exposed to a wider variety of choices, enabling them to key in to something that really sparks their interest and enthusiasm. Whether or not you are an individual who has a problem getting focused, the Tarot can help you turn your imagination toward the future, toward a greater range of life's possibilities. It puts dream images out in front of you, so you can imagine yourself exploring many paths of possibility, moving in the direction of your dreams. When you get cards that point to a very appealing future, you can start investigating the pathways that can lead you to that future. If you get cards that are negative or problematic, you can examine the life issues that you need to get a handle on, so you can make improvements and take control of your destiny.

How Is This Book Organized?

Part 1 of *Tarot for a New Generation* provides some basic background information. Chapter 1 takes a brief look at the history and organization of the Tarot, and provides suggestions on deck choice and care. Chapter 2 discusses card layouts and other preparations for reading, while chapter 3 offers some fine points of reading and interpretation. Chapter 4 provides some sample readings in order to show you how interpretation is done. Chapter 5 discusses other uses of the Tarot, including meditation and visualization exercises, as well as suggestions on how it can help with school work and learning disabilities. Part 2, the bulk of the book containing chapters 6 through 11, is devoted to the interpretation of the individual cards, and covers the Major Arcana and the Minor Arcana (Pentacles, Wands, Cups, Swords, and all of the court cards).

This book's emphasis is on card interpretation because interpretation is likely the main thing young adults need to know in order to get up and running. These interpretations are particularly concerned with prediction, because as individuals about to embark on the long and as yet uncertain future ahead of them, I have found that young people are especially interested in discovering what's down the road. They are also interested in knowing more about what is going on around them, and better understanding the motivations of friends, parents, and other people in their lives. The pages on interpretation start with an overview of a given card's symbolism and traditional meanings, followed by very short paragraphs dealing with common concerns such as behavior, character, choices, communications, conflict, creativity, emotional ties, family matters, health and healing, home life, motivations, personalities, protection, relationships, romance, success, and time elements, among many other topics, depending upon the nature of the card in question. These subtopics vary because different cards and suits are concerned with different areas of life, and they show how cards have different shades of meaning in different contexts. When you sit down to interpret the cards in a reading, you should consider which, if any, of these subtopics best seem to apply to your question, based on your knowledge of the situation. Also, more than one of the potential interpretations may apply to you (due to the way that inner and outer realities are interconnected, a certain theme may be repeated in different areas of your life). As with any book on Tarot interpretation, it is not possible to cover every situation to which a card may pertain, and possible interpretations are not limited to the ones that I detail, because individual situations are so complex and unique. However, I hope that by showing you how these cards have different shades of meaning, it will be easier for you to figure out how to apply them to your own situations. By showing how the cards can be sensitive to context, I also hope to help train your intuition.

In these interpretive pages, I generally do not delve into certain things, such as extended discussions of the cards' symbolism, the mythical, astrological, or cabalistic correspondences that have been linked to the cards, their uses in meditation, or other esoterica, because doing so would lengthen this book considerably and isn't essential to a basic understanding of the cards. (Also, correspondences vary with different decks and different systems.) However, there are many excellent books that focus on these and other aspects of Tarot, so I encourage you to read and explore further as you develop your skills.

At the end of this book are appendices that include some suggestions on the use of significator cards and color correspondences, and a description of a special method used to read the cards for advice.

Note: Part 2 of this book features illustrations from *Legend: The Arthurian Tarot, World Spirit Tarot,* and *Universal Tarot.* These decks are built around special themes, so their pictures don't always match the images that I describe as "typical" or "commonly used." *Tarot for a New Generation* was primarily written with the Rider-Waite-Smith deck in mind, because its images are most frequently used in reproductions, imitations, and spinoffs. However, there is still much agreement regarding the basic concepts, and it is interesting to see how different illustrations compare.

Part 1

BACKGROUND AND BASICS

The Tarot's images are part of a meaningful, unified, and uplifting philosophical system; therefore, they can help you to evaluate your opportunities and choices. This is a symbol system that you can work with to help plan your life path and make a place for yourself in the world.

1 A CLOSER LOOK
AT THE CARDS

The Tarot is a collection of picture cards that is often described as a "text." Like a book, it can be read. Yet the Tarot is a book like no other, for though it is at least five hundred years old, it is an interactive medium. You can read the Tarot in order to gain information about the past, present, and future, as well as to study its philosophy and symbolism. As you get to know the cards, you can imagine them communicating with you, relating their ancient wisdom, and also sharing some special messages, just for you. Over time, you will see a story unfolding. By responding to the cards' predictions (sometimes taking action to avoid or alter things you don't like) and using their advice to bring positive new influences into your life, you will find that you are writing yourself into a never-ending story. If you start reading for other people, you will also get to see how their stories compare to your own story and how, in revealing the challenges that we share, the cards demonstrate that we are all interconnected. As you test your readings against your own life experience and against your friends' experiences, you will also discover new insights into the individual cards. In so doing, you can build upon their meanings in ways that are important to you, your times, and your culture.

The Structure of the Tarot Deck

Any good story consists of chapters that are full of ups and downs, surprises, and conflicts, and in the Tarot, these adventures come to life in all the different cards, with their colorful illustrations and many levels of meaning. Most Tarot card decks consist of two sections: the Major Arcana and Minor (or "lesser") Arcana. The word Arcana (which is plural) means a collection of "secrets" and refers to the hidden wisdom within each card, as well as the belief that the Tarot encapsulates the teachings of the ancient world's mystery schools. (The singular form of the word is Arcanum.)

The Major Arcana consists of twenty-one numbered cards, plus the Fool card (which many Tarot philosophers have labeled "Zero"). The Major Arcana cards are sometimes referred to as the "trumps," and they comprise the main body or core of the Tarot. Over the centuries, the content of their twenty-two symbolic illustrations has become fairly standardized, though some decks have some changes or added embellishments. In the card interpretation chapters in this book, I discuss some of the differences between older and modern versions; however, you'll find that the differences in illustrations usually don't alter the cards' most basic symbols, whose fundamental meanings continue to be relevant to human experience. Tarot experts like to point out that, taken in order, these cards represent the individual's journey through life, with (0) the Fool card representing the state of starting out innocent and inexperienced, (1) the Magician emphasizing the need to make use of our personal gifts and resources, (2) the High Priestess teaching that we must open ourselves to intuition, and so on. This journey relates to the process of "individuation," which is about achieving a strong sense of your Self and your life's purpose, being able to understand the significance of your actions and your life's events, and being able to appreciate your place in the spiritual order that underlies and binds all existence.

The Minor Arcana consists of fifty-six cards; it is unclear whether they developed along with the Major Arcana as part of the Tarot, or whether they started as a separate system that afterward was incorporated into the Tarot. The four suits of the Minor Arcana resemble the suits of ordinary playing cards. In addition to having cards numbered from one to ten, these Tarot suits are similar to those in ordinary decks of playing cards because they have court cards—with Kings, Queens, Knights, and Pages. In fact, fortunetelling systems have also been developed for ordinary cards, though they and the Tarot sometimes have overlapping interpretations, with the Cups corresponding to Hearts, the Wands to Diamonds, the Pentacles to Clubs, and the Swords to Spades. It is possible to read the Tarot using only the Major Arcana cards, but the Minor Arcana is useful because its cards' meanings pertain more to the experiences of everyday life. The Major and Minor Arcana work harmoniously together to demonstrate how our greater spiritual and developmental issues influence our common problems and concerns.

The cards in the Minor Arcana are divided into four suits of fourteen cards each; they are often referred to as the "pip" cards. In the system that is most commonly used, these suits are designated as Wands, Swords, Cups, and Pentacles. The symbols of these suits correspond to the magical elements of the ancient alchemists, with Wands usually representing the element of Fire, Swords representing Air, Cups as Water, and Pentacles as Earth. (Note that when I discuss these suits and their elements, I capitalize them in order to distinguish them in their role as Tarot archetypes from references to ordinary cups, swords, fire, earth, and so on.) Corresponding to Earth, the Pentacles deal with material world concerns, the Cups as Water relate to emotional issues, the Swords as Air signify mental qualities and conflicts, and the Wands as Fire denote inspiration and the ways that ideas are put into action. There are a few decks that use different correspondences, such as the *Shapeshifter Tarot* and the *The Celtic Dragon Tarot*, which associate the Fire element with Swords and the Air element with Wands. Some of the other decks, especially reproductions of older decks, use different designations for the suits, with Clubs, Staves, Sceptres, Batons, or Rods used as alternative names for the Wands, while Coins or Disks may be used instead of the Pentacles. Some of the modern decks that are designed around special concepts have renamed the cards so that, for example, in the *Native American Tarot Deck,* by Magda and J. A. Gonzalez, Wands are Pipes, Cups are Vessels, Swords are Blades, and Pentacles are Shields. Older versions of the Minor Arcana simply portray numbered groupings of their suit symbols, such as groups of swords, cups, and so on, but many of the more modern decks use pictures that portray situations and events relating to the cards' popular meanings.

It is important to know the numerological principles in order to understand the meaning of both the Major and Minor Arcana cards. I will have more to say about the numerical associations of the cards in chapter 3, which deals with some fine points of interpretation, and in the chapters about the cards themselves.

History of the Tarot

It is not within the scope of this book to provide an in-depth discussion of all the theories regarding the origins of the Tarot, but following is a brief rundown of its history.

The exact beginning of the Tarot is not known, because there are no direct links to lead us back to the original source; however, the earliest Tarot decks we know about emerged during the Renaissance. One of the oldest specimens of the Tarot consists of seventeen cards that reside in the Biliotheque Nationale in Paris; Stuart Kaplan believes that this set of cards is probably of fifteenth-century Venetian origin.[1] These cards have no numbers or labels, but they include such familiar figures as the Lovers, the Hanged Man, the Hermit, the Valet (Page) of Swords, and so on. Other decks that have been preserved in museums also date from the fifteenth century. One of these, the Tarocchi of Mantegna, which dates from around 1470, has many additional cards, including representations of figures from classical mythology such as the Muses and the planets. Others, such as the Tarocchi of Venice and the Visconti-Sforza decks, are similar to modern decks in that they have the same number of Major and Minor Arcana cards. By the 1700s, Tarot designs had become more standardized, with designs in the family of decks related to the *Tarot of Marseilles,* some of which are still reproduced. Their illustrations are often crude but brightly colored. They had no special illustrations for the pip cards, only pictures of arrangements of the Swords, Wands, Cups, and Coins.

Although some of these earlier decks have been preserved, we unfortunately do not know who originally designed them. The use of allegory, which represents cosmic forces, human character traits, and other abstract concepts in picture images—usually personified in human form—was an essential part of ancient, medieval, and Renaissance artwork. The people of these earlier societies were also very comfortable with allegorical *thinking,* picturing concepts like love, hope, or charity, for example, as living entities who were active in their daily lives. Because allegorical images were so common, the idea of portraying a whole system of philosophy through card pictures may have been a very natural development.

Because the use of allegorical figures to represent philosophical truths was so integral to the cultural expression of the people of the past, they were used not merely in high art and religion, but also in popular literature, entertainment, and civic ceremonies. The most spectacular of these were the "triumphs," which were lavish processions and pageants featuring costumed people who posed as living tableaux while they rode through the streets in chariots (and later on parade floats).[2] They represented allegorical figures such as Victory, Strength, Eros, Temperance, the Sun, the Moon, and so on. This custom was started by the Etruscans (an early Italian tribe) and taken up by the Romans to reward their victorious generals; it was later copied by Italian and then other European nobles. Triumphs also captured the imagination of Renaissance artists such as Andrea Mantegna, who spent seven years painting *The Triumphs of Caesar.* (*Note:* Stuart Kaplan argues that Andrea Mantegna did not actually design the Mantegna deck;[3] otherwise, we would have a possible link between the cards and a painter of triumphs.) Artists also had a hand in staging the triumphs. As Robert Payne has noted, "The greatest painters of the time were employed to design the triumphs, and their range was extraordinary."[4] For these reasons, some scholars have suggested that the Tarot cards' designs derived from these triumphs. In fact, the earliest Tarot cards were known as "Triumphs" (in Italian, *Trionfi*). It was not until the sixteenth century that they came to be called *Tarocchi,* translated into the French as "Tarot." The popularity of triumph-type processions spread across Europe. Thus, the pageants that celebrated the installation of London's Lord Mayors on October 29 featured some of the characters we know from the cards: Death, Fortune, Justice, and Temperance, as well as some of the characters included in the *Tarot of Mantegna,* such as Philosophy, Poetry, Fame, Charity, Hope, and Faith—among many other allegorical personifications.[5] Allegorical figures also found their way into printed matter, such as the widely read emblem books of the late sixteenth and early seventeenth centuries; their pages resembled Tarot cards, featuring virtues and vices illustrated in human form, as well as characters from classical mythology.

Despite the evident connection with the triumphs, many Tarot users believe that the cards must have different origins—though they disagree about the Tarot's beginnings. In its motifs they see survivals of the mystical traditions of such varied cultures as ancient Egypt, India, China, Korea, Persia, and that of the Gypsies, as well as Hermetic, Cabalistic, Gnostic, Neoplatonist, Catharist, Knights Templar, and Albigensian philosophical teachings. Many of the influential thinkers of the Renaissance were familiar with these and earlier metaphysical teachings. In fact, in the periods that extended from classical times into the Renaissance, a number of mystery schools (which were associations of scholars dedicated to exploring and developing distinct systems of mystical knowledge) flourished in Europe, Asia Minor, and North Africa, and their members traveled widely, corresponded with each other, and sometimes tried to reconcile each others' systems. They certainly had the opportunity to spread the idea of the Tarot, if indeed it originated with or was further developed by one of these groups. Perhaps some of them influenced the selection of cards that we know today (since there were so many other allegorical figures they could have chosen from). It does seem that the contributions of different groups have resulted in the Tarot's being a synthesis of different wisdom traditions.

Just as there are disagreements over the origin of the Tarot, there are also varying opinions on the meaning of its name. The word Tarot is closely tied to the history of cards and the design features of cards, for the words *tarocchi* and *tarocchino,* which are used in Italian Tarot decks, are also the names of card games; Parisian playing card makers of the late sixteenth century called themselves Tarotiers; the word *tarotée* is applied to the criss-cross designs on the back of early cards; and spiral dot patterns on the margins of some playing cards were called *tares,* while the cards featuring such designs were called *tarots* or *tarotées.*[6] Some students of Tarot have suggested more exotic roots for the word: in her book *Tarot Handbook,* cross-cultural anthropologist Angeles Arrien cites different theories, including some that assert (1) the name is derived from the Egyptian *Tarosh,* meaning "the royal way," (2) it might be related to *rota,* the Latin word for "wheel," or (3) it might have Cabalistic associations related to *Torah,* the word for "the law." She also mentions that the word "tar" means "a deck of cards" in the Gypsy language, and derives from the Sanskrit word *taru.*[7] Personally, I favor the possible Latin association because the Rota Fortuna is pictured as one of the cards, Fortuna is the goddess-presence behind the Tarot, and the old Roman cult of Fortuna had a practice of inscribing fortunes on tablets. However, Tarot may well be one of those words that caught on because of several different traditions coming together, thus making it all the more meaningful.

I've heard the word "Tarot" pronounced several different ways, though because it is a French word, people usually don't enunciate the last "t." It is most commonly pronounced [Ta-roh'] or [Tair'-oh], the first being a more European pronunciation, the latter the Americanized version.

Whatever the meaning of the word Tarot and the origins of the cards, the Tarot recaptured the imaginations of scholars in the late nineteenth and early twentieth centuries, and led to the abundance of designs that are available today. The designs and interpretations of many of the more modern Tarot decks have been influenced by the Golden Dawn Society, a Victorian magical order that was established around 1887. Among its associates who advanced their theories on the Tarot's meanings were Samuel MacGregor Mathers, Aleister Crowley, Arthur Edward Waite, Papus, and Paul Foster Case. Around 1910, Waite conceived and commissioned a deck that was illustrated by Pamela Colman Smith and printed by the Rider company (therefore known as the Rider-Waite-Smith Tarot deck or variations thereof). Waite and Smith made the Major Arcana cards more elaborate by incorporating many additional symbols into their graphic design. They also came up with picture concepts to illustrate the Minor Arcana cards, and thereby fixed their own set of meanings to these cards. The Rider-Waite-Smith deck became very popular, and its illustrations and interpretations became the standard on which many or most of the newer Tarot versions have been based.

Aleister Crowley also designed a Tarot deck, the *Crowley Thoth Tarot Deck* (often referred to as the Thoth deck), but his illustrations and concepts for the Major Arcana made some departures from tradition. In collaboration with the artist, Lady Frieda Harris, Crowley also used elaborate symbolic detailing in his reconceptualized images.

Contemporary Decks

In recent years, the Tarot has blossomed into many versions from an extremely wide diversity of sources. Some of them are modeled after the early Renaissance versions, while others take some interesting new directions. Decks have been designed to reflect all kinds of personal tastes and interests. For example, people attracted to Celtic lore may enjoy the *Legend: The Arthurian Tarot* deck by Anna-Marie Ferguson, which is illustrated with haunting images from the old legends, or the *The Sacred Circle Tarot,* a collaboration by Anna Franklin and Paul Mason that combines scenes from Celtic pagan culture with natural world emblems such as plants and animals, and uses specific sites in the British Isles as background. *The Mythic Tarot,* by Juliet Sharman-Burke and Tricia Newell, uses scenes and characters from Greek mythology. Those attracted to African traditions may be interested in *The Tarot of the Orishas* by Zolrak and Durkon, which uses images from the Afro-Brazilian Candomblé religion, while people with affinities for American Indian cultures may want to look into the *Native American Tarot Deck* by Magda and J. A. Gonzalez. Multicultural and feminist images are portrayed in the *Motherpeace Tarot Deck* by Vicki Noble and Karen Vogel; the Barbara Walker deck also has a feminist orientation and draws from ancient mythologies. (Both of these decks are also interesting because they associate new images with the individual Minor Arcana cards.) There are special theme decks, such as the *Tarot of the*

Cat People by Karen Kuykendall, which has inserted a cat into each card illustration, or *The Celtic Dragon Tarot,* by D. J. Conway and Lisa Hunt, which features dragons in each card. And some decks emphasize magical traditions, such as *The Witches Tarot Deck* by Ellen Cannon Reed and Martin Cannon, which unites Pagan and Cabbalistic symbolism, or the *Shapeshifter Tarot* by D. J. Conway, Sirona Knight, and Lisa Hunt, which contains eighty-one cards that blend human figures with animal spirits and other shamanic imagery. Numerous other beautiful and delightful card decks are currently available, but, unfortunately, too many to describe here.

With so many new Tarot design varieties, we have the luxury of being able to seek out decks that have a strong personal appeal; this is something that was not really possible prior to the seventies and eighties. You may have to conduct a long search of catalogs, bookshops, and websites before you find the Tarot deck you like the best, but the quest is part of the fun. Don't worry about whether you'll know the right deck when you see it, because when you do find it, you will probably experience an instant attraction. In the meantime, you can still get fine results by practicing with other decks that are available. However, I do think it is helpful for beginners to work with one of the decks that include illustrations for the Minor Arcana cards, because the pictures help you to remember and assist in interpreting their meanings.

Although most Tarot decks and systems are fairly compatible, with the differences in meaning being only minor, sometimes you may encounter cases where a system, deck, manual, or interpreter does seem to have some significant differences. Chapter 3, which expounds on some of the fine points of reading and interpretation, includes some thoughts on how to deal with different decks and systems of interpretation.

Even though there are many fascinating and exquisite new renditions of the Tarot deck, there is undoubtedly room for many more artists and creative people to come up with additional versions. Furthermore, since any given Tarot card has many levels of interpretation and is able to apply to many different areas of life, there is no reason why inspired artists couldn't come up with hundreds of different picture concepts to convey the different shades of meaning of these cards. In fact, I hope that more will, because having alternative takes on the cards can help us avoid dogmatic attitudes and the habit of thinking inside conceptual boxes. If you are interested in art or design, let this inspire you to think about alternative picture images as you use your own deck. Such exercises will help you achieve new insights and make the sort of connections that enable you to see how the energies of the Tarot operate in your own life.

Caring for your Cards

Once you acquire a pack of Tarot cards, you will probably spend some time thumbing through your new deck, looking it over. This begins the process of imprinting the cards with your own energy nature, creating a bond between you and your cards. However, there are additional things you can do for them. For example, to perform a small ceremony of attunement, rub your hands together briskly and imagine golden energy building in the friction between them. Then, place the deck between your two palms and imagine the cards being suffused with this sparkling energy as you warm them with your hands. You can also say a silent blessing prayer, such as, "May these cards be blessed as they warm to my body and spirit. May they always speak truly and wisely for the good of all around me." (Before you do this, it is helpful to put them in numerical order—such as the order they came in—as this order has its own integrity.) You do not need to repeat this ritual every time you take out your cards, but there may be occasions when your intuition tells you that it would be good to give them a little recharging.

Many readers wrap their cards in silk when not in use. Black silk is traditional because its impenetrable color is believed to keep out unwanted vibratory influences. However, you can use any color that appeals to you. I am a great believer in the intuitive correctness of individuals' responses to colors and other things that "feel right" to them, and the color that you prefer can help attune your cards to your personal energy patterns and other psychic needs. I used to keep my own cards in emerald green silk, but now I have several decorative pouches of various types of cloth, and all work very well. Certain types of camera cases, makeup cases, and small evening bags make good storage cases for the cards, too, and are easy to carry in your purse or briefcase. Other readers store their cards in decorative tin or wooden boxes, as well as many other types of containers.

Some Tarot readers are very fussy about their cards, and don't allow other people to handle them. Some will allow others to handle them, but they feel a need to "clear" or "cleanse" the cards afterward, to dispel any vibrations that the other person or people have left behind. Some clear the deck after every reading, whether someone else touched the cards or not. Cleansing the deck does not mean that the other person is a bad or psychically unclean person. Rather, it is a way to reattune the cards' energies to your personal vibratory state. Cleansing is also something that you can do if you've done a reading for yourself to enquire about a disturbing matter, or if you've had an unsettling experience (for example, if a family fight has left you in a nervous state) and you don't want to transmit bad energy to your cards. One of the simplest ways to clear a deck is by reshuffling it. For this purpose, some readers shuffle more vigorously than they would otherwise, using a snapping motion. Putting the cards back into some kind of order also helps restore their normal state. And you can always refresh and recharge your cards by using the hand warming and golden energy visualization mentioned previously.

Personally, I don't mind other people handling my cards, and I have never really sensed any trouble with other peoples' vibrations lingering in my cards, even when I've been reading for large numbers of strangers. It seems that whatever vibrations there are may get bumped out by the next person or issue to come along. Also, I think that when you use the same cards regularly over a long period of time, your own energy patterns become so ingrained that they are not easily jarred by someone else's. Therefore, I feel that the act of cleansing has more value as a ritual for maintaining a respectful, mindful relationship with your cards.

2 READY TO READ

As I mentioned in the introduction, individuals can start working with the Tarot before they have memorized all of the cards' meanings because their symbolic images are already linked to patterns within the unconscious, the deep mind. Nevertheless, there are some reasons why a beginner should take it slow and easy, and proceed with common sense.

Once you've acquired your first deck of Tarot cards, you will probably be eager to get started. It's quite natural to want to sit down immediately and do a reading to find out what sort of great destiny awaits you; however, some people believe that reading for yourself can present problems because you may not be objective, and you could be overly influenced by wishful thinking. Also, it seems that sometimes a person's emotions can be so strong that instead of accurately predicting future events, the cards will instead reflect his current mood. However, I think that you can train yourself to become more objective as you learn how to check your interpretations against your observations of the events that unfold. I believe the greater danger is that you could draw some cards that are disappointing, and without the right sort of experience in testing for accuracy, putting things into perspective, and keeping the positive aspects in view, you could become depressed. (I elaborate on the subject of accuracy in chapter 3.) Therefore, I think it's best to start by doing small, daily readings. (The Three-Card Spread, described in this chapter, is ideal for such readings.) By reviewing your readings at the end of the day, comparing the cards' meanings (as described in this or other books) to your intuitive impressions and your daily happenings, you will develop a good understanding of how the cards relate to the people and happenings in your life. In this way, you will also become familiar with a good number of cards, fairly quickly. It's best to hold off doing more complex readings or asking questions in which there is a lot at stake emotionally until you've developed more experience.

Also, anyone who plans to study Tarot should have confidence in her ability to deal with life's problems. If the Tarot cards give you some bad news, you must be able to face it with an "I can manage it" attitude. For one thing, readings can be wrong, perhaps due to misinterpretation, psychic interference, and other factors that block the cards' clear expression. For another thing, there are many variables that can influence future outcomes. You may be familiar with Charles Dickens's oft-filmed story *A Christmas Carol,* in which the character Scrooge, warned by a spirit about the bleak future ahead of him, frantically asks, "Are these the shadows of the things that *will* be, or the shadows of the things that *might* be?" Although the ghost doesn't reply, we could answer Scrooge with a quotation from Yoda, the Jedi master of the *Star Wars* series, who says, "Always in motion is the future." The Tarot cards and other forms of divination (fortunetelling) can show you the potentialities that exist at a given moment, and what would happen if you were to continue on the path that you are on, being the person that you are at this time. However, if you don't like the reading, you may be able to change the course of events. Sometimes the reading itself will provide clues as to which changes need to be made, and you can also do additional readings to get more information and ask what you can do to counteract the problems predicted. (See appendix C on consulting the Tarot for advice on courses of action.) Sometimes you may have to work hard to alter your circumstances, but sometimes a simple change of attitude is enough to make the difference.

You must also bear in mind that bad things do happen as part of the normal flow of life. All human beings experience their share of hurt, heartbreaks, disappointments, and setbacks, but we all have to learn to deal with them and move on. If you are not prepared to take the bad along with the good, you should stay away from the Tarot and all other forms of divination. But if you are willing to face whatever the future may bring, the Tarot can help you to think about your different courses of action, and to prepare physically and mentally to take on the challenges.

And that brings us to another issue—the problem of fatalism. Sometimes people who read Tarot cards or daily horoscopes, for example, are thought of as people who are afraid to go out of the house if they get a bad reading, or who give up too easily if they think fate is against them. Although I know many people who use Tarot, astrology, runes, the I Ching, and other forms of divination, I don't know anyone like that. When the cards warn me of potential problems or dangers, I just become more cautious; I check my memory to make sure that I'm not forgetting something important and I try to be extra nice to my relatives (in order to avoid quarrels), but I never let the results of a Tarot reading stop me from going about my daily life. In fact, when I get a bad reading, I become energized because I want to prove that I can beat any problem that is about to crop up—just as when I get a good reading, I get more active so I can get the most out of my anticipated good luck.

Now, let me say a little something about fortunetelling in general: fortunetelling is also called "divination" because ancient people believed that God or the gods wanted their will to be known. Divining the future and seeking other information in this manner can therefore be a way to maintain a special relationship with the forces that animate our universe. For this reason, I consult the cards or other divinatory systems on a regular basis, even when I don't have anything special to ask, because it is pleasant to uphold my end of the relationship and give respect to these forces.

Incidentally, some Tarot people don't like the word "fortunetelling" because they feel that it has become cheapened through its association with frivolous games and con artists. I don't mind it because I associate the word "telling" with the idea of constructing a personal narrative—that is, learning how the Tarot symbolism plays a role in your unfolding life story.

Once you're ready to get going, you might think about whether to study with friends. Whether or not you begin your studies alone depends on your personality and the ability to find friends who share an interest in the Tarot and are mature enough to deal with potent archetypal symbols. However, when you have someone with whom you can discuss the card meanings, you can both learn them faster. What's more, you can take turns reading for each other. Friends add energy to a reading, and you will also be amazed at the new insights you can bring to each other's readings. I advise that aside from your study buddies, you should avoid reading for other people until you are fairly experienced and confident, because in your earlier stages as a learner, you may be hurt by the negative comments that some people might make if they are hostile or skeptical.

Mental Preparation

Whenever you're ready for a reading, there are a few things you can do to attune yourself and create a harmonious atmosphere. Try to set aside a quiet time and find a place that is pleasant and free of distraction. You can create ambience by

playing soft, mystical music, such as classical, New Age, Celtic, or tribal composi-
tions, and by burning candles and incense. Relax, and breathe deeply, until you
feel calm and focused. As you bring out your cards, try to achieve a respectful rapport with them by thinking about how they act as friends and teachers who can
offer insight into your ordinary concerns, while also helping you become more
aware of the spiritual dimensions of your existence. Also, think about how Tarot
and other divination techniques work because of the interconnectedness of all
things, and how they can help us achieve the right relationship with the order of
the cosmos. You can say a prayer for inspiration and guidance, and you might also
want to perform a short ritual. For example, as you bring out your cards, you
could light a candle and recite the following lines:

> As I lay out these cards,
> I honor the ancient wisdom traditions
>   that have taught us that we are all interconnected,
> and the spiritual forces
>   that urge us to recognize
>   our responsibilities to all beings.
> Please help me to read the Tarot
>   so that I may interpret well and wisely,
>   acting as an agent for good
>   in this living universe.

Or compose a prayer or ritual of your own that you think appropriate.

Choosing a Significator

Before you begin to read, you might also want to go through your deck to choose
a "significator." Some Tarot systems or spreads call for the use of a significator,
which is a card that is chosen to represent the person for whom the reading is to
be done (whether that person is the reader or someone else); the significator is
either placed in a central position in the layout or laid face up on the table before
shuffling the cards and doing the reading. Some systems routinely select the
Magician as a significator if the questioner (also known as the "querent" or "subject of the reading") is a male, and the High Priestess if a female. Others use the
court cards for this purpose, selecting a Knight to represent a young man, a King
to represent a mature man, a Queen for a mature woman, and a Page for a young

woman or child. Certain traditions additionally select by physical appearances: for example, using the Wands court to denote blue-eyed, blonde-haired people, the Cups court to denote people with light brown hair and hazel eyes, the Swords court for people with dark hair and brown eyes, and the Pentacles for people with black hair and black eyes. I don't use this system because, aside from the problem of promoting racial stereotypes by linking personality to appearance, it is impractical because it lumps the populations of almost entire nations into narrow categories.

In fact, I have fallen out of the habit of separating a significator from the deck because most layouts have positions to indicate the role that a person is acting out, or that otherwise reflect his status and state of mind. Also, I don't like to take the Magician, the High Priestess, or other cards out of action, because they might have something important to say if allowed to come up on their own, in another position. However, if you would prefer to use a significator—and this can be helpful in getting focused and tuned in to the person for whom you are reading, even if yourself—you can use the Magician or High Priestess as previously mentioned, or you can read through the descriptions of the court card personalities and choose the one that you feel is the closest fit. For more suggestions on significators, refer to appendix A. The process of choosing a significator can be very revealing, because in going over the court cards' personality types and making a decision to choose one over another (since most people have some character traits that will fall into different categories), you really have to think about yourself or your subject, and how the personality relates to the matter in question. Also, instead of a significator card, you could substitute a photo—this can be especially helpful if you are reading for a person who is not present.

By the way, when I am not using a significator, I have found that whichever card would otherwise be chosen as significator for the subject of the reading will often pop up somewhere in the spread—surprisingly often as the first or central card! When this happens, it helps verify that the Tarot is on target, that it is indeed speaking to the subject of the reading. Whether this significator is upright or reversed reveals whether circumstances allow the person to be herself. Whenever a person is able to be herself, she is also in a position of greater strength, so things are more likely to go her way. I sometimes use the word "significator" in a very general sense; when a card seems to denote a known person (possibly recurring in a series of readings), it can be referred to as a significator for that person.

Posing the Question and Shuffling the Cards

Your next step is to think about how to phrase the question or questions you want to ask. Framing the question is important, both in helping to sort out your thoughts and in getting a clearer answer from the cards. The nature of the question can also determine the type of layout (also called a "spread") you choose.

Sometimes you may not have a special question in mind, but would like a general overview of your life situation—where you're at, what sort of past events are still influencing you, and where you are going. For this type of question, more elaborate spreads such as the Celtic Cross (included in this chapter) are very good, although you can also use simpler layouts. When I'm doing readings for friends, I usually do an "overview" reading first, using the Celtic Cross, followed by a series of Three-Card spreads to answer whatever additional questions are on their minds. I also do overview readings for myself at regular intervals during the year, or when I feel that some significant milestone or turning point has been reached. For an overview reading, you can address the cards by saying, "Please show me the energies at work in my life," "Please show me the course my life is taking," or "Is there anything special that I should know at this time?" and other questions to that effect.

You can also ask questions about specific concerns, such as, "Could you tell me about such-and-such a person?" or "Could you please comment on such-and-such a situation?" With more specialized concerns, it is helpful to think first about the best choice of wording. Learning how to pose your questions clearly and concisely takes a little practice, but also provides good training in mental organization. The process of formulating a question is in itself therapeutic because of the mental work involved. Posing the question can also be a magical act, because the heightened focus can start your unconscious to work on solutions to problems or changes to be made. Also, as the authors of *Spiritual Tarot* have pointed out, "Asking the right question creates resonating energy in both your psyche and the greater universe, making it possible for you to draw those cards that give you the information you need." [1]

There are times when it is good to be very specific. Suppose, for example, that you are wondering whether to apply to a certain college. Unless you have a very strong mental image of your idea of a good college, it is best to avoid questions like, "Should I go to State University?" It is more to the point to ask, "Will getting my degree at State University help me to get a good job?" or whatever your most important criterion is in choosing a college. "Should I go to State University?" is too complicated because State University may be good for your family life, but not so good for career connections. (In the case of a question about whether State University's degree program will lead to a good career, you would look for positive cards, cards that foretell general success, and cards pertaining to career success.) If necessary, you could ask a series of questions about different concerns regarding this college, noting whether the majority of your readings are positive or negative. On the other hand, if you are fairly satisfied that the college appears to meet your criteria but are just wondering what your life will be like attending this school, you could ask broader questions, such as, "What will my life be like at State University?" or "Will I be happy at State University?" Again, note whether you draw strong positive cards that point to happiness and well-being. If you are trying to choose between several colleges, you could ask the same question in relation to each institution, and then compare to see which one produces the strongest positive cards.

If you do readings for other people, you will often find it necessary to spend a few minutes talking with them about their hopes and concerns prior to the reading in order to find out exactly what they want to know and how to word their questions. (If you've ever listened to call-in advice shows on the radio, you've probably noticed how difficult it is for many people to put their questions into words.) Occasionally querents may wish to keep a question private; in that case, it is not necessary for them to state the question out loud. Naturally, if you know what the question is, it is easier for you to interpret the cards in its context; but if not, you can give generalized interpretations using the cards' basic meanings, and leave it to the querents to silently consider how they apply to their personal situation.

About the same time that you are articulating your question, you will also be thinking about which layout to use (see the discussion on layouts, which follows). Of course, before you lay out the cards, they have to be shuffled.

If you are a beginner and are reading for yourself, you might want to first pick up your cards before you begin to shuffle, and riffle through the deck in order to quickly review some of their images. Then, start shuffling, maintaining a relaxed state of mind while holding the question in focus. You can shuffle in any manner that is comfortable to you, as long as you keep the cards facedown until you lay them out. Many readers prefer gentle shuffling techniques, because methods that bend and snap the cards can disrupt the cards' energies. However, I do not know whether this holds true for everyone. If you plan to include reversed cards in your reading, be sure to turn some of them while you are shuffling, so a certain number will be upside down. (Some people prefer not to use reversed cards—I will discuss reversed cards further in chapter 3.) Readers differ as to how they handle the shuffling when they are reading for another person. Some shuffle the deck themselves, especially if they have strong feelings about not allowing other people to handle the cards. Some ask the querent to lay her hands on the deck for a moment while concentrating on the question, then take the cards back and shuffle them. Some shuffle the cards a little, then hand them to the other person to shuffle a bit; they may then cut the cards themselves or ask the other person to cut them. I have used all of these methods at different times—sometimes the decision is entirely intuitive, depending on the person for whom I am reading at the moment. I believe that these methods have worked equally well for me.

By the way, sometimes a card will fall out of the deck while you are shuffling or handling the cards prior to reading. When this happens, make note of the card, then put it back into the deck to see if it reappears when you lay out your spread. If not, you may go through your deck after laying out your cards, find the card, and set it out on the table, somewhat above your layout. If spiritual forces or the ordering patterns of the universe influence the cards that come up in a spread, we must assume that cards that present themselves in this manner are also significant. Consider what this extra card may mean to your reading. It could represent some outside influence that may act as a variable; that is, something unexpected that has the power to alter or shed a new light on events. (You might also pull out whichever cards came before and after the rogue card when you locate it in the deck, and interpret them as a Three-Card Spread.)

As you shuffle, continue to concentrate on your question. Remain shuffling until you feel "moved" to stop and "cut" the deck; that is, until you feel that the cards are ready. If you are uncertain about relying on your intuition, it is okay to shuffle a specified number of times—for example, thirteen or fifteen . . . however many times you think appropriate.

Following the shuffling, it is common to cut the deck into several piles, which are then reassembled (although some readers omit this step). There are different methods for cutting, but the technique with which I am familiar involves dividing the deck into three piles with the left hand (because of the left hand's traditional association with the personal subconscious), taking the piles from off the top of the deck, and putting them in a row from right to left. The piles do not have to be of equal thickness. Then, still using the left hand, the pile on the right (the one that came from the bottom) is put on top of the one to the left, and then that pile is placed on top of the remaining pile to the left. When I'm reading for another person, I usually do this part myself because I can do it faster than I can explain it. However, some readers prefer to have the other person cut the deck.

Laying out the Cards

You are now ready to lay out the cards. Start with the card on top, and lay the cards out in front of you, turning them faceup, but taking care not to flip them in a way that would now reverse them (all the necessary reversing will have been done during the shuffling). I am in the habit of laying and turning the cards with my left hand. Set out the cards so they can be viewed from your own position if you are the reader, even if you are reading for another person. I try to do readings at a table or on the floor in a way that allows me to sit next to the other person, rather than opposite her.

As mentioned earlier, the layout is something you usually decide upon when you are thinking about which question to ask. There are many common spreads and creative readers are devising new ones. With experience, you may well invent some layouts of your own, suited to your interests. However, following are some good basic layouts that can be applied to most of your questions, plus a few specialized ones.

The Basic Three-Card Spread

I have found the most practical and versatile of all layouts to be the Three-Card Spread. When I was an eighteen-year-old student, I was exposed to this technique when, at a psychic fair, I had my cards read by Maria Gracietta; she impressed me with the way she could quickly answer a series of questions with three-card spreads. (Gracietta used the *Lenormand* deck, which is not actually a Tarot deck, but the same principles apply.) There are a number of different ways you can interpret the Three-Card Spread, depending on your intentions and the nature of your question. For an overview of a situation, you can shuffle the cards with the intention that they will represent past, present, and future, and then read them as follows.

Past	*Present*	*Future*

For a closer look at a present situation, you can shuffle and interpret the cards with the intention that the central card will represent the basic situation (the focus), and the cards to either side will explain more about circumstances that influence this situation.

Major *Influence*	*Focus of Present* *Situation*	*Major* *Influence*

If your intention is to look into either the past or the future, the same principles apply, with the central card representing a focal situation of the past or future.

Influential *Circumstance*	*Focus of Past or* *Present Situation*	*Influential* *Circumstance*

However, you can also interpret three-card spreads for the past or future in terms of a time line.

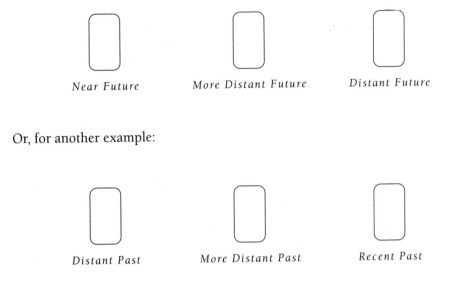

Or, for another example:

I also find the Three-Card Spread to be very useful for daily readings, with the central card representing a focal lesson or event, and the flanking cards as other significant events or influences. They can also be interpreted in terms of morning, afternoon, and evening.

Sometimes, when I review the cards at the end of the day, I'll find that both frames of interpretation apply.

In her book *Tarot for Your Self*, which teaches how to use the cards for greater personal analysis, Mary K. Greer offers a number of variations of the Three-Card Spread, where the layout can represent the body, mind, and spirit; child, parent, and adult ego states; and subconscious, conscious, and superconscious motivations—among many other things.[2] As you work with the Tarot, you will probably think of additional Three-Card variations, because so many of our cultural concepts are expressed in threes. No one of these is more "correct" than the others. Rather, you will find that different arrangements are suited to different types of questions.

The Nine-Card Spread

A natural extension of the Three-Card Spread is the Nine-Card Spread, in which you draw three cards to represent the past, three for the present, and three for the future. Depending on your personal preference (something that you can discover with practice), the cards can be shuffled and laid out with the intention to represent a time line: *distant past / more recent past / recent past / present influence / present focus / present influence / near future / more distant future / distant future;* or as a series of threes representing focal events and the influences that accompany them: *past influence / focus of past / past influence / present influence / focus of present / present influence / future influence / focus of future / future influence.* In either case, you can lay the nine cards out in a straight line or in three rows.

Note: The number Nine is the mystical number in the ancient Celtic and Teutonic magical traditions, as well as among different African groups.

The Nine-Square Spread for Clarification

If you feel that the cards in a Three-Card Spread do not explain enough, you can turn the reading into a Nine-Square Spread. To do this, reshuffle your cards while mentally requesting more information on the reading you just had. Then, go through the reshuffled deck to locate the three cards from your original reading. Pull them out, along with the cards that are immediately in front of and behind each of these cards. Next, lay them out in three rows of three, with the original cards that represent past, present, and future (or whatever you choose) in the central position and flanked by the two cards that were alongside them in the reshuffled deck—but arrange the rows so the original focal cards appear in the same order as they were previously. If the originals are no longer upright or reversed, that's okay, just consider what this might mean in their new context.

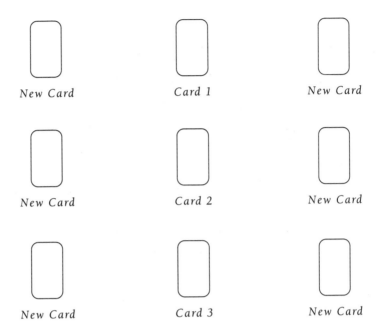

Now you can learn more about your original reading by analyzing the way that the flanking cards modify or expand the meanings of the original cards.

Seven-Card Spread

I like the symmetry of threes in the Nine-Card Spread, but a seven-card technique, which has the advantage of pointing to a more specific outcome, is in common use. As described by Stuart R. Kaplan (the president of U.S. Games Systems, Inc., which prints many Tarot decks), the cards are laid out in a straight line from left to right, with the first two cards representing the distant past and the immediate past, the next three representing present influences, present obstacles, and the present outlook, respectively, and the final two representing future influences and the ultimate result.[3]

Twelve-Month Spread

On New Year's Eve, I often entertain friends by doing a layout of twelve cards to reveal the highlights of each month in the year to come. However, there is no reason why a person couldn't do this on any day, for any twelve-month period. As you shuffle, concentrate on your desire to look into the year ahead. Then, cut the deck as usual and lay out twelve cards; they can be in two rows of six, three rows of four, or in whatever arrangement you prefer. The first card represents the month of January, the second is February, and so on. Each card is interpreted as displaying either a special event or the general character of the month in question. If cards pertaining to certain people that you know (their significators) come up, the focus of those months will be on those people. Sometimes you will also notice relationships between cards, where the pictures or traditional meanings may tell a story that unfolds over a period of months.

Thirteen Moons Spread

As a variation of the Twelve-Month Spread, you can lay out thirteen cards, using the same process as described in the aforementioned spread, but with the intention that each card will represent one of the year's full moons. A full moon represents the culmination or fulfillment of some matter, so look at your calendar, find the date of each full moon, and interpret the corresponding cards as representing things that will have materialized or influences that will be strongly felt around those particular dates. Because of the way the thirteen moons of the year are squeezed into our twelve-month solar calendar, in most years there is one month that will contain two full moons (but it is a different month each year). The second full moon of that month is sometimes referred to as the "blue moon." Make note of which of your thirteen cards represents the blue moon, because it might have a special, magical quality to it. An additional advantage of using this spread is that it helps you become more aware of the lunar cycles.

The Ten-Card or Celtic Cross Spread

The Celtic Cross is the most popular spread for detailed Tarot readings. Around 1910, Arthur Edward Waite described it as "an ancient Celtic method of divination," but offered no additional historical background.[4] Stuart Kaplan calls it the "Ten-Card Spread," claims that it "dates back several centuries," and "is one of the earliest and most effective methods."[5] The shape of this spread is reminiscent of the cross within a circle that is an icon of Celtic spirituality, reminding us that our material world (symbolized by the cross of the four elements) is part of a greater spiritual order (symbolized by the circle). Most Tarot readers assign fairly similar meanings to the cards' positions on the cross, though, as always, there are some individual variations. My own system is laid out as follows:

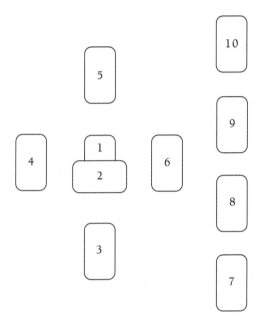

Many readers first put a significator card under card number one. If you want to use a significator, pick a card out of the deck that, to you, best represents yourself or the person you are reading for, and lay that card down first. Next, lay down card one (it should be on top of the significator). If you are reading for someone else, it is traditional to say out loud, "This covers you." The first card is the Tarot's summary of the matter in question; that is, it describes the basic situation that has influenced you to ask this question. It can also provide information about your state of mind in this situation, and the major forces at work.

Lay card two across the first to make a cross, as indicated in the diagram, and say out loud, "This crosses you." This card usually reveals countercurrents at work in your life. These can be areas where you are divided on an issue, pulled in two directions. They can also be outside forces or circumstances that are complicating your problem. However, when strongly positive cards show up, they can represent opportunities, or they may show that you are fairly well centered and focused, so you have a pretty good handle on the situation.

Place card three below the crossed cards, and say out loud, "This is beneath you." This card tends to represent psychological issues that have led you to ask this question, motivations that may be at work on a subconscious level. These issues often relate to past events that have made a major impression on you. This card may also point to important secrets or other hidden influences.

Card four is placed to the left of the crossed cards, with the words, "This is behind you." This card tends to represent events of the recent past; their influences may still be felt, though they will probably fade with the passing of time.

Card five is placed at the top of the cross, with the words, "This crowns you," or "This goes above you." It relates to your conscious goals and long-range plans, especially to the ways in which you hope to be seen, to make a difference, and to be a presence in the world. When this card is positive, it increases your chances of a successful outcome, despite whatever obstacles may be indicated in the reading. If it is a weak card, you may need to give yourself an attitude adjustment.

Card six, which forms the right arm of the cross, is placed down with the words, "This is before you." It shows the direction in which you are currently headed, and may predict things that will manifest (appear in your life) in the near future. (You may already have some sense or premonitions of the impending events that this card represents.) This may be viewed as the next paragraph or chapter in your life story.

This completes the basic cross; with the next card you start laying out the remaining vertical column, as shown in the diagram.

Card seven, the bottom card in the column, represents the role that you are acting out in relation to your question or situation. This is different from your significator, which represents your more basic character.

Card eight represents the environmental influences that are acting upon you. It often reveals pressures or acts of encouragement that are coming from your family and friends, though it can also say a lot about the material circumstances around you.

Card nine pinpoints your main issue areas, that is, your hopes and fears surrounding the matter in question.

Finally, card ten, known as the outcome card, points to the probable future, and is sometimes the answer to a specific question. Its predicted result arises from all of the other factors indicated in your reading. If you like the result, it is a good idea to continue to develop the positive qualities that are indicated in the reading. If you don't like the result, you can think about whether you can change your attitude, the circumstances around you, or any problems that may have been revealed in the reading.

Card Searches as Alternatives to Layouts

In the paragraph describing the Nine-Square Spread for Clarification, I mentioned that if you want a fuller understanding of the cards that come up in a reading, you can reshuffle, find the same nine cards in the deck, then look to the cards on either side of them for more information about the situations to which they pertain. This method of going through the deck to find specific cards has many other uses. For example, if you are studying a card a day to better familiarize yourself with the individual cards, you can ask the Tarot, "How does such-and-such a card operate in my life?" Shuffle, then locate the card you are studying in the deck. The cards to either side can show the areas of your life in which some of the influences that this card represents are active or significant. If you would like more specific information about a certain person (including yourself), you can locate that person's significator in the deck, and the cards that accompany it will reveal things about his personality and state of mind. If you want to know more about the quality of a relationship, look for the Lovers in questions pertaining to people who are or want to be romantically involved, or the Two of Cups for questions pertaining to friends. The cards on either side can show you what each person brings to the relationship. If you are wondering about career choices, you might try digging out the Three of Pentacles; see if the images in the cards to either side of it suggest any special types of jobs to you. If you are wondering how to change your luck, look to the Wheel of Fortune. The cards that accompany it can model qualities that you could bring into your life, or courses of action that you can take to make a change for the better. I could go on and on about the different types of questions to which this technique can apply—there are probably hundreds. However, as you become familiar with different cards' meanings, you will begin to see how you can build questions around them.

Multiple Readings

After doing a layout, you may want further information or clarification of the meanings of some of the cards, or of the general sense of the reading. Also, you may have additional questions that you want to ask. It is okay to do multiple readings in one sitting. If you want a more detailed answer to your question, you can ask things like, "Please tell me more about such-and-such," or you can pose other questions related to the topic. However, be aware that after a while, the cards may get "fatigued," especially if you're trying to pursue a single question because you don't like or understand the first reading. If after several readings your cards don't seem to make as much sense, it is better to wait and return to them another day. Perhaps after a few days, some things will have gotten sorted out in your unconscious, allowing the meanings to come through with greater clarity.

Daily Practice

The best way to familiarize yourself with the Tarot is through daily practice. I like to start the morning with a Three-Card Spread, phrasing my question something like, "What's in the cards for today," or "What is my day going to be like?" As mentioned earlier, you can look over the three cards for a general sense of the reading, and also consider the cards separately as indicating the conditions of the morning, afternoon, and evening. At night, I review the cards to see what they can tell me in retrospect. Another very common daily practice is to draw a card at random while asking questions like, "What wisdom will you share with me today?" or "What is the theme for today?" After reading your manual to refresh your memory on each card's traditional meanings, you can meditate on what it means to you, then spend the day looking for ways that the qualities and energies of this card are reflected in the world around you.

Recording your Readings

Whenever you complete a reading, it is a good idea to write down the questions you asked and the cards you drew. In fact, you might want to keep a special Tarot journal so you can return to your notes to refresh your memory and check the cards against unfolding events. It is helpful to include the date and describe some of the background, such as why you asked this question and what major things are going on in your life at the moment. When you reread these journal entries years later, you'll be able to understand what was most significant about them. I always regret it when I am too lazy to record my readings, because eventually things come up that seem to be very pertinent, but by then I can no longer remember the details of the reading. An advantage of keeping a journal is that by recording the context of each reading and then revisiting those readings from time to time, you can determine to what extent and in which areas of your life the cards' predictions are coming true. Often, a reading that was difficult to interpret at the time will make more sense after the passage of time has revealed how the cards' meanings play out in your life. Keeping a journal will help you get an idea of how certain cards can have very personalized meanings for you.

You can also compare readings that you do over a period of time to discern which cards come up repeatedly (some of them more frequently than chance would normally allow), because with such cards the Tarot is trying to tell you something significant to the cycles of your personal life. Then, the next time one of these "regulars" shows up, you can greet it as an old acquaintance (whether welcome or not), and say, "Aha, we're back to this again!" You can keep track of card recurrence by listing the seventy-eight cards in the back of your journal, then putting down a date or check mark by the ones you draw, each time you do a reading.

3

POINTERS ON READING
AND INTERPRETATION

There are certain things to bear in mind once you get started with the Tarot. Questions may come up while you're reading and studying the cards regarding differences between card decks and systems, concerns about accuracy, and reading for other people. This chapter addresses these issues and also details some of the fine points of interpretation, including how to spot major themes in a reading, observations on reversed cards and gendered cards, and suggestions on timing and on gaining "yes" and "no" answers.

Tarot Decks and Systems of Interpretation

In starting out, I want to emphasize that due to the intuitive, highly personalized way that Tarot cards work, no single Tarot deck or system of interpretation is superior to all the others. Eventually, you will find the system and decks that work best for you; at the same time, your friends may find that other systems work better for them. That's okay, because there is no right or wrong deck or method of reading, as long as you are satisfied with the insights that it offers you.

Because of the wide variety of Tarot decks now in print, you may have the opportunity to work with many different systems besides the more common ones that are based on the Rider-Waite-Smith deck and the *Tarot of Marseilles* decks. (The card interpretations in this book mainly use the Rider-Waite-Smith system, as that is the most popular, as well as the most accessible to beginners.) A common alternative is the *Crowley Thoth Tarot Deck,* which was one of the first to bring in new design concepts; among other things, Strength is renamed as "Lust," Temperance as "Art," and Judgement as "The Aeon," and the illustrations also incorporate many new sets of symbols. Some of the newer decks use a conventional system—primarily the Rider-Waite-Smith system, as their jumping-off point, keeping the basic meanings, but using new picture-scenarios to illustrate them. For example, the Six of Cups can represent periods of peace and harmony that promote a sense of emotional well-being, so the Rider-Waite-Smith illustration shows two children in a garden; this suggests the nostalgia that many of us have for an idealized childhood. In designing the *Motherpeace Tarot Deck*, however, Vicki Noble dispensed with the image of children and illustrated this card with six women riding the ocean waves upon horses and seahorses, in order to emphasize the "mythical, imaginative side to their pleasure."[1] On the other hand, Barbara Walker's deck labels this card "Childhood" and portrays an antinostalgic reaction to Waite's idea of childhood: she illustrates this card with a small child looking up toward a giant, monstrous mother figure that looms over him or her. In her book, she explains that "the universal experience of childhood is that of living among people much bigger than one's self," and uses this idea to launch a discussion of the archetypal meanings of mythical giants.[2] Some decks, such as the *Shapeshifter Tarot*, have even greater variations and use their own systems based on the imagination of their designers.

Card decks may also assign different numbers to the cards—especially to the Strength and Justice cards. In the family of old French decks that includes the *Tarot of Marseille* deck, the Strength card is "Eleven" and the Justice card is "Eight," whereas it is the other way around in the Rider-Waite-Smith deck and its spinoffs. And in one Tarot deck from the sixteenth century, Strength and Justice are both assigned the number "Eight."[3] Proponents of these different numbering systems have well-reasoned arguments for their choices. Also, these numbering systems haven't always been fixed: some of the earliest decks didn't use any numbering. The oldest Tarot numbering system comes from the fifteenth century, and while its cards have the familiar pictures, much of the sequence is different: the Popess (which corresponds to the High Priestess) is "Four," the Hermit is "Eleven," Justice is "Twenty," and some of the other cards have different numbers as well. Because the numbering and sequence of the cards make philosophical statements about the individual's journey through life, Mary K. Greer suggests that "variations in tarot order reflect variations in world view."[4] Fortunately, I haven't found this to be a stumbling block in my own practice, and allow myself to be guided by whichever deck I am using.

You will also find that while most of the people who write books on Tarot tend to agree on most of the cards' meanings (especially if they are writing about the same deck), there are cases where even the most respected authors and other interpreters may assign different meanings to a given card. In the chapters of this book on the interpretation of individual cards, I discuss the reasons why certain people may see different things in a given card, and suggest ways to reconcile different systems. Because any Tarot symbol can apply to many different aspects of human life, different readers key in to different things, based on their own intuition and experience. They bring different insights, opinions, and training to interpretation, and they may adhere to different theories about systems such as the numerological significance of the cards. Tarot artists add to this diversity because their own biases are reflected in their artwork, creating positive or negative impressions of certain cards, which are then perpetuated by the authors who work with them.

So how should a person, especially a beginner, deal with so much variety?

Although card decks and systems of interpretation can differ, the differences are usually fairly minor. When you do encounter a new system, especially one that is substantially different, take things slow and easy; trust your intuitive responses to the cards. For the time being, you can lay out the cards according to the methods suggested in this book, the book that came with your cards, or any other book you have at hand. Once you've laid out the cards, try to analyze your first impressions: what do you think about the images before you? How do they make you feel? Then, you can look up the meanings of the cards you've drawn in this or any other book. Think about how the card meanings in your book correspond to your own impressions, and how it all relates to the question that you have asked. Also, don't worry if everything doesn't make sense right away. Accept that your mind is going to work on other levels, and eventually card meanings will become more obvious to you; you will also develop the ability to understand how their meanings apply to specific questions.

In my case, I sometimes work with new and different systems when friends ask me to read with their decks, or when I'm studying them for purposes of comparison. At such times, I do a little mental reconciliation. I will think about the general meanings of the cards as I have learned them and try to understand why the cards' designers chose to illustrate them with certain images instead of others. I look for ideas that the old and new systems hold in common, but I also try to be open to the new concepts that the deck's designer has introduced, as this is one of the best ways to achieve new insights. Because I believe in a cosmic ordering principle, I pay attention to significant differences in a card's images and its designers' interpretations, considering whether they have unique messages for me at this time. In other words, I believe that I may have been guided to a certain deck on a certain occasion because it has something special to say to me or to the person for whom I am reading.

Don't let the existence of all the different Tarot decks make you worry about whether you've chosen the right one. In keeping with the idea of cosmic ordering principles, I believe that whichever deck first falls into your hands is probably good enough until you come across one that you like better. If you decide to switch to another deck that is quite different, you will find that it's not difficult to learn a new system because you will already have had practice learning the principles of interpretation. You will also be able to carry over a number of the insights you've gained with earlier packs of cards. For example, I believe that my experience with the *Tarot of Marseilles* deck has added new dimensions to my understanding of the Rider-Waite-Smith deck. It is sometimes in the process of comparison that some of the best insights are gained.

It's important to be aware that none of the Tarot cards' meanings are fixed or limited to what you might read in the manuals. There is no one, true, right, and only way to interpret a given card. The images within the cards have many different nuances and shades of meaning that will change with their context or apply to different aspects of a person's inner or outer world. Because different people will react to a given symbol differently, readings must also be interpreted with the reactions of both the reader and the person receiving the reading in mind. This is part of the fine-tuning process that everyone who reads the Tarot will develop over time.

Accuracy in Reading and Prediction

As I mentioned in the introduction, I believe that the Tarot and other methods of divination work because our inner and outer realities are connected in such a way that they mirror each other. Because of this interconnectedness, this cosmic ordering principle, the cards come up in personally meaningful patterns. For this reason, you don't need to be psychic, or experienced with the cards, or even having a good day to get an accurate reading. Nevertheless, this ordering principle doesn't work the way we want it to 100 percent of the time, so it is possible to get inaccurate or impenetrable readings. Because readings aren't totally reliable, you should never allow yourself to become frightened or upset, make life-altering decisions, or form a bad opinion about someone just on the basis of a Tarot reading. Rather, the Tarot should be viewed as a tool to be used in combination with your own intuition and common sense, in helping you to analyze all of your possibilities. You have to evaluate the reading in the light of what you already know from your feelings and experience, and then look for other information to help confirm it. Even experienced readers can be baffled or draw wrong conclusions from a reading. I read my own cards practically every day, and I still get some readings when, even though I understand the basic meanings of the cards, I can't always see exactly how they apply to me, or what it is they are predicting. Sometimes the meanings only come out with the passage of time.

However, there are a few ways that you can judge potential accuracy while you are reading. For one thing, some readings just feel "hot," and you experience a lot of "Ahas!" On the other hand, some readings feel "cold." It may be that some days, more physical and psychical forces are aligned, and your own senses are more attuned, while other days things are not working together as well. Although your reading may still be accurate, it may seem more strained—and sometimes a reading can be flat-out wrong. But don't let this worry you. Use good judgement, and trust that for your bad days there will also be very good days, and that you'll achieve greater precision with practice.

Also, some layouts, such as the Celtic Cross, have card positions relating to events of the past, present, and future; if you are doing such a layout and the cards dealing with past and present represent things accurately, then chances are that the whole reading is on target. When a card that often serves as your significator comes up in a reading, this is a good sign that the Tarot is speaking directly to you. If the cards you are drawing seem to speak to your question, that is, cards about relationships come up in response to a question about relationships or cards about career areas come up in response to a question about career choices, that, too, is a good sign that your reading is on target. (However, cards that don't seem to answer your question, that seem to deal with something else entirely, can still be accurate—sometimes the Tarot has a will of its own, overriding your questions when there's something else it wants to tell you.)

When readings seem to be inaccurate or their predictions don't come true, there can be a number of other factors involved: some readings are just difficult to interpret because they point to things with which you may have little experience, or else their meanings correspond to aspects of your life that haven't been covered in any of the Tarot manuals. To give you an example, when I was a very busy young mother and housewife, I noticed that the Seven of Swords, which shows a man sneaking away from a tent with a load of swords in his arms, often came up in my daily readings. A common manual describes this card as denoting, "unstable effort, partial success . . . The seeker finds someone trying to make away with that which is not his."[5] I had a hard time figuring out how that applied to me until I realized that it came up on days that I did the household shopping. I assure you that I am not a shoplifter—rather, in relation to my case, the card's picture-image of a person with his arms full suggested a person carrying bags of groceries. In retrospect, I must admit that the part of the text describing "unstable effort, partial success" also applied to this situation: as a very overworked young woman, I didn't enjoy shopping because it was a hassle that was never finished (since I just had to go back for more the next week), and I was accompanied by two small children with a penchant for running off in different directions or misbehaving in public. However, this card could just as well apply to someone who enjoys shopping and sees bargain hunting as a creative challenge. These days, now that I am able to devote more time to reading and research, the Seven of Swords can come up on days when I go to the library, so the image is more suggestive of me when I'm walking out the door with a load of books in my arms. This is an example of how the cards can take on highly personalized, "idiosyncratic," nonstandard meanings. Over time, you may discover that certain cards have taken on special meanings for you.

Sometimes readings can be influenced by a type of interference. A person's emotions can be so strong that instead of accurately representing a situation or predicting the future, the cards will instead reflect the reader's or querent's current mood (especially if reader and querent are the same person). A person may also find it difficult to sort out all of her questions or personal issues. This is why little focusing rituals, such as those described under "mental preparation" in chapter 2, can be very important. Another type of interference can occur when something is distracting the reader. A memorable example of this happened when I was reading the *Lenormand* deck (not a Tarot deck, but the cards do have very pretty pictures), doing a series of three-card spreads for a friend. I had difficulty concentrating because my baby son was crying in another room, even though other friends and family members were looking after him. I didn't want to continue the reading, but my friend was insistent. However, the cards' responses didn't apply to his questions. Instead, the card that represents a child kept coming up in the central position. My concern for my child evidently took over the reading.

Another thing that may affect the quality of a reading is the deck you use. Although I mentioned earlier that most people usually find fairly good decks to work with, there are exceptions. It seems that some decks just don't work well for certain people, perhaps due to a subconscious incompatibility, even though their cards may have artistic quality and use conventional imagery. Therefore, if your readings seem to be a bit "off," experiment with another deck.

When a reading doesn't come true, it is possible that your foreknowledge of an event caused you to change your behavior in some way, thereby altering the future. Of course, this is one of the main reasons for doing fortunetelling in the first place—to be warned of potential problems so you can avoid them. Also, many outside influences can bring about change. Sometimes the cards themselves can provide clues as to whether the predicted outcome is more or less likely to be subject to change. As mentioned in chapter 2, the future is mutable. Because some cards point to more mutable situations, they open the possibility for more changes and unexpected turns of events. Odd cards represent movement and change, while even cards represent balance and stability, so there is more of a potential for surprise when the odd cards come up. (Likewise with some Major Arcana cards such as the Fool, the Wheel of Fortune, Death, and the Tower.) There also tends to be more activity with Wands and Swords, so readings with more potential for the unexpected are those that feature odd-numbered Wands and Swords cards. Because reversed cards can show situations that take more effort to bring into reality, they also deal with more uncertainty.

Reading for Other People

Reading for other people enables you to enter a special quality of relationship with them. It creates a type of "opening up" between two individuals, so that even normally shy people will be surprised and delighted by the rapport that develops and the energy that flows between them. Through the act of reading, you automatically start attuning to other people, receiving startling revelations about how the cards' meanings apply to their personal situations. Among the greatest highs that come from Tarot reading are those that occur when you are able to confirm something that the other person already knows or suspects, but which you could not possibly have known, and when the other person recognizes that the insights you provided have shown him the way out of a problem.

Because of this opening up and free flow of energy that occurs between the reader and the querent, it is, of course, important to read for nice, sympathetic people. If you are still a beginner, you might want to inform the people for whom you're reading, so they will be more patient and understanding.

Also, as a matter of self-protection, it is wise to avoid reading for people who don't want you to read for them. Often, your friends will become so enthusiastic once they know you do Tarot, that they will try to pressure other friends into having you read for them. It's fairly easy to tell when people don't want their fortunes read, because they act tense, reserved, or sarcastic, and there is usually somebody standing behind them, coaxing them to have the reading. Unfortunately, if that person is unreceptive, your energy will flow out, but it won't be returned—leaving you suddenly drained. Therefore, if you believe that someone doesn't want her fortune told, you might tell her, "I sense that you feel uncomfortable about having your cards read. Because the ethical rules of Tarot reading require that I not read for anyone who is uncomfortable, let's call it quits for today. We can always do this another time, if you feel different about it later." Alternately, if you think that would offend her, you could tell a little white lie, begging off because you've developed a headache or something.

Because of this energy flow, this vibrational resonance, the energy body of a sensitive reader can become synchronized with that of the querent, which is why I must also insert a warning about reading for people with serious drug or alcohol problems: their energy bodies have become deranged, you could say "reformatted," by their substances, even when they aren't momentarily under the influence. (Although I mentioned in chapter 1 that I've never had a problem with bad vibes getting into my card deck, I have been directly, physically affected by people with the wrong kinds of energy.) By attuning to their energies, you may experience a yucky feeling, like having the flu, feeling tired, queasy, confused, irritable, or being out of kilter. I have never read for anyone with a severe mental or physical illness, but I suspect that a reader could develop similar problems in such cases, or possibly have a temporary experience of some of their symptoms. It's best to avoid reading for certain people; however, if you should have such an experience, it's important to restore your equilibrium by bathing, going for a walk in nature, getting a massage from a friend, diverting yourself by watching an entertaining film, or doing other things that help clear your mind and refresh your spirit.

As you read for other people, you will find that they have many different ways of reacting to you. Some will be very enthusiastic, getting actively involved and discussing what each card could mean to them. (I encourage people to discuss each card, because it is often in the act of talking over their symbolism that the greatest personal insights are achieved.) Others will sit silently and give you no indication as to whether they're enjoying the reading or finding it meaningful. For such people, you must try to interpret the cards to the best of your ability, and have faith that they're getting something out of the experience. Usually, once the reading is over, they will admit that they found it very helpful, even though they may have given no signs of interest. In fact, after the reading their expressions will often change, and then they will become more talkative. They probably had personal reasons for sitting so still, including the desire to test you or to avoid influencing the reading. On the other end of the spectrum are people who practically take over the reading by trying to tell you a thousand details about their life stories with every card that you draw. You may possibly find this embarrassing because it doesn't leave you with much to say, and you may worry that other people will think that you don't know much about the cards and are just encouraging your subjects to talk so that they will spill all their own secrets. Do not be concerned about this, because for these people, just having the opportunity to talk about themselves is what they find most pleasurable and therapeutic about having their cards read. It doesn't matter whether you're able to wow them with your stunning insights—they will go away thinking that you're a terrific reader, even if they didn't allow you to get a word in edgewise.

While you are doing a reading for someone, don't worry about whether you'll be able to remember every important thing that there is to say about each card that comes up. After the reading, you may realize that there were additional things you would have liked to have pointed out, but either you forgot or didn't get a chance. Nevertheless, you will find that there was still plenty to talk about, and your querent will have had more than enough to do with processing the information that came up. Readings tend to take their own courses and have their own momentum, so trust that the things that you do discuss will be very meaningful for the person for whom you're reading. Despite all of my experience, I still overlook certain things; although I blame this on a learning disability that causes weird shifts of focus in my mind, I suspect that other readers probably can't think of everything all the time.

Another important thing to remember when reading for others is that because of the nature of human life, sometimes there will be bad readings or bad news. Most people understand that life is full of setbacks, and appreciate your being direct with them—though, of course, you should word things carefully so that you don't scare someone with warnings of disaster. If a reading predicts a disappointing outcome, you can discuss things the person can do to make changes, and you can follow up with an advice reading (see appendix B) for further suggestions on how to counteract the problem. Furthermore, you can remind your friend that sometimes a reading can be in error, or that other things can change. Always emphasize the positive aspects of any reading, and encourage your querents to leave with a "can do" attitude.

Now, let's go over a few things to remember about card interpretation.

Reversed Cards

The interpretation of reversed cards is a bit tricky, so some readers prefer not to use them—they shuffle their decks carefully so that all the cards remain upright. Some readers have philosophical reasons for not using reversals; they feel that the Tarot cards contain all the information you need in their upright position, with different cards showing the positive and negative aspects of life. Those who do use reversed cards have different systems for interpreting them: some believe that a reversed card represents the opposite of the situation or personality type depicted, while others believe it shows the more negative or the most extreme expressions of a card.

However, with a number of other readers, myself included, reversed cards have pretty much the same meaning and potential as upright cards, but they are interpreted as being more questionable, more uncertain—as having some difficulty in fully expressing their energies. Often their expression is milder, more low-key. Sometimes they may represent forces that are working on more of a subconscious level, and there may also be some resistance on the part of the person who is experiencing them. They may denote events that are unfolding on a slower timetable; they may also be more subject to change or vulnerable to disruption by outside factors. Depending upon the situation, a reversed card could denote either a situation that is just starting to develop (and is therefore not yet fully expressed), or an already existing situation that is now beginning to break up and fade away. Generally speaking, if you get a reversed card, it means that you have to work a little harder at bringing its qualities and predictions into full reality—unless it depicts something that you don't want to happen, in which case there is a better chance of preventing it.

In the case of court cards and other cards representing peoples' personalities, I often find that a reversed card denotes someone who is not comfortable or experienced in the role that he is acting out. For example, a reversed King or Queen of Swords could denote a normally "soft" person who has been placed in a position in which he has to get tough with other people. I differ from some other interpreters in that I tend not to see the reversed card as representing a bad or corrupted person unless it's accompanied by other negative cards, or unless it confirms what you already know to be true of the person in question.

I admit that I do sometimes find reversed cards annoying, and sometimes it seems that they come up more often than uprights. They come up frequently in readings for young people. I believe that this is because teens and young adults are still starting out in life, so they haven't had a chance to develop all of their potentials, and aren't free to pursue all of their interests. What's more, most human beings, both young and old, seldom reach the states of transformation or perfection that are represented in certain cards, such as Judgement or the World, nor the highest expressions of different cards, such as the adepthood implied in certain versions of the Magician or the High Priestess. Most of us just struggle along from day to day, trying to improve ourselves wherever we can, but not always exemplifying the highest ideals that we would like to reach. But take heart—the fact that a card comes up at all, whether upright or reversed, means that its gifts are there for you if you want to go after them!

Gender in Cards

Most Tarot decks portray male and female figures in the illustrations of different cards, but it is important to remember that all of the cards are meaningful, regardless of a person's sex. Although, for the sake of convenience and clarity, I may use language like "the Magician . . . he . . . ," or "the High Priestess . . . she . . . ," a girl or woman can identify with the Magician's desire to assert his personal power in the material world, while a man or boy will benefit from cultivating the High Priestess' intuition and desire to understand her inner world.

Also, because our society's ideas about fixed gender roles are changing, the Tarot can provide ways for people to explore both their inner feminine and masculine natures. Thus, the appearance of the Queen of Cups in a man's reading may stand for an important woman in his life, but it could also denote his ability to show concern for other peoples' feelings. By the same token, the appearance of the King of Wands in a woman's reading could denote her ability to model "kingly presence" by asserting her ideas in a leadership position. Note that some people, particularly certain groups of feminists, are challenging the whole idea of an inner masculine and feminine, asserting that leadership and intuition are sex-neutral qualities, and that we only perceive them as masculine or feminine due to our cultural conditioning. I will sidestep that debate, but perhaps we can agree that many people in our society tend to view certain traits as being inherently more feminine or masculine, and that traditional Tarot interpretation reflects these beliefs. By the way, when reading for men, I have found that Queens may come up when the men are displaying traits they inherited from their mothers or grandmothers, and Kings can come up in women's readings when they are modeling traits belonging to their fathers or grandfathers.

Changes in attitudes toward gender are being reflected in Tarot interpretation practices. For example, in the past, Knights always represented men, but an increasing number of readers also use them to denote young women (and older women, too) in recognition of the fact that girls now have greater self-determination, and many are involved in important outer-world activities.

Because the standard Tarot uses gendered designations like "kings" and "queens," some sex stereotyping is apt to be present. Although I try to avoid sexism as much as possible, I also want to work within tradition, especially when writing a book for readers who will mainly be using traditional decks. Therefore, I do go along with some conventional sex roles in describing Queens as being more concerned with different modes of nurturing and Kings as asserting power over others, especially in the business world. Of course, large numbers of people identify with these traditional roles and personalities, and most social institutions depend upon them. However, I would argue that the Kings (and all men) do not represent a higher level of mastery and personal development than the Queens (and all women). In other words, the Kings are not automatically "better" than the Queens just because they're masculine and have been assigned a higher number. (There are systems out there that hold the belief that Kings are higher and better.) Other than that, I will leave it to you to decide to what extent you want to go along with tradition, based on the role that gender plays in your life and in your personal philosophy, and in those around you.

Themes within a Reading

After you've laid out your cards, but before you start interpreting them, it is a good idea to look over your spread to see if any major themes are emphasized. This will be the case if you have a large number of cards from the same suit.

Because the Major Arcana comprises about 30 percent of the Tarot deck, a layout in which more than three out of ten cards are Major Arcana cards reveals complex spiritual and psychological issues at work in your life (or that of your subject), even if your question involves some fairly ordinary matter. The situations and events depicted are likely to make more of an impact on you, being more significant to your life path than readings that have few or none of these cards. As it is, Major Arcana cards tend to dominate any reading in which they occur, exerting a strong influence over the situations represented by neighboring Minor Arcana cards, and adding emphasis to whichever positions they occupy.

On the other hand, a layout with all Minor cards indicates that the affairs of everyday life are commanding your attention. A layout that features a good number of Wands cards indicates a flurry of activity in your life, which can include different types of interactions with the outside world, multitasking responsibilities, and the struggle to act upon your ideas. When there is a large number of Cups cards, your spiritual and emotional life is in focus, and there may be an emphasis on the quality of your relationships. A spread with many Swords cards alerts you that much mental and emotional energy will be expended on things like personal causes, the defense of your rights, and ideological conflicts. And with a large number of Pentacles, the main theme may be material world concerns, such as things having to do with your money, possessions, business, and personal security issues; your work and study, as well as your values, may also be areas where you will be concentrating your energy.

Take notice of the cards' numbering, as numbers repeated two or more times can also point to certain themes. Thus, many Aces would indicate that you will be experiencing all kinds of new energies, new projects, and other new beginnings. The Twos highlight relationships and choices: you may be in the process of trying to make adjustments in your life in order to get along with another person, or your interests, ideas, and responsibilities may be pulling you in different directions. Threes point to creative activities and exchanges; community relations may also be prominent in your reading. With Fours, your ability to build solid foundations and enjoy material things is important to the matter in question, and there could also be a focus on things having to do with your home life. A layout featuring several Fives shows forces of change at work, sometimes leading to the destabilization of a formerly secure situation. Along with this, you may be taking risks and seeking stimulation, competition, and challenges. Sixes reveal that you have come to a point in a cycle where you can relax somewhat, enjoying peace, harmony, and social pleasures. A reading with a number of Sevens is characterized by challenges that arise while you are trying to live your dreams or plan for the future. Multiple Eights place importance on the way you've got different areas of your life organized, and they show your energies in a tight holding pattern. Nines show the multiplication of possibilities in your life, but they can also point toward the completion of cycles. Tens signal the end of one cycle and the beginning of another. Tens can also show that your family responsibilities are important to the matter in question.

It is also significant when a number of court cards come up in a spread. Court cards require some thought in order to determine whether they represent other people, or whether they illustrate the different roles that you have to play in your relationships to other people, and in your need to deal with different areas of life. Of course, in the way that outer world things mirror inner-world issues, the people in our lives often mirror different stages of our personal development. Consequently, the presence of many court cards can reveal that your situation requires having to interact with different types of people, and that these other people will exert some influence over the outcome. Court cards also place emphasis on your "relational Self," that is, your need to be different things to different people, and to shift into different modes of relating.

Sometimes you will draw several of the same type of court card. Two or more Pages could mean that you are concerned about some children or young friends, but they could also highlight your role as a learner, and as someone who is opening to new experiences. Pages also have a traditional association with messages, so they could denote an activity or period of time with numerous communications going back and forth. With two or more Knights, the layout may signal the arrival of friends who will get you involved in many activities, or it could show your ability to get out into the world and start putting your skills to the test. Knights also have a traditional association with travel, so a lot of movement could be indicated. The appearance of Kings and Queens can show different aspects of your relationship with your parents—the same parent can be many different things to you. It can also denote influential men or women who have the power to help you. Alternately, several Kings or Queens may indicate that you are empowered to take on a number of different responsibilities, possibly where you will be in charge of other people.

Occasionally, you will draw several court cards belonging to the same suit. The appearance of several members of the Wands court may characterize a reading focused on your relationships with action-oriented people, or your developing different ways of acting on your ideas. The Cups court can denote interactions with friendly people who are particularly interested in your well-being, or it can show your developing realization of a need to relate to others in more personal ways. With the Pentacles court, your dealings with other people may involve practical matters, or you may have different types of work or study responsibilities. Cards from the Swords court may point to some conflicted relationships in which you feel challenged to defend your values and ideas, or they may suggest that you approach different areas of life in an argumentative or problem-oriented manner.

Clues in the Graphic Designs

Although you should first consider a card's conventional meanings (along with your own intuitive reactions to the card), there are times when normally insignificant elements within a card's illustration can take on some special meanings. In one of my memorable daily readings, I did a Three-Card Spread, and two of the cards that came up had pictures of boats and stretches of water in the background. As it happened, I was invited to go sailing that day. Therefore, although incidental things in the illustrations, such as animals, buildings, mountains, and so on, are usually just symbols that enhance the overall meaning of a card, you can observe unfolding events to see if any of these symbols come up in other areas of your life. Colors may also be meaningful in this way, with the predominant color scheme of a card playing a role in your day. (See appendix C for more about color symbolism.)

Another way that the elements in the graphic designs can take on special meanings is when figures within a card illustration are facing in a certain direction or pointing to some element within a neighboring card. For example, if the significators of a boy and girl come up facing each other, it can be a good sign that they like each other, but if their significators are facing in different directions, it could mean that they have had some differences of opinion. The direction that figures are facing could also indicate whether they are coming or going, or whether they are oriented to the future or the past. For this reason, reversed cards can also sometimes have special significance in addition to or instead of their normal meanings.

Positive and Negative Cards

Some cards, such as the Sun, the Star, and the World, are especially positive, and they also soften the meanings of any negative or disappointing cards in a reading. On the other hand, a card like the Devil is usually perceived and experienced as bad news. However, most cards have to be evaluated in the context of your question and circumstances, and also analyzed in association with any cards that accompany them, in order to determine whether the outlook is good or bad. For example, the Five of Swords usually has more negative implications, but because it can relate to competition, challenges, and issues of inclusion and exclusion in groups, it can be good news if you're wondering whether you'll make the team—especially if it is accompanied by more traditionally positive cards. However, it could also denote exclusion and the types of cruelty that cliques often inflict upon outsiders, especially if it is accompanied by negative cards, or if that makes sense in relation to your question.

Yes and No Answers

When a question asks for a yes or no answer, sometimes the response is evident from the cards that come up. For example, if you ask, "Will I have fun staying at my friend's house?" and you get cards showing people enjoying themselves, such as the Three or the Six of Cups, or other very positive cards such as the Star or the World, the answer would be "yes." However, another common technique for eliciting yes or no answers is to count the number of upright or reversed cards, with the idea that a majority of upright cards answers yes, while more reversed cards mean no. This is something that you might want to try if a reading is hard to interpret. For example, if you ask, "Will my friend pay back the money she owes?" and you get some cards that don't make a lot of sense in that context—such as the Four of Cups, the Two of Wands, and the Six of Swords—you might try to interpret it from this perspective, noting whether more of these cards are upright or reversed. You can also apply this method more directly by simply asking your question with this in mind, then drawing a single card and relying for your answer upon whether it is upright or reversed.

Timing of Events

When using the Tarot for predicting future events, you will often wonder when certain things are likely to take place—and there are different systems of timing that you can use. However, I must confess that I haven't found them consistently reliable, perhaps because the Tarot deals largely in the language of the unconscious, and as such, it resonates to the premodern, preindustrial mind, which is more concerned with the unfolding of its own psychological timetable, and is not well oriented to fixed calendar dates.

The method that I prefer links the Tarot cards to the seasons. (If you study preindustrial people, you'll notice that they tend to structure their lives around cycles and events in nature, reminiscing, "It happened during the year of the great windstorm," or planning, "I'll return in time for the grape harvest.") For general philosophical reasons, I equate Wands with spring, Cups with summer, Pentacles with autumn, and Swords with winter. Sasha Fenton,[6] Trish MacGregor, and Phyllis Vega[7] also make these associations (although Anthony Louis uses a system derived from astrology, which links the Swords to autumn and the Pentacles to winter).[8] To use this method, ask a question about the timing, such as, "When will the event indicated in the last spread take place?" Then shuffle and draw cards until you get one from the Minor Arcana. Aces represent the first week of the season, Twos the second week, and so on up into the Queens, which represent week thirteen. (There are fifty-two weeks in a year, with thirteen weeks in each season.) I use the leftover King to represent the most significant holiday within that season, while MacGregor and Vega suggest that the Kings represent seasonal transitions (which, being solstices and equinoxes, are also ancient holy days).

A more common way of seeking the approximate date of an event is to ask a question like, "When will love come into my life?" or "When will the event predicted in the last reading take place?" and then draw one card. Don't pay attention to its conventional meaning, but look at its numbering—having decided in advance whether the numbering will represent days, weeks, months, or years, depending on what seems most probable for your question. Thus, if you've decided to interpret the cards in terms of weeks, an Ace would represent one week, as would the Magician. A King would stand for fourteen weeks, as would Temperance. The highest you could go is twenty-one weeks, represented by the World. Since the Fool card is designated "Zero," I would let this card be an indicator that due to unknown or as yet unformed factors, the timing cannot be foretold. With reversed cards, the timing would be less certain, more subject to forces of change.

Some even more refined methods for timing designate different suits as representing days, weeks, months, and years. For example, Laura G. Clarson assigns Cups to days, Wands to weeks, and Pentacles to months. In her system, Swords mean that the timing is undetermined (although a person could let the Swords stand for years). Major Arcana cards show events that are already in the process of unfolding.[9]

Note that certain cards give clues as to what kind of time element is involved, related to their graphics and other traditional associations. Thus, the Hanged Man can denote a period of stasis where nothing seems to be happening, while the Chariot shows movement toward a goal. Also, in her book *Tarot Handbook,* Angeles Arrien tends to assume a timing factor that is built into the cards, so in addition to everything else it stands for, the events denoted by a card like the Three of Cups are likely to be experienced over a period of three weeks or three months, the events in the Star in seventeen weeks or months, and so on.

4 SAMPLE READINGS

To demonstrate the use of some of the layouts described in chapter 2, as well as some of the reading techniques in chapter 3, this chapter provides reconstructions of readings that I've done for young friends. Most are three-card spreads, but I also include a reading done with the Celtic Cross. To respect privacy, the querent's names and certain other details have been altered.

Sharon wanted to know what was in the future for her romance. She was dating a young man named Jonathan, who seemed fairly nice, but there were some inequalities in their relationship and differences in their backgrounds that could lead to problems. At that time, their relationship was becoming more intense, although Sharon seemed to be more serious about it than Jonathan. We did a Three-Card Spread in order to show the general state of the future, and used The Witches Tarot *by Ellen Cannon Reed and Martin Cannon. The cards drawn were the Sun, the Ten of Cups, and the Seven of Wands.*

The Sun   *Ten of Cups*   *Seven of Wands*

The Sun is a card of happiness—often predicting love, marriage, and children—and the fact that it is a Major Arcana card adds emphasis. The Ten of Cups is also very much a traditional card of love, marriage, family, and happiness. Although *The Witches Tarot Deck* does not use an illustration of a happy family group for this card, as is most common, its striking picture of a woman with a crystal and glowing cups creates an instant impression of romance and emotional fulfillment. Based on these first two cards, the reading strongly pointed to a happy and committed relationship. The meaning of the third card, the Seven of Wands, was more difficult to apply because it can have mixed meanings. Generally, it denotes the creative challenges as well as the social struggles involved in living according to your ideals. Its most common illustration depicts a young man fending off a number of staves that are thrust upward toward him, showing that he has a lot to contend with; however, it generally implies that he'll hold his own. *The Witches Tarot Deck* has taken a different tack: its picture of an artist working at his easel emphasizes the creative potentials in this card. We interpreted this card as predicting that some problems were likely to come up, but that difficulties might be managed with cleverness and cooperation, since the other cards were so strongly positive. Sharon and Jonathan did get married about a year later. They had some early difficulties with resistance from families, as well as getting started economically. However, Jonathan got a good job, which enabled Sharon to stay home when their baby came along. They are now enjoying the type of traditional family life hinted at in the cards.

Note: Although I have included Sharon's reading to provide an example of a positive spread about a relationship that proved successful, I must point out that many questions about young romance do not get such favorable responses. Most young people find that the cards bring up outer-world issues that have to be dealt with before relationships can develop into something more serious.

> *Joe wanted to know why his father seemed irritable and remote. A past-present-future reading using the Rider-Waite-Smith deck and a Three-Card Spread featured the Seven of Cups reversed, the Nine of Cups reversed, and the Knight of Cups reversed.*

Seven of Cups
Reversed

Nine of Cups
Reversed

Knight of Cups
Reversed

This reading was all Cups, which put the emphasis on the father's emotional life. The fact that the cards were all reversed revealed that the father was going through emotional difficulties, and the combination of so many reversed cards also brought out their more negative potentials. The Seven of Cups reversed showed that he had experienced some disillusionment, even a loss of his dreams. The Nine of Cups reversed depicted a loss of material as well as emotional comforts. Because the Nine is the "wish card," its reversal can also reveal disappointment in pursuing dreams. The reversed Knight of Cups showed the father retreating inward emotionally, which made his family feel like he had withdrawn his affection. Also, the fact that the Knight of Cups came up instead of his normal significator, the King of Pentacles, showed the father in a less empowered position, acting out a role that he was not comfortable with. Joe already knew that his father was worried about something, but this showed him that the situation was possibly worse than he had been aware of. It turned out that office politics had created what is called a "hostile work environment." Things got worse before they got better—his dad didn't get a promotion or the raise that he deserved, and had to get counseling for depression. At least this reading helped Joe to have a better understanding of his father, and encouraged further communication.

Two sisters thought their family pet, a canary, looked ill, and wanted to know whether or not he would get better. A reading using the Three-Card Spread featured the Nine of Pentacles reversed, the Hermit, and the Seven of Wands reversed. (Note that this was more of a situational reading; it did not specify whether the cards would represent past, present, and future, although we considered that possibility as a secondary level of interpretation.)

Nine of Pentacles
Reversed

Hermit

Seven of Wands
Reversed

This is an interesting example of how graphic elements within the cards can be very literal. Many versions of the Nine of Pentacles show a woman with a bird. Since this was a question about a bird, we can see that the Tarot had chosen this card as the canary's significator, and it also showed us that the reading was on target. Because this card was reversed, it showed him in a position of weakness. Under some circumstances, the Hermit can stand for an elderly person, and as far as anyone knew, the bird was fairly old (he had belonged to someone else previously). When the Seven of Wands—which shows a man fighting off some poles that are aimed at him—is reversed, it can mean difficulties holding one's own. Since the overall reading shows old age and weakness, the outlook was not good. Despite their attempts to nurse him back to health, the bird died a few days later.

Sean was frustrated because his teacher had assigned group projects (they didn't get to choose their group members), and was planning to grade these projects on the collective success of the group, rather than on each person's contributions. Unfortunately, the other people in Sean's group weren't putting in much effort or coming up with good ideas, so he was worried about how things would go. He had a three-card reading to learn about the near future, and the cards drawn were the Three of Wands reversed, the Seven of Swords, and the Knight of Wands.

Three of Wands
Reversed

Seven of Swords

Knight of Wands

The Three of Wands reversed can show problems with a group project; this was the existing condition that was continuing into the very near future. However, it can also show that the group's creative energies are there to be tapped, and indeed, this group soon started to cooperate and communicate somewhat more, and better ideas were developed. The central card, the Seven of Swords, shows a person who takes his own initiative to solve a problem, though it may point toward only partial success. Perhaps partly due to the encouragement of this card, Sean took on more than his share of the work, with the consequence that the grade/project was better than it would have been, but not as good as it could have been had everyone carried his own weight. The final card, the Knight of Wands, is Sean's normal significator. Because it was upright, it showed him in a position of strength, and receiving recognition for who he is. Even though the project wasn't everything it could be, Sean had made the teacher aware of his extra work, and this may have made a difference when the teacher was calculating his final, overall grade.

Now, here's an example of the card search technique discussed in chapter 2.

Arthur was studying the Tarot, trying to learn a card a day. On this day, he focused on Strength, the eighth card in the Major Arcana, so he posed the simple question, "How does Strength function in my life?" After shuffling, he went through the deck until he found the Strength card, which was accompanied by Justice and the reversed Knight of Wands.

Justice   Strength   Knight of Wands
                                                   Reversed

The Justice card would indicate that his strength manifests through his fair-mindedness, his concern about doing the right thing, and his ability to see both sides of a matter, weighing the pros and cons of different questions. On the other hand, the reversed Knight of Wands seems to indicate areas where he is not as effective as he could be, suggesting that he could assert his personal power more skillfully if he were more clear and decisive about going after his dreams, acting on his ideas, and interacting with people. This requires adopting a "ready for action" type of mindset, which Arthur tended to resist, being more of a quiet, introverted young man.

By the way, this reading was done with *The Celtic Dragon Tarot,* in which the Wands are associated with the Air element (instead of Fire, as is more common). However, since the Dragon deck retains the same basic interpretations for the individual cards, it can still be used with this and other standard manuals. The general meanings have not been altered, but people interested in exploring elemental energies can ponder how some of the cards might have different nuances.

Now here's a longer, more involved reading, using the Celtic Cross Spread.

> *Evelyn, a seventeen-year-old woman, wanted an overview reading to get an idea of where her life was headed. She was looking forward to high-school graduation and making plans to attend a small college. She would live on campus because, although her new school was in the same state, it was not an easy commute. However, it was close enough for her to visit her family and friends—as well as her steady boyfriend—on weekends. Her boyfriend, Dan, was in the same grade as she, but he was still undecided about his future career, so he planned to take some classes at a local junior college. Although they had talked about marriage, they had put off any plans for the indefinite future.*

For the significator, Evelyn chose the Page of Pentacles, because she saw herself as a quiet, diligent student type. This reading was done some years ago, before it became more common to let Knights represent young women as well as men; if we were doing this reading today, we might have a discussion about whether she related more to the Knight of Pentacles or the Page.

Then, the first card in the spread, the one that "covers her," was the Chariot. This showed movement in her life, and as a Major Arcana card, it told us that great energies were carrying her forward on her life path. This card may have also pointed to her anticipated move to college in another town.

The second card, the card that "crosses her," was the Two of Wands, and it was reversed. The Two of Wands can denote the need to lead a double life or divide your energy two ways, so it could pertain to Evelyn's plans to divide her time

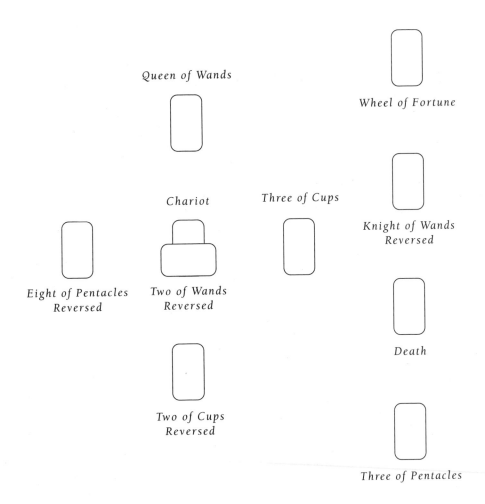

Queen of Wands

Wheel of Fortune

Chariot   Three of Cups

Knight of Wands
Reversed

Eight of Pentacles
Reversed

Two of Wands
Reversed

Death

Two of Cups
Reversed

Three of Pentacles

between weekends at home and weekdays at school, with their different sets of people to relate to. The Twos can also apply to personal relationships. When a person is in a close relationship, she must be willing to work around the needs of another person. All of these interpretations applied, because Evelyn was concerned about how her going away would affect her relationship with Dan. The fact that the Two of Wands was reversed showed a problem maintaining two lifestyles, as well as potential problems in the relationship. Evelyn admitted that she and Dan couldn't agree upon a shared vision for their future. (Once she was attending college, she found it difficult to go home every weekend because she had too much to do.)

"Below her" was the third card, the reversed Two of Cups. Notice the interesting coincidence of two reversed "Two" cards, emphasizing the fact that relationship issues were an important basis and crosscurrent of this reading. The card in this position reveals major motivating factors, including the reason for doing the reading; often these factors are below the level of consciousness. The reversed Two of Cups especially points to emotional difficulties in a relationship, and upon further discussion, Evelyn admitted that some aspects of her relationship with Dan were very unsatisfactory. In later years, she suggested what would, at the time, have been a very shocking thought—maybe she was actually looking forward to college because it would give her a chance to slowly end the relationship.

"Behind her," representing the influences of the recent past, was the fourth card, the reversed Eight of Pentacles, a card that can deal with getting things organized. This could apply to the preparations she'd been making for college: she had done a lot of planning and was doing a fairly good job of getting everything organized; however, there were still some things that needed to be done, including lining up more financial aid.

The fifth card, which "crowns her" or goes "above her," was the Queen of Wands. It is always significant as well as amusing when a King or Queen appears in this position, because of the pun on the word "crown," as well as this position's association with the inner King and Queen archetypes, which order personal growth priorities in the psyche. Cards in this position show our long-range goals, so this could indicate a desire to achieve the energy, creativity, and self-confident maturity that the Queen of Wands embodies. We had some discussions about this; because Evelyn envisioned herself as developing into more of a Queen of Pentacles type, we thought that the Queen of Wands just represented certain ideals of female empowerment. However, in the years that followed, Evelyn got into a major and then a profession that enabled her to "shine," so she did come to embody more of the fiery Queen of Wands qualities.

Card six, the Three of Cups, "goes before her." These are influences that are coming into being in the near future. This card's picture of dancing maidens was very reassuring, showing her that she would be among friendly, stimulating people.

At this point, let's pause to look at the human figures in the first six cards, which form the "cross" part of this reading. We see images of single individuals as well as couples (including the Two of Wands, which can represent couples) and trios; these cards show the need to develop as an individual, issues pertaining to one-on-one relationships, and a turning toward participation in somewhat larger groups—all common but important themes in many young adults' lives.

The seventh card, which reveals the role that she was acting out in this situation, was the Three of Pentacles, a card that stands for creative work and interactions with a productive community. Although Evelyn wasn't an art student, she took a craftsmanlike approach to her studies, and also looked forward to college as a means of identifying with a more creative crowd of people. In this latter respect, the Three of Pentacles echoed the previous card, the Three of Cups. Note that the second card and the third card (the Two of Wands and Two of Cups) also have shared themes. I find that this kind of "mirroring" or "doubling" happens a lot in readings—and not just in larger spreads like the Celtic Cross, but also in simple three-card spreads. It gives a reading a "holographic" quality, by which I mean that themes and images that come up in one part of the reading are reflected in others, emphasizing the importance and interconnectedness of those themes in the querent's life. This can also be another clue that a reading is on target. Common themes can also come up in cards that have similar graphic elements, or that are close to each other in meaning.

The eighth card, which represents her environment, was Death. The sight of this card is always alarming, but here we have an example of Death as denoting change, rather than someone's demise. (No one close to Evelyn died, either before or after the reading.) Rather, Death seems to have been foreshadowing the transformation that Evelyn would soon experience in her surroundings and in her way of life, as well as revealing that some separation was already taking place on a deeper level. She, Dan, her friends, and her family were already sensing this impending change, and there were also some other changes going on in some of their lives (though that would be too involved to discuss here).

The ninth card was the Knight of Wands, which was reversed. This position reveals the querent's hopes and fears—which I call her "issues." The Knight of Wands can represent involvement in major activities, but it can also represent a passionate romance coming into the querent's life. Evelyn had reasons for being concerned about both potential interpretations; she knew she would be attracted to many extracurricular activities, and realized that this would create problems with dividing her energies between home and campus; however, she also knew that college would open opportunities to meet interesting men—this is something she both feared (because she didn't want to be unfaithful to Dan), and also secretly looked forward to (because her relationship with Dan was already cooling). Her ambivalence regarding these issues was revealed in the fact that the Knight of Wands was reversed. Interestingly, because the Knight was reversed, he faced toward the right rather than the left (in the Rider-Waite-Smith deck), indicating movement toward the future, and also echoing the Death card below him, because the skeleton on horseback was also headed in that direction. Evelyn did indeed become involved in more activities than she could easily manage, and she eventually met another man (although that was somewhat later, toward the end of her college years). It is also significant that this card was another member of the Wands court; along with the Queen of Wands, this showed identity development that brings out more Wands-type qualities.

The tenth card, which was the Outcome card, was the Wheel of Fortune. This is a very complex and mystical card, portraying the workings of a person's greater destiny through special decisions, opportunities, and cycles of change. At the time, we took this to mean that college would bring some major changes in Evelyn's life, offering new opportunities that were significant to her life path. This was a reasonable prediction for someone in her position. However, it turned out that the Wheel would take several more spins, because in the years that followed, Evelyn also changed her major and transferred to a larger institution, and then went on to grad school at a university even farther away.

Now, having presented the high points of this reading, we can take another look at the big picture to consider its dominant themes. Among the main impressions that emerge from this layout are the themes of movement and change. Major changes are certainly portrayed in the Wheel of Fortune and Death, and these cards also show movement, as do the Chariot, the Knight of Wands, and even the Three of Cups with its lively, dancing maidens. In fact, these themes are so strong, it's like there's a big neon arrow pointing and saying, "Look at this." Sometimes the messages of the Tarot come in very loud and clear.

5   OTHER USES FOR THE TAROT

Before we get into the interpretive section of this book, I want to demonstrate some other ways that the Tarot can be an important resource. This chapter discusses the Tarot's use in meditation, visualization, and Tarot spells, as well as ways that it can help you with school work and certain types of learning disabilities.

Meditation

One of the most important traditional uses of the Tarot is in meditation. In fact, some scholars consider this its greatest value and believe that the Tarot was designed for this purpose and only later was applied to fortunetelling. As focal points for meditation, the cards' images can help you think about paths to spiritual self-improvement, broaden your understanding of the human conditions that we all share, and highlight the workings of archetypal forces in your life.

Among Tarot users, a common practice is to pull a card a day, then contemplate its meanings. You can actively think about it, read what different authors may have to say about it, and look around you for ways that its energies are expressed as you go about your life. This is essentially the traditional Western (European) approach to meditation, which is to think about something at great length.

Another way to meditate on a card is to find a calm, quiet place, then relax and hold the image of the card or one of the symbols within the card in your mind. (Beginners might try to see if they can sustain such an image for ten minutes or so.) After concentrating on this image, other images and impressions may flow into your mind, increasing your understanding of the card or symbol. However, don't try to force any images—just relax and concentrate. Even if nothing happens, your deep mind will go to work on the image, and meaningful revelations may pop up at a later time. The meditation may also trigger some interesting dreams that reveal more about the mysteries of the Tarot.

Two other techniques that I classify as meditative are called *Free Writing* and *Deep Description*. Free Writing is a term that is current in writers' workshops, and is a stream of consciousness technique. To do a free write on a Tarot card, select a card and then write down everything that comes to your mind about the card, including any chains of thoughts that may arise, even if they seem silly or unrelated. It doesn't matter whether you already know anything about the card in question. *Trust your intuition.* You know more than you think you know. It's a good idea to set a kitchen timer for ten minutes, and do not permit yourself to lay down your pen (or take your fingers off the keyboard) until the timer has rung. Do not stop to read and edit what you've written until the time is up, and pay no attention to "the critic within." It doesn't matter if it seems that what you're writing makes no sense, or whether it looks like it was written by a second grader. You will be surprised at the insights that emerge. *Trust the process.*

Deep Description also involves writing, but the discipline is quite different. For this type of exercise, set one of the cards in front of you and then write down everything you see in the card, noticing things like the colors used, incidental objects in the background or foreground, whether or not there is a border, what kind of lettering is used if there is a label, whether any of the objects or arrangements of objects form geometrical shapes, whether any of the human figures look out at you, what sort of gestures they are making, and much more. The trick here is to avoid blending description with speculation or analysis. In other words, write down *only* what you see; do not permit yourself to write down any other thoughts about what you see until afterward. Do not make any guesses about anything that is not actually featured in the picture, or form any opinion about the meaning of the card until you are done. This is very difficult to do because most people can't separate description from analysis—analysis always contaminates perception. But if you trust the process, revelations will arise once you have completed the exercise. By the way, if you can get a friend to try this using the same card, you may surprise each other with all of the things that one of you saw and the other did not, even when you both thought you couldn't possibly describe anything else.

Visualization

Tarot imagery can also be used in visualization exercises. Visualization practices can be similar to certain types of meditation in selecting images to hold in your mind. However, rather than trying to gain extra impressions about these images, you are trying to influence your unconscious mind by showing it the changes that you want to make, altering your reality to mirror the images you desire. Visualization is based on the theory (supported by clinical research) that the unconscious mind responds to vividly imagined mental pictures as if they were the real thing. It is best known for its role in alternative healing. For example, some cancer patients practice visualizations portraying their white blood cells as hungry birds or cats, gobbling up the cancer cells, which are imagined as bird seed or cat food.[1] As more doctors and patients invent some particularly good healing visualizations, they pass them around, thus building up a collection of usable images (a "cultural repertoire"). Visualization exercises are also being used to help people concentrate on studies, break bad habits, summon creative inspiration, and improve athletic performance.

Because the Tarot has such a rich supply of images, it is ideal for use in many types of visualizations. For example, suppose that you are someone who is preparing to take your driver's test, or perhaps someone who already has a license, but would like to improve your driving performance. You could get out the Chariot card, think about its different meanings, and carefully look over the image itself. Think about how the charioteer embodies the archetype of calm, superior performance. Concentrate on the image of the charioteer, and hold it in your mind. Now, imagine yourself as the charioteer. Envision yourself controlling the two horses (or sphinxes) as you race across some ancient desert (or drive along in some other fantasy scenario). Imagine what it feels like to have his knowledge, his experience, his discipline, his presence of mind. Now, change your mental image, merging into the present. Picture yourself getting into your car and driving confidently and skillfully. If you are going to take a test, picture yourself with the instructor, perfectly carrying out all of her directions. Since the Chariot is also associated with the "triumphs," the ancient victory processions, picture your own sense of triumph as you pass the test. If you need to build your confidence, you can regularly repeat this visualization. Whenever you go for a drive, or if you encounter a difficult situation in traffic or whatever, you can identify with the charioteer and call these images back into your mind. If you like, you can keep a copy of the Chariot in your car as a charm to help you reconnect with this image.

Now that you understand the idea behind Tarot visualization, you can probably come up with hundreds of useful images, tailored to your own interests and challenges. There's plenty of room for new people to invent new visualizations, because different individuals prefer different ones, and some like to use a variety of visualizations to tackle a particular problem. In fact, there is a big advantage in trying out a number of visualizations to deal with a particular problem or goal, because this activates different areas of the brain. As Jeanne Achterberg has said in relation to imagery and healing, it's a good idea "to recruit as many neural patterns of health as possible."[2] No doubt, this philosophy can be applied to many of the other things that you'd like to achieve. Because coming up with creative visualizations depends more on imagination than experience, this is an area where young people can contribute to our cultural repertory.

Tarot Spells

Tarot "spells" are a more elaborate form of visualization: you select a group of cards that tell a story, showing step by step what you want to achieve. You could describe spells as multimedia or multisensory techniques for focusing both the conscious and unconscious minds on bringing about change, because you can bring in candles, crystals, incantations, and so on. If you look at spellworking techniques, such as those you may find in traditional forms of folk magic or in such excellent modern works as Silver RavenWolf's *Teen Witch*[3] or Dorothy Morrison's *Everyday Magic,*[4] you will notice that they often involve visualizing a desired goal, saying incantations that are also "affirmations" that repeat verbal images (stating your desires as if they were already true), going through certain motions that act out the desired goal, or working with things like herbs, crystals, and handicrafts that are in some way connected to the goal. Experiments with visualization have revealed the scientific basis for spellworking: we can change our reality by sending strong positive images to the unconscious. These other spellworking techniques are other ways of communicating to the unconscious. They also work through the same cosmic ordering principles that enable Tarot patterns to be meaningful—making use of the interconnectedness of all things.

Because the Tarot has so many detailed images, it is a superb tool for use in spellworking and in combination with other magical techniques. The principle is very simple: to construct a Tarot spell, you go through your deck to find cards whose images relate to your goal, then string them together to tell the story that you want to unfold in real life, while also visualizing the action you want. To bring extra focus to your spell, you can tell this story out loud, in the form of affirmations. You can also use candles, gemstones, and other accessories in colors that relate to your goals. (See appendix C on colors.)

To give you an example, following is a blessing spell that you might use to turn the heart of someone who has been mean to you. If you are an average teen or young adult, you have probably had the experience of dealing with someone who doesn't like you—often for no apparent reason. Perhaps this is a class member with whom you're being forced to collaborate on a project, or someone who teases you and turns other people against you, or maybe even a brother or sister who may be resentful. By sending blessings to others, especially to people who don't like you, you communicate spirit to spirit, soul to soul, that you are a person of good intentions, and that you want to relate directly to the good that is within them. So, to perform such a spell, you could first light some pink candles to promote warmth and affection, or white candles for purity of intention, and you could wear a piece of rose quartz as a pendant or in a pouch, as rose quartz opens the energy center of the heart. Then, lay down a card that acts as your significator. (See appendix A on significators.) Next, lay down the Star (a blessing card) on top of your own significator, while saying, "I have the power of blessing, for I can draw from an infinite source of magic and goodness." Visualize yourself receiving the power of the Star (and of the stars); visualize yourself by the pool in the Star, pouring out the water and then refilling it, knowing this is really magical energy. Then, lay down the Two of Cups to the right of the Star. Visualize yourself as having filled two cups from the Star pond; imagine that now you give one to the person whom you are blessing, and hold the other one yourself, while saying out loud, "With the power within me, I extend the life energy of the universe. May it bless you, and may it bless me. Please know that I seek only goodness." Then, lay down a card chosen to be a significator for the other person, picturing him as being kind and friendly—how the person would look at his best, in order to call out the best. Immediately lay the Ace of Cups on top of that, and say, "To you I extend the hand of blessing. May all good things come to you, and may the power of goodness flow through you." Envision the person taking in the magical energy offered in the cup, causing him to feel warm and good and friendly. Hold these images in your mind for a few minutes, then close the spell by putting out the candles and saying, "So it is and so shall it be." You can put your cards away, or you can leave the arrangement sitting out for a while, if you have the space.

By the way, if you would like to learn more about this technique, I have written a book called *Tarot Spells*,[5] which contains over seventy positive spells similar to this one, though dealing with different subjects like love, health, prosperity, protection, and so on. However, if you understand the principle behind Tarot spells, you can learn to design your own.

Note: When you get a really good Tarot reading, you can treat it like a Tarot spell, doing a visualization for each card or burning candles by the layout, for example, to help stretch the good energy it brings. When you get a bad reading, rearrange or change some of the cards to make it a good reading, and then do the same.

Help with your Homework

In addition to using visualization techniques to improve concentration and skill, there are a number of ways that high-school and college students can use these and other types of Tarot visualizations to aid memory, to generate inspired ideas for essays and other projects, and to deal with certain types of learning challenges.

One way that you can use the Tarot is by identifying with card characters that exemplify different qualities of discipline, focus, concentration, and love of learning. When you need help with your studies, you can visualize yourself embodying these Tarot archetypes. Because the Magician is a very resourceful, quick-witted character, his image can be summoned for inspiration when taking an exam or giving an oral presentation. The High Priestess is concerned with probing the deeper mysteries of life, so she is a good image for anyone needing to go deep within some area of research. The Hierophant is a good model for people who identify with the very institution of learning and handing down traditions of knowledge, while concentrating on the Hermit can help bring resolve to students who know that they must cut back their social life in order to devote more time to their work. Many of the other cards also model different skills, types of discipline, dedication, and focus. In fact, you could use several cards in combination—for example, the Magician combined with the Eight of Pentacles can show you summoning your powerful will to get your work organized. There are effective images for students with other interests, too, such as Strength or the Chariot for athletes, or Temperance or the Star for artists.

Imaginative interactions with the Tarot characters can also help you with school assignments. By engaging in imaginary conversations with the figures pictured in the cards, you can better learn and remember the material you must study. This technique won't work on all assignments, but it may be able to help if you are studying a subject that can be broken down into blocks of information and ideas. For example, suppose that you are reading a science assignment on cell structure. As you start the chapter, the first paragraph is describing the protoplasm that cells are made of; after you read it, imagine that you are discussing the nature of protoplasm with the Fool (the "Zero" card), explaining it to him in your own words. Since he's the Fool, he will probably respond by making a joke about it, but that's okay. The fact of having had this conversation with him will sharpen your understanding and memory of protoplasm. Now, the next paragraph that you read is about the contents of the cell—its nucleus and cytoplasm—so imagine yourself discussing this with the Magician (card One of the Major Arcana); perhaps he will respond with some thoughts on how this is essential to the magic of life. Then you go on to the next paragraph, about the cell membrane, imagining that you are discussing this with the High Priestess (card Two). Proceed through your reading, bringing in the other Tarot characters, in numerical order. As you proceed, stop from time to time to review: "Let's see, the Fool comes first, that had to do with protoplasm; then there was card number One, the Magician, which was about the nucleus and the cytoplasm . . ." This may seem rather time consuming, but it will pay off because you will remember more. On test day, if you find you can't remember some of the terms or facts, try to recall which cards they were associated with. If you can think about the card, the contents of the conversation are likely to come back to you.

Here are some other examples of this technique: suppose you're studying angles in geometry—you could imagine the Fool drawing and then explaining (or joking about) a right angle, the Magician explaining obtuse and acute angles, the Priestess explaining complementary angles, and so on. If you're studying something that is debatable, such as history, literary analysis, or philosophy, you could actually imagine different Tarot personalities arguing the different sides of the debate. Again, it may not be possible to use this technique on all fields of study, but where you can, it's a good way to organize things in your memory.

These techniques are, in fact, inspired by a very ancient practice called the *Ars Memoria,* the Art of Memory, where you link things you need to memorize with a sequential set of images.

Sometimes students are required to write essays about their own lives. In such cases, the Tarot can help you probe the meanings of your experiences. For example, suppose that you have been asked to write about a major turning point in your life. As you look back over significant events—possibly a move to a new town, the beginning or end of a friendship, a birth, death, or divorce in the family, becoming involved in a sport, social club, or hobby, and so on—you can ask the cards questions like, "What did I get out of this experience?" or "What sort of forces were at work in this experience?" By contemplating the ways that the cards you draw might apply to your experience, you may gain some philosophical insights that will add extra layers of interest and meaning to your paper. Also, the layout of your cards may even suggest ways of organizing your thoughts in sections or paragraphs. For example, using the Celtic Cross spread described in chapter 2, you could organize your paper in terms of (1) a prominent theme of the experience, (2) conflicts or crosscurrents that were present, (3) how your underlying motivations influenced the situation, (4) the influence of the past, (5) long-term goals that have been affected by this experience, and (6) how this experience has influenced the present or your expectations for the near future.

Another way to bring the Tarot into your studies is to think about the general meanings of the cards and the personalities of the card characters in relation to people, events, and settings in literature, poetry, history, and so on. For example, suppose you're reading *The Great Gatsby*, by F. Scott Fitzgerald. You could think of Nick, the narrator, as the Fool, because he traveled to New York and into a new situation as a total innocent. Jay Gatsby may be considered a failed Magician because he reinvented himself and built up this fabulous life, but it's based upon an illusion. Tom and Daisy could be the Emperor and Empress because of their wealth and power (though they use their power carelessly). Daisy could also be the High Priestess, at least from Gatsby's point of view, because of the ideals and mysteries she embodies for him. It has been pointed out that Gatsby's car and American car culture are central to the story, so you might think about how all of this relates to the Chariot. Other characters and situations may be applied to other cards. Among others, the Lovers, the Devil, the Tower, Death, and Judgement certainly fit into the plot. Another example: you could look at a complex literary and historical personality and analyze the different archetypes that were contending within that person. Most people have a number of activated archetypes within their personalities, and more interesting literary characters will also be more complex. Thus, you could study the life and character of someone like Napoleon, Winston Churchill, or Abraham Lincoln, and ask yourself, *To what extent was he a King of Swords? a King of Pentacles? an Emperor? a Magician?* and, *What roles did the archetypes of the Chariot, Justice, the Tower, and so on, play in his life?* While not all literary or historical personalities will correspond neatly to the Tarot card types, thinking about the ways that they do apply will help you to develop a greater knowledge of the cards at the same time that you will be gaining new insights into your subjects of study.

You can probably think of additional ways that Tarot images, even those in the Minor Arcana, may be of help in your studies. For example, they can serve as sources of inspiration for art and poetry. Try to keep a running list of associations for each card, and note how individual cards may relate to situations in your life, scenes from movies and television programs, lyrics from songs and passages from poems, famous quotations, events in history, principles of natural science, theories in psychology and philosophy, and so on. In this way, you will eventually be able to make connections between a number of seemingly unrelated things, and you may even get some fresh ideas for essays and term papers. What's more, this will enable you to become part of what is known as "a community of discourse," which means that when you meet people who are doing the same thing, you'll have plenty to talk about. People in the Tarot community are always eager to learn new card image associations, so this, too, is an area where young people can make original contributions.

Tarot and Learning Disabilities

The above discussion on how to bring visualization into your studies offers suggestions that would be helpful for anyone, but they may especially be of use to two types of people (1) they can provide learning shortcuts for people who have a visual learning style and therefore don't respond well to traditional academic methods, and (2) they can help students who have the opposite problem (a weak visual memory) by helping to build strong visual associations.

I designed some of these techniques for my younger son (a college student at the time of this writing) who has been diagnosed with Asperger's syndrome, which is an autistic spectrum disorder. Like many other young people with this problem, he "thinks in pictures," which makes it very difficult to read printed words, due to the tedious process he has to go through in translating words into picture images and back again. (For visualization and study purposes, he likes the Cannon-Reeds' *The Witches Tarot Deck* because of its bold, action-oriented figures.) Many of his friends also have forms of autism, ADD (attention deficit disorder), dyslexia, and other sensory processing problems, so my familiarity with their special challenges has also influenced my interest in alternative learning techniques, and it has informed some of my writing about the Tarot's messages for young adults, since those with cognitive difference may be especially attracted to things like the Tarot. (Cognitive difference refers to different ways of perceiving, experiencing, and interpreting the world, whether due to differences in brain structure and chemistry, upbringing, or other factors.)

Some of the conditions referred to as learning disabilities don't just influence learning, they can also exert control over a person's behavior. Whether or not you have one of these disorders, Tarot imagery can help you make sense of situations that come up and form strategies for self-improvement, so you can be the one in control.

For example, suppose that you have ADD, or are a person who sometimes has trouble controlling impulses, and that you recently got in trouble for talking back to a teacher—even though you felt that you were telling the truth, and were justified in what you said. You could go through the Tarot deck and pull out cards that seem to describe your situation. You might come across the Page of Wands, and recognize it as one of the main cards dealing with communications. (The *Hanson-Roberts Tarot* deck does a good job of illustrating this, because it has a close-up portrait of the page with his mouth open.) With this card before you, you could think back over your own history as a communicator, about where you have communicated skillfully, and where you have gotten yourself in trouble. You might consider whether a reversed Page of Wands might represent this unskillful aspect of your nature, and whether its appearance in future Tarot readings might warn you of the need to be more tactful. Now you might pull out the Hierophant, which can represent teachers and institutions of learning; you contemplate this card while you think about the history of your relationships with your teachers, and your general attitudes toward school authorities. Perhaps you feel that they've been making all kinds of rigid and unreasonable rules that don't take account of human needs. Nevertheless, they exert a lot of power over your life and over your future. Finally, as a summary of the trouble you're in, you pull out the Devil. The Devil could stand for the punishment you may be suffering, or the sense of enslavement you may experience in your school. However, this card also represents the things we do to sabotage ourselves and keep ourselves in bondage, so it can help you understand the ways in which you are a prisoner of your own habits and impulses. So, what should you do about this situation? First of all, recognize how these cards apply to your life; the next time they appear in a reading, they may be forewarning you against similar outbursts. The next time you are tempted to speak out, the images of these cards might suddenly appear in your mind's eye, warning you to stay in control. Also, as discussed previously under Tarot visualizations, you could set out cards to help you focus on managing your behavior. For example, you could lay down the Page of Wands to represent the impulsive side of you, and to either side of it set the Chariot for cool-headedness and control, and Temperance for self-modulation. Also, you could set the Two of Cups above this layout (not on top of it, but above it in a way that creates a pyramid shape) to remind yourself that good relations with other people are important to succeeding in life, and that creating harmony can be more important than saying whatever you feel like.

Social awkwardness is an additional problem that often goes with some of the conditions labeled learning disabilities. Again, whether or not you have a disability, the practice of Tarot can help you learn to relate to other people in a more direct, genuine, and meaningful manner. Here I can use myself as an example: as a teenager and as a young woman, I was clueless about many subtleties of social interaction, and I was pretty much a loner, though I was lucky to have a few good friends. Part of the problem is that I have delayed reactions, due to distortions in seeing, hearing, and other mental processing functions. Some people think that Tarot readers get their information by looking people over and making guesses based on their appearance and body language, but I couldn't even look people in the eyes, and anyway, I certainly couldn't think that fast. For people like me, it is easier to memorize a stack of books on Tarot, palmistry, and astrology than it is to decipher other peoples' gestures, expressions, or intentions, for example. However, as I have discussed in chapter 3, when you interact with other people by reading their cards, there is an almost magical "opening up" that causes energy to flow between reader and querent. Not only does this help develop your intuition, it promotes empathy, which is the ability to sense and appreciate other peoples' feelings. I'm not trying to say that reading Tarot will develop social skills overnight, because learning to get "in sync" with other people can be a lifelong process. But reading for your friends and acquaintances does open new lines of communication, new ways of connecting. It creates a better basis for relationship because you come to take more of an interest in peoples' life stories, and you have something to talk about when you meet them.

Part 2

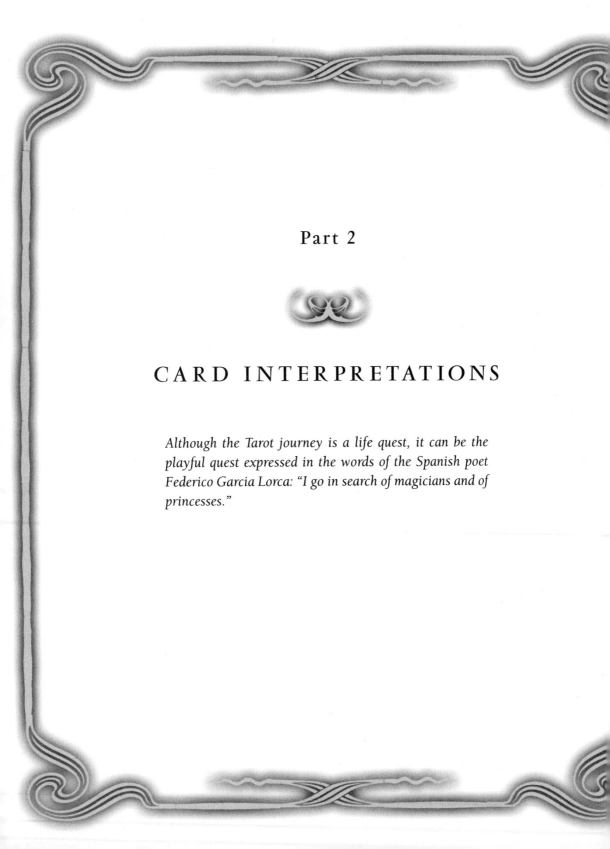

CARD INTERPRETATIONS

Although the Tarot journey is a life quest, it can be the playful quest expressed in the words of the Spanish poet Federico Garcia Lorca: "I go in search of magicians and of princesses."

6 THE MAJOR ARCANA

The twenty-two cards of the Major Arcana comprise the core of the Tarot deck. They are often referred to as the "Keys" for their ability to unlock profound mysteries, or as the "Trumps" or trump cards, deriving from the word for triumph (the earliest Tarot cards were known as "Triumphs"). In most modern decks, the Major Arcana images, as well as their number and sequence, have become somewhat standardized, although different artists have added their own special touches. These cards depict archetypes that are important to human development, though different individuals experience them differently, and the manifestation of an archetype is also influenced by cultural factors. (As mentioned previously, archetypes are symbolic patterns that correspond to significant human personality types, situations, and events.)

As an example of an archetype acting through a social role or personality type, the Hierophant is an archetype of teachers as well as teaching and religious institutions whose purpose is to pass down information, traditions, and values. You may have a positive experience of this archetype when you are befriended by an influential teacher or mentor who is good at explaining things and inspires you to achieve or to find personal meaning in a philosophy, but then you might have a negative experience with the archetype of the Hierophant when you encounter a school or religious official who insists on following meaningless rules and won't consider the needs of individuals. (Of course, some of the positive and negative characteristics of any Tarot archetype can be embodied by the same person.) Also, because the archetypes have different cultural expressions, you would find the image of the authoritative teacher to be quite different, say, between a colony of Amish people and a group of jazz musicians. However, if you got to know those people, you would soon be able to recognize the type and say, "That's one of their respected teachers," because archetypes are so fundamental to human experience.

You will also find archetypes manifesting through your own personality. For example, when you are passing certain types of information and traditions along to your friends or others, or when you feel a strong sense of identification with a religious or teaching institution, then you, too, are embodying the Hierophant.

Because archetypes express themselves not just through character roles, but also through situations and events, if you are in a love relationship, the Lovers can raise archetypal issues focused on the state of being in love and being in a relationship, as well as the way you act out the role of a lover. This card also has broader implications relating to being in a position where you have to make a choice.

The cards in the Minor Arcana (the rest of the deck) can also portray characters, situations, and events that are recognizable types, but they don't have the deeper archetypal significance that those of the Major Arcana possess, because they are not as rich in their layers of spiritual and psychological symbolism, or personal and social importance. Thus, the King of Pentacles is a recognizable authority figure (a practical, realistic person who insists on facts and results). However, in terms of the things that he represents, the areas of life where he may be experienced, the social power with which he is invested, and the weight of the symbolism attributed to him, he does not have as wide a range of meanings as the Emperor. Because the King of Pentacles embodies some of the Emperor's qualities (both are concerned with structure, and with the reality principle), we could say that the King of Pentacles is a subcategory of the Emperor archetype—but not the other way around.

Because of the greater importance of the Major Arcana cards, they are preferred for use in meditation, and it is possible to use just these twenty-two cards for divinatory purposes. However, when the Major and Minor Arcana are used together, they can show us how the great archetypes represented by the Majors are expressing themselves in the daily life roles and situations represented by the Minors. That's where we can appreciate the interconnection between our physical, mental, and spiritual worlds. The Major Arcana also exert more influence in a reading because their energies are more strongly experienced, they speak to a person's deeper spiritual and psychological issues, and the situations and events they denote or affect are often life-changing, or at least they have a more lasting effect.

If you are asking the Tarot a question about a very ordinary matter, such as how many candy bars you hope to sell for a club fundraiser, and one or more

Major Arcana cards comes up, you would do well to ponder the deeper significance that this may have for your life path. For example, if the Magician comes up, even if you don't do well in sales, the experience might enable you to develop skills that you can carry into other areas of life, and also boost your confidence in your ability to interact with people. On the other hand, if the Devil comes up, you may still be able to sell a lot of candy bars, but you might find the job of selling (as well as the other responsibilities of club membership) to be personally oppressive, and that might influence you to consider career and life paths that will enable you to have more individual freedom.

It is often pointed out that the sequence of the cards in the Major Arcana tell a story. Since the Fool is generally considered the "Zero" card, this story could be labeled "The Fool's Journey," showing a person who starts out in life with little wisdom and experience. He has to learn the lessons of the first card, the Magician, in order to gain mastery of his outer-world conditions, and of the second card, the High Priestess, to explore his inner life. He has to deal with parental/authority figures like those in cards three and four, the Emperor and Empress, and also learn to internalize their best qualities and assert his own authority, and so on and so on, until he finally achieves the state represented in the last card, the World, where he has developed his best qualities, found ways to come to terms with or transform his negative traits and experiences, and is now standing in a right relationship to others, and to the larger world around him. However, because the Fool card is un-numbered, he can be thought of as coming at the end of the sequence, too, which can relate to the idea that life moves in cycles. We may start out as beginners in one area of life, go through all sorts of lessons, and then achieve a degree of harmony and fulfillment, only to have to start out as beginners again, in a new area of life.

Through these cards you can also illustrate your own life story. If you were to make a time line of your own life, listing the events that had the greatest impact on your personal development, these events could likely be linked to the different Major Arcana cards. Of course, your life story may not fall into the same neat sequence as the Fool's journey, but you can be sure that you will meet all of the Major Arcana archetypes time and again as you also deal with recurring themes and go through a series of cycles.

PERCIVALL

0 THE FOOL

IL MATTO   0   THE FOOL
LE FOU   EL LOCO

DER NARR   DE DWAAS

0. THE FOOL

The Fool card is said to represent every person in her original state of innocence and inexperience. In its positive expression, this card is about learning new things and opening yourself to new possibilities and opportunities—a mode of acting that enables you to be playful, curious, and enthusiastic. The Fool card also has to do with the natural learning process that takes place when life dumps us into unexpected situations. Many scholars of the Tarot have pointed out that the Fool is going on a journey of self-development; on this journey he will explore the wisdom of the other Tarot cards. (This is one reason why the Fool is sometimes considered both the first and the last card in the Tarot deck.) Although this journey is a life quest, it can be the playful quest expressed in the words of the Spanish poet Federico Garcia Lorca: "I go in search of magicians and of princesses."[1]

Character

The Fool card can refer to a person with both positive and negative character traits. This may be a person who is innocent, trusting, fun loving, and ready for adventure, but possibly also one who is inexperienced, easily misled, and likely to take senseless risks. When this card is reversed, it may denote a person who finds it difficult to be open with other people, or who is afraid to try new things. This person may have been made fun of or had his feelings hurt in the past. When reversed or surrounded by negative cards, the Fool can also represent a number of negative personality types or ways of acting. Among others, it may refer to a person who displays "learned helplessness," that is, a person who messes up out of fear or an unconscious desire to get other people to take care of him. It may sometimes refer to a person who puts himself down or acts goofy as a way of saying, "I'm going to make fun of myself before someone else gets a chance." Such people need to find things that they can do successfully, which will build their self-esteem. Because the Fool's journey is about self-development, the reversed Fool could also indicate those times when people are not being themselves, perhaps because they want to impress other people.

To determine which side of the Fool's character is indicated in your reading, you can look for clues in the surrounding cards. It also depends upon the question; for example, if you are asking whether a certain person is qualified for a position of leadership, the appearance of the Fool would indicate that she is not savvy or experienced. On the other hand, if you are wondering whether a certain person has done something wrong, the Fool card would point to her innocence.

Embarrassment

"I'd rather die than make a fool of myself." Many teenagers are afraid of looking stupid in front of other people, and for some of us, this is one thing that doesn't change as we get older. Unfortunately, the appearance of the Fool card may point to a situation in which embarrassment is unavoidable. This is not always a bad thing—if we want to learn new things, try new things, develop our interpersonal skills, and reach out to others to make relationships, we must risk asking seemingly stupid questions, making really big mistakes that can waste time and money, and being laughed at and rejected. When this card is reversed, it can indicate a person who does strange things because she lacks awareness or self-control. It could also denote a person who is viewed as strange because she is different in some small way. Many young people who have been labeled as class clowns, nerds, geeks, and so on act impulsively or weirdly due to learning disabilities such as ADD or mild forms of autism, while others simply haven't had the socialization experiences one needs in order to know how to behave in different types of situations.

Fooling Around

If you've come to the Tarot for a report on your own or other peoples' actions, intentions, or progress, this could be the answer: just foolin' around. If reversed, the foolishness may be more unconscious, as in cases where people sabotage themselves, messing up because their inner beings are not in harmony with their work or whatever it is they have to do.

Romance

Because the Fool signifies new adventures, it could denote the start of a new love. However, it does not bode well for the long-term stability of the relationship, because it can imply that the people involved may not be ready for commitment. On the other hand, if this card is reversed, it may indicate people who avoid getting romantically involved because they are afraid of making a bad choice, being rejected, or looking foolish.

Opportunity

This card often denotes special opportunities, but you have to be willing to act quickly if you want to take advantage of them. The reversed card may refer to missed opportunities, though the Fool's eternal going forth suggests that you will get second chances.

Travel

One of the traditional divinatory meanings of the Fool is adventure and travel, as we can see that the Fool has gone out into the world, out onto the open road. If reversed, this card may indicate that you have a strong desire to get away, go somewhere, even see the world on your own, but circumstances are holding you back. However, it is likely that you will get a chance to get away in the not-too-distant future.

Warning of Danger

The little dog that yaps at the Fool's heels in some versions of this card (in some older versions the dog is biting at his butt) represents the voice of instinct, which warns us about walking into danger. A Tarot layout may emphasize the element of danger if the Fool is surrounded by cards like the Moon, the Devil, the Ace of Swords, the Five of Pentacles, and so on, or it may be graphically highlighted if a figure in an adjacent card points to the Fool's dog (for example, if in the Rider-Waite-Smith deck, the page of Swords is reversed and to the immediate right of the Fool). Generally, it is important to cultivate common sense (as well as the wisdom lessons of the other Tarot cards) so you know when you should be cautious, and when it is safe and appropriate to let go and enjoy the playful and spontaneous side of the Fool.

I. THE MAGICIAN

MERLIN

I THE MAGICIAN

IL MAGO / LE BATELEUR — THE MAGICIAN / EL MAGO — DER MAGIER / DE MAGIER

The Magician card is about taking charge of your life so you can craft your own destiny. Most card illustrations depict a magician standing before a number of instruments that symbolize the elemental powers of Fire, Earth, Air, and Water. In older versions of the deck, these symbols are disguised as trifling objects such as little cups and peas, whereas most of the modern versions represent them as powerful magical tools. The older versions labeled this card the Juggler and disguised the elemental powers in order to make the statement that although these great powers are available to us—virtually at our fingertips—most of us don't realize it and don't make much out of them. Therefore, this card suggests making the most out of what you have around you (and inside of you). Whenever I draw the Magician card, no matter which deck I am dealing with, I keep both the old and the new interpretations in mind. I reconcile them by viewing the qualities of the Magician as being on a continuum, and looking for clues in the reading to determine whether it designates a person who is skillfully using her resources, or a person who is still learning. Although you may experience the Magician's energies in many ways, following are some of the conditions to which this card may apply.

Character

In this world, few people reach the levels of attainment suggested in the modern graphic renditions of this card, which portray a magical adept. Therefore, when the Magician refers to a person, it is more likely to denote someone who is acting on a strong desire to achieve mastery over his world. This is a person who is in the process of discovering inner powers, gifts, and resources; a person with a positive outlook; a proactive person who takes charge and acts independently; a person who is using his creativity to make things happen; a person whose sense of identity is defined by an active interest in everything. When this card is reversed, it indicates that the person in question has the natural ability to build a good life and achieve a higher level of success, but lacks self-confidence and awareness.

Destiny

The Magician signifies the ability to recognize the destiny that is right for you, so you can work to make your dreams come true by seeking out the right experiences, the right education, the right work, the right people, the right places, and so on. (See the glossary for a discussion of the term "destiny.") It is important to remember that although the Magician can shape reality, he can do so because he is reality-based to start with. When this card is reversed, it may denote the problem of not knowing what to do with your life. This can lead to a period of experimentation as you drift from one interest or activity to another. However, unless accompanied by negative cards, it implies that you will find your path eventually.

Education

Education is a major area where the Magician's energies manifest in the lives of young people, and this card is a suitable significator for the dedicated student. The reversed Magician may indicate a person who is doing some self-searching to help decide which educational choices are most meaningful to her life path.

Romance

If you are a girl or a woman, the Magician can represent your ideal man: the powerful, charismatic type of man who can make things happen for you. If you are wondering whether you will ever find love, this card may promise that Mr. Right is out there. If you are enquiring about a man or boy that you already know, it indicates that he is interested and can be a good match for you. When this card is reversed, it could warn that your expectations are unrealistic; perhaps you have criteria that no one can live up to, or perhaps you are building your hopes around someone who is uninterested or unworthy. For both males and females, the Magician advises that you will find the right person by being the right person.

Magic

In line with this card's title symbolism, it can refer to a person who is interested in magic and metaphysics, or to some type of magical influence in his life. When reversed, it may indicate the misuse of magical energies.

Position of Advantage

When the Magician card is in a position that signifies your status in a reading, it generally indicates that things will go your way because you are in a position of strength, and you are doing the right things. On the other hand, this is bad news if it pertains to a rival, because it means that she is the one who holds the cards, so to speak. If this card is reversed, it indicates a position of weakness: you or whoever is in question don't have "the right stuff," at least not at this point, so it may be a good idea to find a way to compensate for what you may lack.

II. THE HIGH PRIESTESS

The High Priestess represents an individual who is training herself to achieve a higher level of awareness and being. Because she is concerned with underlying patterns and hidden meanings in the world around her, the High Priestess is associated with the intuitive and reflective qualities of the moon—which is why most Tarot artists depict her with a lunar crescent on her forehead or at her feet. She often holds an open book or a closed scroll, representing the desire for understanding. Because the High Priestess card also has many layers of meaning, its mysteries may be experienced in many areas of life. However, following are some of this card's possible expressions.

Character

The High Priestess depicted in the Tarot is a mysterious figure—maybe a wise woman—who radiates inner peace and gently guides us to look within ourselves. Although we may encounter few women or men who are able to devote themselves as fully as the High Priestess to penetrating life's wonders, this card can represent intuitive, receptive individuals with a love of wisdom. Such people are often attuned to the rhythms and cycles of nature. They believe in submitting their egos in loving service to higher ideals, and hold a deep reverence for the spiritual world. The High Priestess personality type may seem inscrutable, for although she feels deeply, she often keeps her feelings to herself. However, she is good at giving advice and protecting confidences. The reversed card may indicate a person who is strongly attracted to mystical philosophies but hasn't achieved depth of understanding.

Influence on Reading

The appearance of the High Priestess card affects the interpretation of any Tarot spread (even if the other cards are Minor Arcana cards dealing with mundane matters) by emphasizing that the situation depicted has deep meaning for the development of your soul and psyche. This card also tends to affirm any intuitive feelings you have about the matters depicted in the other cards. When this card is reversed, it could indicate problems because the affairs depicted in the other cards are not in harmony with your inner being.

Inner Work and Personal Spirituality

The High Priestess card signifies dedication to "inner work," using religious and psychological means to understand yourself, your role in life, and your relationship to the spiritual world. Techniques that can help you develop intuition and understanding include meditation, dream analysis, and, of course, Tarot—among others. Such techniques help you better understand your own motives or actions, but they also contribute to the quest for wisdom by showing you how the patterns of your life are mirrored in the archetypal symbols that have inspired people in all cultures through all times.

Romance

In traditional Tarot interpretation, the High Priestess can often represent a man's ideal woman or "dream woman"—the sort of woman who anticipates his needs and has the ability to be whatever he wants her to be. If you are a man or boy who is wondering whether you will ever find love, the appearance of this card may predict that the right woman or girl will enter your life. If your questions pertain to someone you already know, it indicates that she is probably interested in you, but the situation requires more understanding. While you cannot have a relationship with a person who does not fulfill some of your fantasies in some way, it is important to be able to make a separation between what you can realistically expect from a real woman who has human imperfections, and what has to stay in the realm of fantasy. The reversed High Priestess card may point to unrealistic expectations about love.

Relationships

The High Priestess can signify the need to understand your "relational Self." Although you have a certain core of Self, at the same time your sense of who you are can change from moment to moment, depending upon who you are with. For example, perhaps you have noticed that you are a different person when you are with your parents than when you are with your friends. You can let the High Priestess' intuitive wisdom guide you in the appropriate ways to relate to different people at different times and achieve an empathic understanding of other people that gives you insight into their issues, needs, and behavior. High Priestess–style intuition also enables you to make a spiritual connection with another person— as Jungian psychologist Jean Bolen has pointed out in her book, *Ring of Power,* you are in "sanctuary" when you are in the presence of someone who recognizes the soul in you.[2] When this card is reversed, it may warn of problems connecting with another person, perhaps because he does not value spiritual ideals.

Secrets

One of the traditional meanings of the High Priestess card is the possession of secrets. In a reading, this could mean that someone is keeping a secret, or that all of the information you seek just isn't available at this time. When this card is reversed, the situation is all the murkier. In symbolizing hidden knowledge, the High Priestess also teaches us that there are times when we have to deal with and be comfortable with the fact that we can't know everything. Sometimes we may have partial knowledge of a situation (including what we can learn from consulting the Tarot), but we have to be willing to wait and to continue studying the matter until more is revealed. Generally, the High Priestess advises against taking action on a matter until more information can be gained. However, sometimes we have to accept the fact that we may never know the full truth of a matter (this might be the case if this card is reversed).

Thoughts on the High Priestess

As mentioned in the previous paragraph, the High Priestess card sometimes deals with states of "not knowing"—those times when we may have to accept the fact that we don't fully understand everything. My own experience with this aspect of the High Priestess influenced my writing of this book, when I had to make decisions about what information to include and how to phrase it. While I have tried to write this book in what (for me) is informal language, I have made a decision not to "dumb it down," even though certain terms used could be new to my younger readers. But even if you don't understand particular terms, you can begin to get the gist of them, and your unconscious mind will also go to work for you so they will come to mean more over time. I believe that most Tarot readers learn as they go along. This involves going into "High Priestess mode" by examining your own intuitive responses to the cards, then checking your feelings against the interpretations in your manual as well as what you already know about a situation, then looking for other ways to corroborate your interpretations by the things that show up in your life. If you still don't understand the meaning of your cards, if some of the words or chapters in this book don't make sense to you, or if they don't answer your particular question, then accept it and let it go, having faith that you will become more attuned, that you will come to understand more, and that more will eventually be revealed to you.

III. THE EMPRESS

GUENEVERE

The Empress is often portrayed as a throned woman in a long, richly embroidered gown, holding a scepter and wearing a crown of stars. Her beauty and femininity are sometimes accentuated by her long golden hair and the sigil of Venus on a heart-shaped shield by her feet. This association with Venus emphasizes a state of harmony and well-being based on generosity of imagination, emotional openness, love, and concern for others. The Empress may be surrounded by fields of ripening grain, or she may sit in a garden of flowers and trees, signifying her connection with the life force of nature. In some older versions of this card, she holds a shield emblazoned with an eagle with upturned wings, symbolic of her soaring spirit; this reminds us that a combination of physical and spiritual, and earthly and heavenly qualities is necessary to human happiness and wholeness. Following are some of the meanings that the Empress may hold for you.

3 THE EMPRESS

Abundance

The Empress traditionally signifies the growth and abundance of good things, including material goods and wealth, gifts and favors, productivity, success, security, health and healing, fulfillment, happiness, affection, a peaceful home life, and pleasure. She also represents people who use their resources to create beauty and harmony, and to aid and comfort others. When this card is reversed, all of these blessings are probably within your reach, but you may have to work a little harder to develop your potential, as well as to cultivate Empress-style creative vision, nurturing energy, and social grace.

Authority

This card may pertain to unique or conventional expressions of feminine power and authority, or to authority in general. Depending on the question and context, you may have to deal with an authority figure who has the power to help you, or you may assume a leadership position yourself. When this card is reversed, problems may arise from resistance to authority. In some cases, reactions may be based on negative beliefs about women's rights to be in leadership positions.

Femininity

The Empress can represent traditional feminine values and interests, as well as the ability to take pride and pleasure in our bodies. Some elements of our society have denigrated womens' concern with feelings and intuition as weak-mindedness, and womens' role in looking after human physical needs as trivial. However, many women (as well as men) are now rediscovering the value of these qualities, and honoring their special blend of strength and wisdom. Likewise, there is a movement to honor the body by rejecting superficial standards of beauty, and by attending to bodily needs for health and comfort. Therefore, when this card appears in a reading, whether upright or reversed, your situation may require you to examine your own attitudes toward these things.

Fertility

The Empress is often depicted as pregnant, highlighting this card's qualities of fruitfulness. In a reading, this could predict a pregnancy (especially if this is desired), although it has also been linked with fertility of the mind—the ability to bring forth creative ideas. As such, it is a lucky card for artists and others developing their talents and seeking creative success. The reversed card could indicate infertility or creative block; however, because the Empress card is so auspicious, these problems may be temporary.

Matriarchal Roles

This card can denote a woman who is strongly identified with her position as the head of the family. She may be active in the lives of her children and grandchildren (and possibly nieces, nephews, and the children of friends and neighbors) throughout her life. The reversed Empress can represent the condition of a woman whose family is fragmented, either due to divorce or the dispersal of her adult children.

Mother Figures

The appearance of the Empress may indicate that the matter in question involves your mother, or perhaps a woman who serves as a mother figure. It is a blessing to have many mother figures in your life, for as Clarissa Pinkola Estes, author of *Women who Run with the Wolves,* has said to her own daughter, "You are born to one mother, but if you are lucky, you will have more than one. And among them all, you will find most of what you need." She points out, "Your relationships with *las todas madres,* the many mothers, will most likely be ongoing ones, for the need for guidance and advisement is never outgrown . . ."[3]

Parenting Issues

When the Empress card comes up, especially if it is reversed or accompanied by negative cards, it can stir some emotionally charged issues involving our mothers and our own maternal instincts. People who have troubled relationships with their mothers may find it difficult to relate to and embody the archetypes of good mothering. If this is the case for you, it is important to seek and emulate strong, positive models of motherhood, whether they be people around you, historical figures, or religious figures such as the many ancient mother goddesses, because a negative internalized mother image can taint your life and relationships. Also, work through your issues and then let them go, so you can understand and forgive your own mother. (Your compassion will grow if you become a parent yourself.)

Romance

This card may predict love, passion, romance, marriage, children, and family life. For male querents, it can also represent an ideal woman. The reversed card could point to the type of problems that arise when a person has an overidealized image of marriage and romance, or of what the feminine should be, so she does not learn to deal with human imperfection, or to maintain and appreciate a genuine relationship.

IV. THE EMPEROR

The Emperor is usually portrayed as a bearded older man, crowned, seated upon a throne, and wearing robes over a suit of armor. He usually holds a scepter in his right hand to symbolize his ability to manifest desires, and an orb in the left to signify his worldly power. The Emperor card corresponds to several major archetypes, including the archetypal Father and King, and it combines many of the qualities of the Minor Arcana cards' Kings. The archetype of the King is active in people and institutions when they create, defend, and maintain the structures and systems that make it possible for us to enjoy peace and freedom, so that we can pursue our own creative and productive interests. As Robert Moore and Douglas Gillette have said in their book *King/Warrior/Magician/Lover,* "This is the energy that seeks peace and stability, orderly growth and nurturing for all people—and not only for all people, but for the environment, the material world. The King cares for the whole realm and is the steward of nature as well as of human society." [4] The range of this archetype also includes an "inner King," which is an important ordering principle within our psyches. As Robert Bly has stated in *Iron John,* his book about masculine psychology, the inner King knows our best interests, so "he can make clear what we want without being contaminated in his choice by the opinions of others around us. The inner King is connected with our fire of purpose and passion." [5] Following are some of the ways that the Emperor archetype may express itself in your reading.

Authority

The Emperor is a card of authority and rulership. You may have to deal with an agency of worldly power, such as a branch of government or corporate bureaucracy, or perhaps an authority at school or work. Alternatively, you may achieve a leadership position. When this card is reversed, you may have negative reactions to authority, or you may need to develop confidence and experience in asserting your personal power. If negative cards are present, the matter in question may involve a lack of leadership or an abuse of power.

Blessing

Moore and Gillette point out that one of the traditional roles of the good king was to give blessing by providing presence and guidance, and by rewarding and acknowledging the merits and accomplishments of others. Although they emphasize that this type of blessing is a crucial psychological as well as physiological need, they state that due to the nature of our society, "Young men today are starving for blessing from older men, for blessing from the King energy," and that "they need to be seen by the King, because if they are, something inside will come together for them."[6] Thus, for young men (as well as young women), the appearance of the Emperor card may suggest that this is the time to seek out male mentors who have the power to help you.

Father Figures

The appearance of the Emperor may indicate that the matter in question involves your father, or perhaps a man who serves as a father figure.

Intellect

Tradition emphasizes the logical nature of this card, which denotes intelligence, will power, mental organization, and the ability to think on a large scale and plan for the future. People who cultivate Emperor-style consciousness can see things as they are as well as how they should be, and they know how to get things done. They have the ability to assert the rule of reason over runaway emotions and other disorderly behaviors. The reversed card might indicate a person who has difficulty achieving a working balance between logic and emotions, leaning to one extreme or another.

Parenting Issues

When a parent embodies the Emperor's positive qualities (or when any person has achieved the maturity that this card represents), he is generous with love and attention, ensuring the growth needs of everyone in his care, because he wants them to achieve their full potential. He puts the needs of his loved ones first, and works hard to provide comfort, security, stability, order, structure, discipline, and protection. However, the Emperor's negative expressions—something that may be indicated by the reversed card or the presence of negative cards—tend to be very rigid and authoritarian, often denoting a parent who has to have everything his way, who insists that everyone in the family serve his interests, and who doesn't empower his children to exercise their own choices when the time is appropriate. The negative Emperor may also represent a parent who is absent, uninvolved, or immature.

Responsibility

The situation at hand may require you to step in and take charge, even if you have to shoulder all of the blame, as well as all of the responsibility. However, you should, if possible, try to delegate some of that responsibility to competent people, giving them some direction, but also motivating, encouraging, and rewarding them. The reversed card could indicate some resistance or hesitance in taking on responsibilities.

Success

The level of confidence, competence, and drive that the Emperor embodies suggests that you will achieve your goals and along with that, success, prosperity, stability, and respect. The reversed card can indicate that these things are within your reach, but more experience and discipline may be needed to accomplish them. Also, if you have feelings of inferiority, you must realize that you have the *right* to reach out for more of everything good.

Thoughts on Patriarchy

The Emperor card is sometimes connected with patriarchy, which the dictionary broadly defines as "control by men of a disproportionately large share of power."[7]

Some Tarot readers have negative reactions to this card because patriarchal societies have treated women like slaves, and they have historically also carried out the conquest and subjugation of other people, and the vicious persecution of anyone unwilling to conform to their social hierarchies.[8] Even today, patriarchal elements within our society have denigrated women's intelligence, interests, and values, and they also look down upon men whose interests and inclinations aren't considered important or masculine according to a certain rigid set of standards. These are among the reasons Moore and Gillette assert that "patriarchy is *not* the expression of deep and rooted masculinity," but is, "in part, the shadow—or crazy—side of masculinity."[9] Fortunately, many men and women are promoting more positive models of masculinity that use male strength to help rather than hurt people, and they are also demonstrating that men and boys have deep and genuine aspirations for love, peace, relatedness, and interconnectedness. However, because many people and institutions are still loyal to patriarchal ideas, you may sometimes have to deal with them. Whether you are male or female, you may find this to be the case when you are not receiving the recognition or advancements that you deserve. This problem may especially be indicated if the Emperor is accompanied by cards of conflict.

V. THE HIEROPHANT

The Major Arcana card number Five is commonly called the Hierophant, which is a Greek word for the high priest of a mystery religion, and has since been used to describe a person who explains things—especially the mysteries. (To give you an example, in his essay "Defense of Poetry," Percy Bysshe Shelley states, "Poets are the hierophants of an unapprehended inspiration, the mirrors of the gigantic shadows which futurity casts upon the present.")[10] The older versions of this card labeled it the Pope, but the designers of most modern decks have found this term too narrow. Some recent decks have simply labeled it the High Priest. The hierophant is typically portrayed as a popelike figure who wears long robes and a three-tiered crown, and holds a staff topped by a triple cross. He is often seated on a thronelike chair between two pillars, and raises his hand in a gesture of blessing as two monks or priests kneel before him. This card may stand for religious teachings, or it may be more generally applied to the transmission of knowledge, traditions, and cultural institutions. Due to its concern with the outer expressions of belief, it is often contrasted with the High Priestess, who is concerned with quiet, inner exploration. The Hierophant can be seen to carry on the work of some of the earlier cards, synthesizing the wisdom of the High Priestess, the values of the Empress, and the Emperor's concerns with maintaining social structures; the Hierophant directs their accumulated knowledge outward, while reminding us that our actions must take account of our connection to a larger, spiritual order. Following are some of this card's potential applications.

Blessing

In the previous section on the Emperor, we touched on the need for young people to receive blessing from important authority figures. The presence of the Hierophant also signifies blessing, for teaching and mentoring are among the most direct ways to make a positive difference in another person's life. This card could also indicate that you might receive blessing in the form of special advice, or that someone might help you by pleading your case before a higher authority (for example, recommending you for a scholarship, or asking for leniency if you are in some kind of trouble).

Conscience

Because the Hierophant can represent the internalized Voice of Authority, its presence raises issues that engage your conscience, spiritual values, morals, and sense of duty. This card can also stand for someone who acts as a spokesperson for a philosophical system, or a person who strongly identifies with it and can be counted upon to behave consistently, in conformity with the values of her group. The reversed card may warn of inconsistent behavior or conflicts with conscience; in some cases it could point to an extremely harsh inner critic, while in others, it could reveal an undeveloped code of ethics or divided loyalties. If accompanied by negative cards, it can denote people who have little understanding or tolerance of other spiritual paths.

Education

Because of its concern with the transmission of knowledge, the Hierophant may apply to teachers and teaching, or to educational institutions. In teenagers' readings, it could point to college, and a possible future in academia. As a card of advice, it could indicate the need to seek out the mentor who is best qualified to teach you what you need to know. The reversed Hierophant may indicate some negative experiences with a school or educational institution, possibly due to being at odds with the rules, customs, representatives, and goals of the institution.

Religion

The presence of the Hierophant may indicate that religion or a religious teacher or institution may be exerting a weighty influence on the matter in question. Perhaps you are seeking spiritual guidance; if so, take heart, because the appearance of this card can illustrate the saying, "When the student is ready, the teacher comes." It could also mean that you are thinking about committing to a religious profession or way of life, or you may be teaching or communicating your spiritual philosophy to others. An important religious ceremony may figure in to the reading. The reversed card could indicate that you are struggling with your faith, or questioning the role that religion should play in your life.

Note: Many interpreters have tended to strictly associate the Hierophant with conventional, organized religion. Often they approach it negatively, emphasizing the harmful role that dogmatic religions have played in promoting ignorance, bigotry, warfare, hatred, oppressive social hierarchies, the devaluation of women, and the belief that there can be only one correct solution to any problem or only one true path to spiritual development. However, modern religious diversity complicates the interpretation, as I have often seen the Hierophant come up in the readings of those who practice neopaganism, Asian religions, Native American spirituality, or other ancient wisdom traditions. These same people may be active within their religious associations, and may even play a role in creating new religious traditions.

Traditions

In addition to the educational and religious institutions discussed above, the presence of this card may indicate that a traditional institution, discipline, or way of doing things (or someone who represents such tradition) may be influential in your life. You may have to give some thought as to which one may be represented here, for although our society has its dominant social, political, and religious institutions, there are also subcultural groups that have their own traditions, and even families, local communities, schools, corporations, and other types of group entities have their own body of customs, sense of history, knowledge that they pass along, and expectations to which their members are encouraged to conform. We associate with some of these traditions and institutions due to family and ethnic heritage, but there are also those with which we come to identify ourselves as a matter of choice. The reversed card may indicate a person who is trying to detach from some traditions. If surrounded by negative cards, the Hierophant may indicate someone who rigidly adheres to a set of beliefs and pressures others to do likewise. If surrounded by cards of conflict, the Hierophant could also denote problems that arise from a clash of opposing traditions.

GARETH & LYONES

6 THE LOVERS

DIE LIEBENDEN   DE GELIEFDEN

VI. THE LOVERS

Most modern versions of the Lovers depict a man and woman who may embrace or hold hands while an angel hovers over them in an attitude of blessing. The Rider-Waite-Smith version represents the trio as Adam, Eve, and the angel Raphael in the Garden of Eden. Older versions typically portray a man who must make a choice between two women while a winged cupid aims his arrow at the fairer woman, implying that the man will choose her. Through the Lovers card, the Tarot recognizes the importance of the human drive for wholeness through union with another person, and the way that devotion to another is spiritually uplifting. It also makes the statement that an ideal life depends upon the harmonious interaction of opposites: male and female, head and heart, active and passive modes of being, inner- and outer-world concerns, and so on. In a general sense, the Lovers predicts your ability to go after your heart's desires, enjoy beauty and harmony in your life, and find partners among loving, caring people. Its qualities may also manifest in some of the areas detailed below.

Choices

The Lovers card may reveal that you have to make a choice that is significant to your life path. Choicemaking is implied in older versions of the Lovers, which portray a young man choosing between a woman who is young and fair, and one who is dark and mysterious. Some authors have speculated that the older woman represents his mother, and Rachel Pollack has suggested that the Lovers may point to "the first real choice a person makes independently of his or her parents."[11] Other readers suggest that the two women represent the need to choose between a pure and lasting love and temporary sensual pleasure. You may have to decide which of a number of life choices is the most attractive to you, though the Lovers card traditionally suggests you make the choice with heart, that is, the choice that best fulfills your deep spiritual and emotional needs. When this card is reversed, it can mean a number of things, including indecision, an unsatisfactory choice, a choice to return to the past, a decision to break with a current relationship, or a decision that goes against your outer goals and desires—perhaps in favor of an unconscious need that you don't really understand. It could also represent a choice to give up the pursuit of a desire in order to comply with parents' wishes, or with your own higher goals.

Also, if there are cards to either side of the Lovers, these may reveal something about the nature of the choices involved—likewise when the card is reversed.

Love

The Lovers is the card that best signifies love and romance, and usually points to romantic relationships that involve deep commitment, passion, and possible marriage. These are the type of relationships in which two people share the same desires and are so well matched that each makes the other feel more complete. When it is accompanied by other cards in a reading, the cards to either side of the Lovers may reveal something about the personalities of each individual and their roles in the relationship. The reversed Lovers card can mean many things, depending upon the question and context. It could indicate that two people have been drawn together in a passionate relationship, but they have major personality differences, and will therefore need to work hard to make their relationship successful. There may be some serious inequalities in the relationship, perhaps because one partner is more committed. It could also signal changes within a relationship ranging from one or both partners gaining greater independence, drifting away from each other, or longing to return to past relationships. If a Knight or other card denoting another person appears to one side of the reversed Lovers, it could indicate that the partner is interested in someone else. If reversed and surrounded by negative cards, the Lovers could warn of a troubled or abusive relationship.

Partnerships

I have occasionally seen the Lovers card turn up in readings to denote two people who are not romantically involved (or interested in becoming so), but have a very close friendship or partnership of some sort, which is pertinent to the matter in question. Exchanges of gifts or favors may be involved. It could also signify two individuals or parties who are brought together in a common cause, and implies that everyone will work together to achieve peace and success. If this card is reversed, the partners or parties may not have a shared vision of what they hope to achieve, so there will be major barriers to cooperation.

Self-Development

Interpretations of the Lovers often bring in the Jungian idea of the *anima* and the *animus,* which are the twin selves or (what our culture considers to be) the masculine and feminine natures within any individual. As part of the individuation process, which is the process of becoming whole, unique, and empowered people, we try to integrate these complementary qualities within ourselves. Consequently, the Lovers could indicate that you are making progress, while the reversed card may hint that your problems revolve around difficulties in integrating opposite facets of your character.

Sexuality

Under some circumstances, the Lovers may denote issues revolving around sexuality, particularly the choice whether or not to become sexually involved. (Some of the more recent illustrations of this card emphasize sexual issues by foregrounding the nudity and sensuality of the couple—in contrast to the Rider-Waite-Smith illustration, in which nudity is used to suggest childlike innocence and openness.) Naturally, decisions to become sexually active depend upon many factors, including a person's age, level of independence and personal responsibility, and religious beliefs and ethics. However, in view of the heavy pressure that young people get from peers, the media, and society in general to become sexualized at a very early age, anyone making this decision must be able to handle all of the consequences, including the possibility that other dreams may have to be sacrificed in the event of disease or pregnancy. My own suggestion: keep your decisions in line with the Tarot's values of self-knowledge and mastery, discipline, and spiritual attainment, so that you are not pushed into anything that you are not ready for.

Special Technique for Reading

To learn more about the nature of a relationship, you can shuffle the cards, then go through the Tarot deck until you find the Lovers; look to the cards to either side for information about what each person brings to the relationship.

VII. THE CHARIOT

The Chariot tends to show that you're in control of your life and are moving toward your goals, despite a number of difficulties. Older versions of the Chariot portray two horses (of different colors) who are trying to pull in two directions, while many newer versions feature two motionless sphinxes who sit before the charioteer. In the older versions, the horses represent the conflicting forces and crosscurrents within us, such as the emotions and instincts that can tear us apart by contending with our reason and social conscience. The charioteer's position is an uneasy one, because he must exert an enormous amount of concentration and control. The newer versions would imply a higher level of mastery—as Echols, Mueller, and Thompson have pointed out in their book *Spiritual Tarot,* the chariot is more like a throne.[12] In either case, by setting your heart and mind on images of discipline, excellence, wisdom, and genuine goodness, you will find it easier to get your desires, impulses, and ideals to work together. Listed below are some of the situations that you may be trying to stay on top of.

Control

The Chariot denotes your need to control a situation—managing your moods, thinking clearly, and forming strategies. However, it implies that your situation is one that may require a lot of control, which means that you may have to resist temptations, deal with people problems, and so on. Also, it may be up to you to step in and take charge of a situation when others can't make up their minds or don't want to bother. The reversed card may indicate that you realize the need to take control, but are having problems concentrating, making decisions, and getting organized.

Life Path

The Chariot can represent a person who is focused on studies, career, and life path. When you get your energies harnessed, a good future is virtually assured, because those energies will build momentum that carries you forward. The reversed card may point to problems finding a sense of purpose.

Movement

The Chariot says "yes" to questions about movement, whether they are concerns about traveling or physically relocating, getting your career going, waiting for people or institutions to get moving on a certain matter, and so on. It also indicates that things in general will be moving at a fairly fast pace, and your circumstances will require you to get out into the world to deal with matters of personal business. The reversed card indicates problems or delays, but unless surrounded by negative cards, it should be possible to get things moving eventually.

Success

The Chariot's association with victory hearkens back to the Roman "triumphs," lavish victory parades in which a returning general rode through the city in his chariot. These processions included statues or people dressed as allegorical figures such as Victory, Strength, Eros, Temperance, the Sun, the Moon, and so on—also drawn in chariots. Later, these triumphs were used to entertain European royalty. In keeping with this traditional symbolism, the Chariot foretells honor, celebration, rewards, and success. When this card is reversed, it could denote a partial success; it could also mean that success is within your grasp, but you must take some quick action to secure it.

Other Peoples' Influence

When other people (or things) control your life, either directly or indirectly, you are not "in the driver's seat," so to speak. This situation may be indicated when the Chariot comes up reversed, especially if also in relation to other peoples' significators. Young people are often in a double bind, trying to negotiate between the demands of the peer group, as well as those of authority figures such as parents. Be aware that people can still be "driving" you when you automatically react by doing the opposite of what they want, rather than making your own reasoned decisions. However, the presence of the Chariot card is still a good sign, because it assures you that you do have the power and internal resources to reassert control and get your life back on track.

Travel and Transportation

Sometimes the Chariot predicts that you'll go on a trip, get a new car, or otherwise solve a problem dealing with transportation. Although transportation may seem a trivial concern for a Major Arcana card, many aspects of our lives depend upon our ability to get around. The reversed card could signal problems or delays with transportation, but unless surrounded by negative cards, it implies that they'll get straightened out eventually.

VIII. STRENGTH

The Strength card commonly depicts a maiden in a flowing gown who casually leans over a lion, her hands around his muzzle. She seems either to be prying his jaws open or else closing them—but in a gentle manner. Sometimes a lemniscate (the symbol of eternity and inner harmony) appears over her head. Some of the earlier versions of this card also feature the woman with the lion, but she was more often portrayed holding up or standing by a marble pillar. Other versions portray a man and a lion; the man often wields a club and is identified with Hercules. Many writers have emphasized how this card portrays the triumph of our more civilized or refined qualities over the lower drives, showing the power to assert wisdom and self control over the animal instincts, love over hate, and spiritual values over materialism and material power. The appearance of this card, therefore, assures you that you can persuade people by appealing to the good in them, and that goodness and reason will prevail in the matter in question. Following are some of Strength's other potential meanings.

Body Image

Although this is not one of Strength's traditional meanings, this card (because of its explicit physicality) could come up in a reading when you are concerned about your body and your physical appearance. Our culture can be cruelly judgmental about what are considered to be desirable and undesirable body types, and young people are especially subjected to this kind of pressure. The Strength card may ask you to reflect on how

important looks may be to your life path. Attractiveness that radiates from vibrant health is one thing, because greater health gives greater freedom. However, if popular images of beauty or handsomeness are making you feel bad about your own body, you will find them at odds with the images of self-awareness, self-development, will power, and balanced lifestyle that are repeated themes throughout the Tarot. The need to be alert to where our idealized body images are coming from applies to young men and women alike. However, the Tarot's depiction of Strength, which is so often portrayed as feminine, may have additional meaning for girls by reminding them of their right to claim positive images of femininity. There is some urgency here, for as Mary Pipher points out in her book *Reviving Ophelia: Saving the Selves of Adolescent Girls,* the insistence on impossible body images is one of the reasons we live in a "girl-poisoning culture."[13]

Fortitude

The Strength card has often been alternatively labeled "Fortitude," which is the possession of energy, courage, determination, endurance, and the strength of character to face whatever you have to deal with. You may have to make a really big push to get something done, but even when discouraging cards come up, the presence of Strength usually indicates that you will get through your situation fairly well, and you will probably also achieve some success. If this card is reversed, the situation is less predictable, because your energy level or sense of resolve may come and go. This may force you to question your commitment to a goal.

Health

Because of its obvious associations with physical strength and energy, this card is good news for the success of anyone involved in physical activities or athletics, or someone who hopes to recover from illness. It also denotes enthusiastic people who generate a high level of energy by finding joy in life and taking pride in what they do, and it can stand for an interest in vitalism, which is the study of the life force—often explored through things like herbalism, the art of body movement, and communion with nature. When reversed, the subject may still need to work on building stamina, or a longer period of recovery may be required.

Self-Assertion and Defense

Although the Strength card reveals your access to spiritual power that breeds confidence and inner strength, its presence may indicate that such strength is needed. Your situation may require you to make a show of strength—or at least physical presence—in order to protect your rights or achieve other good. In some cases, you might also have to call upon your animal instincts for motivation and drive, or to warn you of danger. Your strength may be needed to help others, too; you may have to allow them to lean on you, while (for the time being) putting your own worries aside. The reversed card can show the use of restraint, especially in a situation where a very soft approach is necessary.

Self-Improvement

Strength expresses itself in peoples' daily lives when they are working on self-discipline and improvement: trying to break bad habits and replace them with good ones. For many young people, this can apply to building study skills, or paying attention to diet and exercise. However, the appearance of Strength might also signal a desire to make a greater commitment to the ethical principles of your religion, or to explore different wisdom traditions, such as the various Asian arts, which teach self-government through the combination of physical, mental, and spiritual disciplinary practices. The reversed card may denote a person who, for whatever reason, is relaxing her level of self-control.

A Word about Numbering

Most of the older decks used Strength as card number Eleven and Justice as Eight (although the earliest decks used other systems in sequencing the cards, and a deck from the sixteenth century assigned the number Eight to Strength and Justice alike). However, Arthur Edward Waite fixed Strength as Eight when he designed his deck in 1910 (using a numbering system favored by a magical order to which many influential people belonged), and many new decks also use this system.[14] I have organized this book with the Rider-Waite-Smith deck and its spinoffs in mind since these are in the most common use, and as I mentioned in chapter 3, differences in numbering have not affected my reading and interpretation.

Further Thoughts on Body Image

It would be too much of a digression to discuss this at length, but Power (with a capital *P* because it acts as an independent entity and can't be traced to any single source) routinely inscribes itself on human bodies, which means that it makes demands about how people should look, what they should wear, and so on, as an effective means of assuring conformity. (For more about what Power is and how it works, see chapter 9.) The fashion trends promoted by different peer groups are a familiar example of how Power displays itself on young people's bodies, but, of course, the reach of Power is far more extensive than that—for old and young alike. By embodying the qualities of the Strength card, however, we can exercise more choice by going along with customs, trends, and fashions only when they serve our own interests.

IX. THE HERMIT

Lancelot in Exile

In the Arthurian legends and others, hermits lived in the wilderness, where they set their minds on spiritual values and pondered mysterious things, but they also acted as guides to those who became lost, or counselors to those who sought them out. Thus, the Hermit card combines the ideas of guiding and seeking. This card usually portrays a robed, hooded man who holds up a lamp to light the path before him. He is often white-bearded and elderly; sometimes he leans on a cane. He is surrounded by a wilderness or desert, often with mountain peaks (representing spiritual elevation) rising on the horizon behind him. As he walks through a landscape of doubt and darkness, the Hermit relies upon divine guidance as well as the light of his inner being (both represented by the star that glows within his lantern). In pursuing the quest for meaning, he ignores all of the pressures and distractions of the social world. From the Hermit's point of view—one could say the view from the mountain—it is possible to get a clear vision of what is truly important. Therefore, when this card comes up, you need to think about where you are on your life path, and where you still want to go. Following are some of the ways that the Hermit's search for wisdom may be experienced in your life.

9 The Hermit

Character

When the Hermit refers to a person, she is likely to be thoughtful, cautious, patient, self-disciplined, and insightful, with an ethic of service to human and spiritual ideals. This person may enjoy spending long

111

periods alone, devoted to meditation, contemplation, and study. She is probably elderly and has gained wisdom from a lifetime of experience, though in some cases this card could represent someone who is an "old soul." You can recognize such people by their calm, philosophical approach to life, and the inner light they seem to radiate. The reversed card may denote someone who recognizes the need to act with greater maturity, self-discipline, and spiritual awareness, but who has difficulty staying mindful and building better habits.

Loners

In folklore, the Hermit separates himself from society because of fundamental differences in values. Sometimes young people find themselves acting out the role of the hermit when they are separated from the crowd, either voluntarily or because they have been excluded (many who keep to themselves do so because of a history of exclusion). If this describes you, take heart, because outsiders have often provided the most valuable observations, discoveries, and critiques of society. Things also get better as you get older, because you may rise through college and on into a chosen career, where you will encounter more people who share your specialized interests; if not, you will still have more mobility to seek out your own people. If you still prefer to keep to yourself, it will be a choice that you have come to terms with. When this card is reversed, it may indicate a person who is trying to fit in to society, but still feels a sense of isolation.

Mentoring

The Hermit card assures you that even if you quietly follow your own path, you will link up with the people who need to be in your life—whether as teachers, students, or fellow travelers. However, it helps to pray, meditate, and set your heart on wisdom in order to attract the right people into your life. One of the greatest blessings you can have in life is a mentor or role model who can show or explain the path that you need to take to get from where you are now to what you ultimately want to become—for truly, in order to achieve certain goals, it is not enough to have the desire—you must be able to clearly envision all of the steps you must take, including the sacrifices that you must make. Because there can be many teachers in your life, and they can take many forms, listen more closely to people you may have been overlooking, as well as others who may show up in your life. Some of them may not volunteer advice (since they have learned that most people don't care), so you must be assertive enough to ask questions. Also, when the Hermit card comes up, think about ways that you can be a light to others. When the Hermit card is reversed, it could warn against following advice that is not suited for you. When the people in our lives do not have the clarity to see us as the individuals that we are, they may give advice that does not take our unique goals and developmental needs into consideration. Therefore, you must look at everything carefully to sort out what is meaningful and what is not.

Orientation to the Past

In some versions of the Tarot, the Hermit lifts his lamp to the left, the direction that Western culture associates with the past. Therefore, this card could suggest that something from the past may weigh heavily on your mind. Alternatively, it may be necessary to go back to look for something that was lost in the past. Also, although most Tarot readers associate the Hermit with self-knowledge and wisdom, Fred Gettings has pointed out that this card may denote a "preoccupation with the past" from which a person needs to be liberated if he wants to move into the future.[15] I think this would more likely be the case if the Hermit is associated with cards of blockage or stasis.

Quest for Knowledge

The Hermit reveals that the quest for knowledge is or will be a dominant element in your life. For many young people this could signify devotion to studies, though it can also denote spiritual and philosophical seeking. In relation to some questions, the Hermit can also denote the search for specific information, possibly the act of uncovering the truth of something. Here the graphics can be significant: if the Hermit's lantern points to an element in an adjoining card (whether the Hermit is upright or reversed) this other image may provide a key to the information you seek. When the Hermit is reversed (especially if surrounded by negative cards), it could denote a course of study that is inappropriate for you because it does not satisfy your soul, or it could mean that you are looking in the wrong places for the information you seek.

Seclusion

This card may denote a period in your life when you need to spend more time alone, perhaps so you can focus on study or spiritual contemplation. You may also find that solitude enables you to gain greater self-knowledge or get a better perspective on a personal situation or problem. The reversed card could denote a desire to come out of a period of seclusion and become more socially active.

Time Element

Related to the Hermit's images of age and patience, this card would tend to indicate that a desired outcome may take a long time to materialize, probably because it will be necessary to develop more discipline or gather special information. With the reversed card, the time element is even more indeterminate.

Travel

Some readers see the Hermit as predicting a journey. If so, it is likely to involve travel for the sake of gaining knowledge or being alone. In keeping with the Hermit's surroundings, it could involve a trip into the wilderness. The cards that the Hermit is facing (whether he is upright or reversed) may provide clues about the destination.

X. THE WHEEL OF FORTUNE

ARTHUR'S DREAM

The card that represents the workings of destiny through cycles of change is the Wheel of Fortune. The Rider-Waite-Smith illustration for this card is elaborate in its mystical symbolism: it portrays a sphinx with a sword sitting atop a wheel that is inscribed with the letters *TARO*, as well as the Hebrew letters *Yod-Heh-Vau-Heh* (the Cabalistic name of God), and alchemical symbols for the elements. A jackal-headed figure representing Anubis (the Egyptian guardian of the dead) ascends the wheel, while a snake representing Typhon (a god of destruction) descends it. The four corners of the card feature an angel, an eagle, a winged lion, and a winged bull, all reading books; Waite identifies them with the four creatures in the vision of Ezekiel, although they have also been identified with the four fixed signs of the zodiac (Aquarius, Scorpio,[16] Leo, and Taurus), and the four archangels (Raphael, Gabriel, Michael, and Uriel). Waite uses this complex design to signify "the perpetual motion of a fluidic universe," with the sphinx demonstrating the attainment of "stability amidst movement."[17] Before Waite, the Wheel of Fortune generally illustrated the mutability of human life, often by showing people at different stages of life, or with different degrees of wealth and power, rising up or being cast down by a giant wheel. Sometimes the people have animals' ears or tails, or they look like strange hybrid creatures, to illustrate the idea that most people spend their lives going around in circles, and because they aren't able to rise above and see beyond their basic drives, they are not substantially different from animals. Many of the older versions also portray the goddess Fortuna, who is the main goddess-presence behind the Tarot. (The word

10 THE WHEEL OF FORTUNE

"Tarot" may signify the Wheel of Fortune, called the "Rota Fortuna.") She is sometimes winged, crowned, or blindfolded, and may stand beside, above, or in the middle of the wheel. Sometimes she also carries a horn of plenty (cornucopia), which was her most common emblem in more ancient eras. Following are some of the turns that the Rota Fortuna could take for you.

Change

A change may be coming up, so prepare for both the expected and the unexpected. Even though the change in question is likely to be for the better, you might experience it as disorienting, and need to find ways to adapt. Things are happening, chains of events unfold, and people are in motion. There is energy here, and now you must determine in which direction the energy is moving. If you like the energy and the direction, you can ride it into the future. When this card is reversed, changes may be taking place on a subconscious level or unfolding on a slower time scale, or there may be some resistance to change; also, more variables may make the course of change less predictable.

Cycles

The Wheel of Fortune encourages us to examine our lives in terms of circles and cycles. Recurring themes enable us to appreciate our continuity with the past and with the future, showing us how we have a stake in both. The ability to identify patterns also allows us to avoid getting into ruts, and to make effective changes and take new directions. It is possible that you have come to a point in a cycle when you can bring something to completion, while carrying other things forward into a new phase of life. The reversed card could indicate the temporary disruption of a cycle, or the need to return to an earlier phase to relearn something.

Destiny

When the Wheel of Fortune comes up, it indicates that the matter in question, even if it is something trivial, may play a role in your larger destiny, either enabling you to make a connection with a significant issue that is being carried forward from a previous lifetime, or guiding you toward something that your soul is set on experiencing in this lifetime. (See the glossary for more information about the terms "destiny" and "life path.") By destiny, I do not refer to things such as events and relationships that are fated and cannot therefore be avoided. Rather, because we are the individuals that we are, with the likes, dislikes, and character traits that we have, we tend to be attracted to certain life paths in order to make certain general contributions here on earth. When we are able to follow a good destiny, our lives are more meaningful, and the things that we need or desire are more easily attracted into our lives. Consequently, the Wheel may denote things, relationships, and events that have been attracted into your life to help you move toward whatever it is that gives you the greatest fulfillment.

Luck

Unless accompanied by negative cards or otherwise indicated, the things that the Wheel of Fortune portends are likely to be lucky for you, in keeping with the ancient Greeks' and Romans' view of Fortuna as a benevolent goddess of abundance. Because this card may also point to an important nexus (connecting link) on your life path, your luck might especially be found in new opportunities that are opening up. When this card is reversed, it could indicate that luck is there for you, but you might have to work a little harder to make it happen. As the German saying goes, *"Jeder ist sein Glückes Schmied,"* which means that everyone forges his or her own luck (is his or her own "luck-smith").[18] Under some circumstances, unexpected growth opportunities may be revealed in a state of being that is the opposite of what you would normally find desirable.

Second Chances

Because the Wheel is concerned with the cyclic process of life, and the idea that we repeatedly come around to the same points, one of the things that this card may promise is a second chance. If you feel that you've really blown an important opportunity, such as a chance to meet or romance a special person, a chance to improve your relationship with someone close to you, a chance to get in on a special offer or adventure, or if you have regrets about another type of missed opportunity, another chance may come up—possibly very soon. Of course, second chances may not always involve the same people, places, and circumstances, but if a certain action, experience, or change of direction is important to your life path, the forces of destiny will work toward your benefit, helping to find another way for you to compensate. When this card is reversed, it could indicate that it is possible for you to make up for a missed opportunity, but you may have to go outside of your normal boundaries to look for a new opportunity.

Some Thoughts on Progress

It is a characteristic of the American mindset that we like to see life's progress moving forward. We expect that next year we should be better off, at least by a small degree, than we are this year, and we also assume that each generation will be more secure than the previous one. When a reversal of fortune sets us farther back, either as individuals or as a society, this is traumatic not merely because of the hardships it imposes, but because it goes against our whole philosophy of the way things should be. In past eras, when social and technological changes were very slow and not necessarily visible to the average person, personal advancement was not seen as everybody's entitlement, so reversals of fortune were often taken more philosophically.

XI. JUSTICE

The Justice card typically portrays a woman holding a sword in one hand (usually her right hand) and a set of scales in the other. She is sometimes portrayed blindfolded, but this is very rare, for her penetrating vision enables her to see to the heart of any matter, and her sword shows that she has the power to back up her authority. The figure of Justice is modeled after the ancient Greek and Roman goddess of Justice, who was named Diké or Astraea. Legend has it that she once came down from Olympus to dwell among humankind, but became disgusted with human contentiousness and ascended to the stars to become the constellation Virgo. Her scales also associate her with the sign of Libra, which seeks to create peace and harmony, establish values, balance the needs of the individual with the claims of society, view issues from both sides, and honor diversity and differences, while Virgo has the powers of discernment, logic, order, objectivity, concern with facts, and intellectual clarity. Following are some of the issues that the Justice card could raise.

Balance

Like other cards in the Tarot deck, such as Temperance and the World, Justice signifies the need to find balance in life. Consequently, it may indicate that you are in the process of making lifestyle adjustments (notice that the *Crowley Thoth Tarot Deck* labels this card "Adjustment") in order to achieve a combination that is ideal for you. This could include finding the right balance between your own needs and those of others, the right mix of work, study, social life, recreation, and so on.

The reversed card could indicate frustrations with achieving a workable combination; you may have a tendency to run to one extreme or another, which gives you a sense of being out of kilter.

Character

Justice can denote a person with honesty, integrity, and a balanced point of view. It can also signify a judge or another person empowered to make important decisions. If reversed, especially if accompanied by negative cards, it may indicate someone whose actions have wounded her integrity; a consequence may be the creation of distrust or trouble with the law. This is a warning to protect your good name, because, as the African saying goes, "You only need to kill one lion to be called a lion killer, and you only need to tell one lie to be called a liar" (or "to steal once to be called a thief").

Decisions

The Justice card may be telling you that you will have to make a heavy decision, and advises you to make an informed choice by detaching from the situation emotionally and gathering the data you need to weigh the pros and cons. Fred Gettings emphasizes this interpretation in *Book of Tarot,* saying that Justice "is meant to represent a warning and indicates a need for proper deliberation."[19] If reversed, there could be problems with indecision or an inability to make an objective decision; it might be a good idea to seek the opinion of a friend in whose instincts and analytical abilities you have confidence.

Education

The Justice card may have a special message for students, as Eden Gray has stated that it denotes "[t]he elimination of useless, outworn forms of education," as well as the need for education "with a well-balanced mind as its aim."[20]

Equality and Fairness

When the Justice card is present, especially if accompanied by favorable cards, it can indicate that you, the people in charge, or other people in question want to act fairly by trying to divide rewards, punishments, goods, jobs, or opportunities, for example, as equally as possible. Even if things don't appear to be "equal," they may be "equitable," that is, taking individuals' needs and differences into consideration. When this card is reversed, it could point to an inequality, possibly because the people involved don't know how to handle a situation fairly. It could also mean that you have to come to terms with things that either God, society, nature, or chance has dealt out to you, seemingly unequally in comparison with other people.

Legal Matters

As the title and imagery make explicit, this card often points to legal affairs. Because Justice is such a strong card, it indicates that justice will be done, and that the law will decide in your favor. If Justice is reversed, but otherwise accompanied by favorable cards, it could mean that there might be complications or delays in the legal process, but eventually things will work out for you. However, if Justice is reversed and surrounded by negative cards, it could warn of bigger problems. You might want to avoid getting involved in any legal actions at this time, and if you are thinking about doing anything illegal, or even associating with anything or anyone that is questionable, *don't!* (My dad has the following saying: "When the black wagon backs up to the door, they take the good girls—or boys—along with the bad.")

Karma

The Justice card is sometimes associated with "karma," a term that is used to describe metaphysical laws of cause and effect that work on a grand scale, often over the course of many lifetimes (although different religious and philosophical systems have different ideas about how karma works). To put it simply, karma refers to a belief that we will eventually reap the rewards of our good actions and intentions, and have to deal with the consequences of our bad ones. Thus, if it looks like someone is getting away with something, this card may warn that he will pay for it later. Also, the Justice card could indicate that karmic factors are involved in the situation in question, so the things that are going on now, whether positive or negative, may be the consequences of past deeds. This may especially be the case with Justice reversed, as reversed cards can show forces at work on a slower or subconscious level. However, since we cannot know for sure which events are karmic and which are not, we should always stand up for our rights and fight for justice whenever we can, rather than passively tolerating injustice to ourselves or others in the belief that it could be karmic.

Relationships

In order to function well within a relationship, a person needs to make some compromises so that both partners' needs are taken into consideration. The presence of Justice may indicate that you are going through this process, but it bodes well for the long-term success of the relationship, because you are conscious of the need for give and take. The reversed card could warn of an inequality that could eventually trouble the relationship.

XII. THE HANGED MAN

The Hanged Man typically portrays a man suspended upside down from a tree or a horizontal pole. Usually he hangs very loosely, by one foot only, with his other leg bent behind him (making something of a crosslike figure). His arms are also folded or tied behind him. He often has a very peaceful look on his face, and the card gives the impression that his suspension is voluntary, and that he could easily free himself. Some of the modern versions of this card differ from the older ones by portraying a halo around the head of the hanged man, which accentuates the spiritual side of this card. Whatever version you're using, this is a card that can have several levels of meaning, so its interpretation is especially dependent upon the nature of the question and the surrounding cards. It can make a statement about the problems of a life in stasis, but it can also refer to life's transitional periods, as well as meditative states and acts of self-sacrifice. Following are some of the conditions to which this card may relate.

Attitudes and States of Consciousness

When accompanied by positive cards, the Hanged Man may show that you have an attitude of acceptance, based on your spiritual faith and the knowledge that now may not be the appropriate time to try to control a situation. You may be taking time out for rest and reflection, and perhaps you are trying to solve a problem by viewing it from new and different perspectives. When accompanied by spiritual cards (such as the High Priestess, the Star, and others), the Hanged Man can represent higher states of consciousness, achieved

through meditation or religious devotion. On the other hand, when accompanied by materialistic cards (such as the Pentacles), the Hanged Man could warn of inertia or apathy, while the presence of negative cards could warn of attitudes that lead to victimization. The reversed card may foretell that your everyday concerns will pull you back to reality, but you may be able to hang on to some of the insights you've gained.

Life in Suspension

The Hanged Man can denote pauses in the normal flow of activity, or periods of waiting, so don't expect quick results or solutions to problems. Sometimes this card may represent a period of indecision during which the train of events could go in one direction or another. When this card is accompanied by positive cards, it may indicate that waiting is the best thing to do at this time, because something good needs time to develop. Accompanied by negative cards, it denotes a lot of frustration and delay. Perhaps a person or institution has left you "hanging" by not giving you the support or information you need. The reversed card tends to indicate that things are beginning to return to normal; the wait is almost over, and you will see some progress.

Punishment

Although this card usually pertains to the other human conditions listed here, imprisonment and punishment are among its traditional meanings, so it should serve as a warning to anyone who is thinking about getting into trouble. The reversed card does not lessen this warning, though under some circumstances, it could indicate a person who is soon to be freed from punishment.

Sacrifice

One of this card's most common interpretations is that of voluntary sacrifice: giving up your plans, your freedom, or a valued object in the service of a greater good. This sacrifice or detachment is often necessary in order to reach your next stage of spiritual growth. The reversed card could mark a realization that it's time to stop making certain sacrifices, perhaps because you have done enough, or maybe you are being taken advantage of.

Young Adult Years

When the Hanged Man comes up in a young person's reading, it may denote some of the frustrations that stem from a relative lack of power, choice, and mobility, and all the other restrictions associated with dependent or underage status (especially if accompanied by cards of restriction, such as some of the Swords or Pentacles). Many young people feel that their lives are "on hold," as they wonder whether they'll be able to go to college or get into careers with a future, while they wait to get a driver's license or a car, or while they look forward to the time that they'll be out on their own. The reversed card may indicate a young person who is making some progress toward personal freedom (though she may remain partially dependent for a while yet).

Transitional Periods

Because it depicts a person suspended between heaven and earth, the Hanged Man sometimes represents a person in a "transitional state" because he is undergoing a significant change in status. This could refer to a biological condition such as adolescence, pregnancy, or the midlife transition, or a transitional social state, such as that of trainee, a person between jobs (unemployed), a person going through a religious initiation, a person in military boot camp, a person in jail, a person engaged to be married, a newly divorced or widowed person, and so on. (Surrounding cards may provide further clues to the person's status or condition.) The Hanged Man can also denote a turning point: a personal realization that you need to make a change, though you may be unsure about where to go from here. Traditional societies often have special ceremonies for transitional periods, but in our own society, some of these may be lonely passages characterized by uncertainty and ambiguity. When accompanied by positive cards, the Hanged Man reversed could denote a person whose transition is giving him a new sense of purpose, though the presence of negative cards could indicate that there is some resistance, secrecy, denial, or lack of social acknowledgment of the changes a person is undergoing.

Although this card usually features a skeleton, it carries philosophical meanings for many stages in a person's life cycle, and is therefore very seldom a warning of real danger. When you read the Tarot for other people, it is important to stress this fact. (You should also avoid reading for anyone who has a difficult time dealing with potentially frightening images.) Some older versions of the Tarot portray the Death figure swinging his scythe as he walks through a field where severed heads, hands, and feet lie scattered; however, blades of grass sprout up around them, conveying the idea that the forces of destruction can clear the way for transformation and new growth. Some of the more modern decks show the skeleton clad in black armor and riding upon a white horse as kings, priests, and youths fall down before him. These depictions may also include symbols of rebirth, such as the mystic white rose portrayed on Death's banner in the Rider-Waite-Smith deck and some of its variants. Following are some of the ways that the transformations associated with this card may be experienced in a person's life.

Character

The Death card often portends a dramatic transformation of character or consciousness, which is why Eden Gray states that it "represents the death of the old self— not necessarily physical death."[21] Sometimes it represents experiences that forcibly eliminate distractions and pretensions from your life, enabling you to better understand your essential self, to get down to the "bare bones." It can also predict transformations brought about by a profound or frightening experience or another event that causes you to review the meaning of your life. If this card is reversed, it could indicate a slow process of personality transformation at work on a subconscious level.

Death

Tarot readers repeatedly emphasize that this card seldom foretells the death of a person. Indeed, if you regularly use the Tarot, this card will come up many times over the course of many years, without denoting anyone's actual death. However, as the years roll by, the inevitable death of family members and friends, and the acceptance of our own mortality, is something we must come to terms with. Therefore, this card could warn of danger for an individual who is very sick or very elderly, though because the future is not fixed, that person may well be able to outlive the threat. The appearance of this card does remind us to cherish our loved ones and improve our relationships while we can. The reversed card may warn of a "close call," or it may reveal that someone's behavior is motivated by the fear or the awareness of death.

Deathlike States of Being

In his book *The Broken Connection*, Robert Jay Lifton describes certain experiences of "separation, disintegration, and stasis" as "death equivalents." (Disintegration is a situation where things—including one's sense of identity—are falling apart; stasis is the inability to make changes or take action.) Under extreme circumstances, losses or traumas can produce psychological numbing in which "life becomes deathlike."[22] Depression is such a condition: Jennifer Barker Woolger and Roger J. Woolger have pointed out that when a person is depressed due to separation from a loved one, the loss of a job, the end of a way of life, or myriad other reasons, it is as if his life energy has followed the lost object into a psychological underworld.[23] Consequently, when the Death card comes up in a reading, consider whether you have been grappling with a "death in life" condition. Sometimes this realization enables you to confront the things that scare you, and to think about ways to recover your vitality. You might also choose to focus on creative activities, improved relationships, spirituality, and other things that give you a sense of connection to something greater than your own life. When the Death card is reversed, it may indicate that a person is dealing with death equivalent issues, but in a deeper, less conscious manner.

Descansos

In her book *Women who Run with the Wolves*, Clarissa Pinkola Estes states, "Women have died a thousand deaths before they are twenty years old. They've gone in this direction or that, and have been cut off. They have hopes and dreams that have been cut off also."[24] Based on the new research presented in his book *Real Boys*, William Pollack indicates that the same holds true for young men.[25] Estes suggests that we honor these symbolic deaths in memory by imagining them as marked with *descansos,* which are the little crosses often seen along highways that mark the sites of fatal accidents. You are not too young to think back over your own life, asking, in Estes's words, "Where are the crosses? Where are the places that must be remembered, must be blessed?"[26]

Endings and Beginnings

The Death card has a lot to do with cycles. Although it may denote something coming to an end—which could be a project, a job, a period of study, a relationship, your current social status, or a way of life, among many other things—it typically also promises a new beginning, an entry into a new state or level of existence. If you are nevertheless afraid of losses, you can usually soften the impact of this card by facing the need to let go of your attachments, especially if you are clinging to things that are unhealthy or outworn, and to make room in your life for new growth. The reversed card may indicate a slower process of transformation, resistance to change, changes that are going on behind the scenes, or a subconscious realization that some form of change is looming. This subconscious awareness could manifest in anxieties, worries, restlessness, and mood changes.

The Fascination with Death

Death images are prevalent in the media, as well as in the fashions of certain subcultural groups, and they especially seem to interest younger people (at least this has been the case since the latter part of the twentieth century). There are probably many reasons why this is so, related to a number of cultural developments. However, the Death figure can also serve as a source of artistic inspiration. In the words of the German writer Heinrich Böll, "The artist carries death within him like a good priest his breviary."[27] (A breviary is a book with prayers for the different hours of the day.) I believe that some young people are attracted to death images because they have an instinct for artistic reverie. Because we are a culture that discourages thinking or talking about death, objectification of death images (for example, a skull and crossbones on a ring or a tee shirt) enables us to get a glimpse of cultural and individual "shadows" (material repressed from consciousness), albeit from a safe and impersonal distance.

XIV. TEMPERANCE

During the Middle Ages and Renaissance, educated Christians listed the capacity for "temperance," which is defined as "moderation in action, thought, or feeling,"[28] as one of "the four pagan virtues" because temperate behavior was so highly respected by the ancient philosophers. (The other "pagan virtues" were prudence, courage, and justice.)[29] This quality of self-control is important to understanding the Temperance card, but so is the related term "temper," which, in the archaic sense, means "a suitable proportion or balance of qualities," as well as the act of "tempering," which refers to softening, strengthening, or mixing ingredients in order to bring something to a suitable state.[30] All of these definitions apply to the interpretation of the Temperance card, which is about making the adjustments needed to achieve an ideal state of being. This card usually features a winged angel who pours liquid from one cup or jug into another. In some of the modern versions of this card, the angel is described as male but has an androgynous appearance. Older versions of this card portray the angel as female, though in some decks she wears parti-colored robes (one side red and one side blue) and pours her fluid from red and blue or gold and silver vessels; this illustrates the idea of blending opposites, such as the spiritual and material, active and passive, conscious and subconscious, and masculine and feminine qualities. By mixing the fluid, the angel circulates the flow of life energies, and sometimes the angel stands with one foot in a pool or stream, to illustrate his or her connection with the greater life source. Following are some of the ways that the principles of Temperance may operate in your life.

Character

This card depicts a careful, thoughtful person who is self-contained and even-tempered (neither too emotional nor too detached), aware of what matters and what doesn't, and dedicated to continual self-betterment. She also performs her work with skill and competence, knows when to be soft and when to be tough, gets along with other people, tries to create harmony in her environment, and is good at managing the details of daily existence. When this card is reversed, it may denote an ordinarily conscientious person who is being overwhelmed by chaotic outward circumstances, making it difficult to stay in control of her life.

Creativity

Temperance is especially meaningful for people in creative work, because the synthesis of many different elements and resources is fundamental to artistic success, as well as to finding unique solutions to problems and bringing something new into the world. (In fact, the *Crowley Thoth Tarot Deck* has relabeled Temperance as "Art.") Emulate the Temperance angel by adding a creative touch to whatever you do.

Equity

Like the Justice card, Temperance is concerned with balance and adjustment; one tradition holds that decisions will be well considered and impartial, so something will be dealt fairly or shared equally.[31] When reversed, problems may arise from some kind of inequality.

Guardian Angel

Some Tarot readers have suggested that this card can point to angelic influences (and other good influences) in your life. A reversed card would indicate that guidance is there for you, but you need to be more open to it.

Health

Health and health management are important to the balance and well-being with which the Temperance card is concerned. Generally, this card points to good health; for a sick person, it predicts healing and the return to an active life. Indeed, Mary K. Greer sees the Temperance figure as an "angel of healing" who offers an elixir that "brings the energies and flow of your body and mind back into balance."[32] This card may also indicate an interest in healing that leads you into a health profession, or encourages you to experiment with alternative medicinal or physical practices such as Ayurveda, yoga, or tai chi, which aim to balance the body and spirit. When this card is reversed, it can point to a disharmony within your body and mind, thus urging you to pay more attention to your needs.

Life in Balance

The Temperance card may depict your efforts to achieve the right balance of elements in your life: the right combination of work, study, rest, and recreation, as well as the right people, the right relationships, the right activities, the right places to be, the right spiritual path, and so on. (For many of us, this is an ongoing, long-term process.) When this card is reversed, it may indicate that something important is missing from your life, or that you have too much of some things and not enough of others. Any cards that accompany the reversed Temperance may provide clues as to what needs to be readjusted, that is, the upright cards may indicate the things that you have too much of, and the reversed cards may show what you need more of.

Self-Improvement

The appearance of the Temperance card indicates that you are working on self-betterment and control—developing virtue, patience, adaptability, and self-esteem that is based on pride in performance. One of the long-term goals is "individuation," a process that involves learning to express all of your positive qualities, while also integrating negative or repressed aspects of your selfhood by acknowledging and understanding them, and, where possible, transforming them into something useful. When this card is reversed, you may need to get some feedback from your friends, because it is possible that you have both positive and negative traits that you are unaware of. (Traits that other people can see in you but you cannot see in yourself are said to be part of your "shadow" nature; we can have both positive and negative characteristics in our shadows.)

XV. THE DEVIL

The Devil card can point to many evils, dangers, and negative influences. It especially makes a statement as a card of self-defeat, as many versions of this card emphasize that evil or suffering can be self-imposed, but also that liberation is possible. For example, in the Rider-Waite-Smith deck, an enslaved man and woman stand before the devil figure. However, their chains hang loosely about their necks, implying that they could slip away if they had the determination or realization that they could do so. Some of the problems that the Devil can represent are discussed in the sections below. Note that I have not attempted to detail every form of evil that you might encounter, because that would get too involved; also, other types of problematic situations are discussed in association with other Tarot cards and their reversals.

Addictions and Self-Limiting Behaviors

The Devil card may warn that your problems are either directly or indirectly of your own making, possibly due to a self-limiting factor within you. Questions to ask when this card shows up include, "What is my biggest addiction?" "What is my most limiting belief?" and "What is my most self-defeating behavior?" Also, be aware of the human tendency to rationalize addictions or other harmful behaviors. Sometimes people will unconsciously create or exaggerate unhappy home conditions or other problems in order to justify negative behaviors because those behaviors give them another type of satisfaction. When this card is reversed, it could indicate a person who is less aware and more

likely to be in denial of her problematic behaviors—though, if reversed but accompanied by very positive cards or cards of revelation (such as the Sun, the Star, the Hermit, or Judgement), it could indicate a person who is becoming aware and starting to work toward breaking free of addictions.

Enemies

According to many traditional Tarot systems, the Devil card can signal the presence of enemies. Do not allow this possibility to create paranoia and cause you to suspect your friends, relatives, and the other people you deal with. However, do take reasonable precautions by being careful about what you say and do, and by working harder to promote harmony. The reversed card could represent people who have hidden resentments that even they may not be fully aware of; their underlying hostilities could come out later.

Human Evil

The Devil card may warn of danger, especially if accompanied by other negative cards. Sadly, there are genuinely evil people in this world, as well as people whose actions lead to evil, so when this card comes up, be very cautious about dealing with people who seem to be up to no good, and avoid potentially dangerous places or situations. If you start to experience fear for any reason, trust your instincts and seek safety. The reversed card could indicate that danger or evil is present, but other forces are holding it in check; however, it is still important to follow commonsense precautions to protect yourself and avoid trouble.

Other Problems

In addition to the other types of problems discussed, I have seen the Devil come up in situations that had no real evil at work; however, various things started going wrong. The reversed card could warn of the potential for things to go wrong, so it is important to make sure that there are no hidden weaknesses in your plans, or important things that you have left undone, or other factors that you have overlooked.

Psychological Complexes

Because the Devil can indicate situations in which you're acting under a compulsion to do things that go against your conscience, it can point to psychological complexes. You may have a complex if you find yourself doing things that you wouldn't ordinarily do, and can't understand why. This can happen when a part of the psyche, where energy has been building up around a deep resentment or unresolved personality conflict, has momentarily taken control. Some complexes affect more areas of life than others, but if they are causing destructive behaviors, it is wise to seek out a mental health professional for counseling. The reversed card could indicate a problem that is more difficult to identify.

Self-Destruction

Some of the self-destructive tendencies that the Devil represents can be attributed to the force known as the *contra naturam,* which means "against nature." Clarissa Pinkola Estes refers to this as "the predator of the psyche," and as "a derisive and murderous antagonist that is born into us . . ." It is a force within us that can prod us to do things that go against our own survival, and though we can psycho-analyze this contrary instinct into infinity, as Estes says, it "is what it is."[33] You may suspect the influence of the contra naturam if an inner force seems to be goading you into behavior that will harm you. It can also act as an inner voice that undercuts your self-esteem or your desire to be creative by discouraging you with its overly critical commentary.

Sexuality

Most versions of the Devil card make use of sexual symbolism, for although healthy expressions of the sexual instincts are integral to a person's sense of wholeness (when that person is ready to take full responsibility in relationships), inappropriate sexual activities do have a destructive influence on many lives. Young people today may especially be pressured by forces in the peer group and the mass media to become sexualized at earlier ages. Consequently, the Devil card may indicate that sexual issues are involved in the matter in question, and you may have to make some decisions about taking control of your own sexuality. When reversed, this card could point to sexual temptations that are not being acted upon, but are nevertheless creating tension.

Social Evil

The Devil card could warn of situations that have you fighting against social evil. Fortunately, many of us no longer live in countries that openly approve of slavery, conquest, genocide, child abuse, the oppression of women, and discrimination against minorities, and we're also making some strides in fighting poverty, cruelty toward animals, and the rape of nature. However, it is disturbing that it took thousands of years to arrive at this stage, with most reforms only having been instituted in the last half of the twentieth century. I believe that history's worst abuses have arisen out of a desire to control people who are different by keeping them "in their place." Indeed, there are many groups within our society who would like to roll back a number of reforms for this reason, and although they lack sufficient political power, their attitudes still manifest in certain forms of social evil. An example of this sort of manifestation that is familiar to many younger people is the school bully. Whatever other personal problems bullies may have as individuals, bullies act out our society's "shadow" nature by targeting as their victims people who are "different" in one way or another. The Devil could also warn of larger events, such as wars, depressions, or famines, for example, when these things loom into our consciousness due to our concerns for world events, or when they touch us or our families in some more direct way. The reversed card could indicate a form of trouble that isn't affecting you in the most direct and open way, but it could be causing worry if signs of it are appearing in your social environment. Social evil may especially be indicated if the Devil is accompanied by the reversed Emperor, Hierophant, or Justice cards (which are cards concerned with social order).

A Comment on Alternative Versions

Because early Christian missionaries demonized the gods of older religions, it is believed that the devil was modeled on one of the horned gods of old Europe. Some modern Tarot designers, uncomfortable with the evil portrayed in the Devil card, have assigned new images and meanings. For example, Anna-Marie Ferguson's *Legend: The Arthurian Tarot* deck portrays "The Horned One—Cernunnos" (the god who protects animals) and relates it to primal instincts.

XVI. THE TOWER

The Tower can represent a massive force that disrupts a way of life or overthrows existing beliefs and ways of doing things. This card typically shows two individuals (possibly a man and a woman) who plummet headlong from a burning tower that is being struck by lightning. It is generally presumed that the destruction of the Tower has been brought on by something in a state of "not-rightness." Young peoples' lives are often turned topsy-turvy by other peoples' decisions (such as parents' decisions to move, divorce, and so on), so many of the events that the Tower can signify—and the conditions that lead up to them—are beyond your control, and the best you can do is try to adjust to them. However, there are also things that are within your control, such as studies, career planning, relationships with friends and coworkers, and the activities you choose for recreation, so you can help to avoid or soften the impact of potential problems by reflecting on the Tower's messages and symbolism. Because the top of the Tower, the part struck by the lightning bolt, is often crown-shaped (representing the intellect), it may denote situations in which mind, body, and spirit are not in harmony, perhaps due to superficial, materialistic values. Other conditions that can lead to Tower-type downfalls may include rigid thinking, isolating oneself from other people, ignoring problematic situations, and risky lifestyles. Therefore, when the Tower comes up in a reading, it's important to examine your life; by making critical changes, you can avert some of the worst effects of the Tower. Following are things associated with this card (both positive and negative).

16 THE TOWER

Accidents

The Tower seldom denotes a physical disaster, but in my own experience, it has helped me avert some potential accidents. For example, the Tower came up on a day that my husband was planning to work on a ladder while doing some electrical wiring; because he was forewarned, he was more cautious, and discovered some bad wiring that otherwise would have given him a shock. Therefore, when you get this card, it is a good idea to be more mindful as you go about your daily routines. If this card is reversed, it is still a good idea to be cautious.

Consciousness

In some contexts, the Tower can represent creative breakthroughs and insights into problems, with the bolt of lightning representing the flash of illumination. In other cases, dramatic events bring about a change in attitude or dismantle illusions. On a higher level (something that may be indicated by the presence of very spiritual cards such as the Star, Judgement, or the World), the Tower can signal breakthroughs in consciousness that enable you to recognize your spiritual nature and your connection to the forces of nature and cosmos. At the very least, it can change your way of seeing things. When this card is reversed, it may indicate that your mind is working on a problem. If reversed and surrounded by spiritual cards, it may indicate that spiritual forces are stirring and pushing for change below your conscious awareness.

Emotions

Sometimes the Tower points to problems caused by people who are temperamental or impetuous. However, even in quiet and peaceful individuals, it can represent a buildup of rage or frustration that can explode in angry confrontations, nervous collapses, and the breakup of relationships. In *Seventy Eight Degrees of Wisdom*, Rachel Pollack says that forewarnings of building pressure may be experienced as disturbed dreams, depression, and arguments.[34] When reversed, building tension may be at an even more unconscious level, which means that if a blowup occurs, it may come as a greater surprise. Alternatively, it could denote an attempt to keep destructive emotions under control.

Events

The Tower can represent chaotic forces and events that disrupt your plans or even alter your way of life. These events, which can be brought on by natural causes, social causes, or human actions, tend to be sudden and unexpected; sometimes they can be rather unusual. Some Tower-type events that may affect young adults include family quarrels, family moves, loss of friends, or disappointments at school (such as discovering that you've carried out a project improperly and have to do it over), among many other things. Also, the Tower can signal events in your inner world that are connected to events in your outer world. Thus, things like accidents, illness, or losses may be mirroring turmoil in your emotional life. When this card is reversed, it can indicate the effects of more unconscious, small-scale, or gradual changes. It may also indicate situations that are still in a state of unfolding.

Foundations

The Tower card often implies that an individual has built the structure of her life upon a poor foundation. This can point to many problems, including unhealthy attitudes, actions, and lifestyles. One of the worst delusions associated with the Tower is the attempt to build one's happiness on top of someone else's misery. We have many large-scale historical and social examples of this, such as the past institution of slavery or the oppression of women and other social groups; when repressive situations persist for too long, they can lead to the overthrow of governments or institutions. However, there are many ways that ordinary individuals pursue happiness by hurting other people, as in the case of people who cheat, steal, put down other people, or break up others' relationships. The consequences may not be revolutionary, but the pain that they inflict may someday flare up in a situation foretold by the Tower.

Liberation

One of the more positive portents of the Tower is the possibility that you'll be cut loose from a situation that you really aren't happy with (for example, being laid off from a job that you really hate). Although this can leave you disoriented and confused, it can open your life to new opportunities. Many Tarot readers feel that when the Tower card appears, something in your life is not as it should be, and that the disruptions are therefore needed to put you back on your rightful life path. If this card is reversed, your new freedom may be of a more limited nature.

Time Element

Events predicted by the Tower usually happen suddenly and unexpectedly, and sooner rather than later. When this card is reversed, things are more uncertain and slower to develop, so it may be easier to avert trouble by attending to neglected problems.

XVII. THE STAR

The Star reveals the channels of energy that flow into your life, bringing inspiration, guidance, and renewed life force. This card generally features a beautiful woman who is portrayed kneeling beside a stream or a pool of water. The lush countryside setting represents fertility and creativity. Her nudity shows her innocence, openness, and essential humanity, and she pours fluid out of two pitchers, nourishing the land and replenishing the water around her. A bird is often shown perched on a tree or bush behind her (said to be symbolic of the soul resting on the Tree of Life). Stars fill the sky above her, with a large eight-rayed star often in the central position. Among the qualities that this card conveys are optimism, enthusiasm, affection, loving kindness, good luck, unexpected opportunities, favors, abundance, health and wholeness, inner peace, freedom, and self-expression. Following are some of the other ways in which you may experience the special gifts denoted by this card.

THE FIREDRAKE

17 THE STAR

Character

When this card comes up in response to a question about the character of a person, it can indicate someone who is kind, caring, gracious, and open to others, but also self-contained and directed by inner values. It can point to depth and strength of "soul force," and may also indicate that he experiences the protection of spiritual powers, and that he is a person who will aid and protect others, and may have a special destiny to fulfill. I see it as relating to certain African beliefs that we all come into this world with a special mission and

141

renewed energy from the ancestor world (the world of spirit) that is expressed in our own unique personalities. The reversed card could denote a basically good person who lacks direction or self-esteem because he finds it difficult to sustain the sense of his specialness and unique spiritual connection.

Creativity

Fred Gettings emphasizes the creative associations of this card, seeing it as denoting creative inspiration and the human ability to act as a creative force.[35] This is resonant of the mystic Meister Eckhart's belief that God expects us to serve as coworkers in the ongoing project of creation. Tradition has it that this card can also predict a person who will bring artistic inspiration into your life. The reversed card could indicate that sources of inspiration are opening for you, but you need to learn to trust the flow of your own creativity.

Heart's Desires

As a promise of wishes and desires fulfilled, possibly through some very serendipitous means, the Star encourages you to develop your talents and believe in your personal dreams, as well as in your visions of a better world. (Serendipity refers to a state of affairs in which things work to your benefit, often in ways that involve strange luck, coincidences, and unusual turns of events.) The appearance of the Star also assures you that your ideals are in harmony with your rightful destiny. As Marcus Bach has stated in his book *The Wonderful Magic of Living*, "One of the secrets is to believe that a good fate is on our side, that the deepest longings of the heart have a special meaning or they would not have arisen within us in the first place."[36] When this card is reversed, it could indicate that although you have some luck, you are not making the most of it because your outer actions are not well aligned with your inner desires.

Regeneration

Because the Star follows the Tower, it can be seen as representing a process of recovery following a period of trauma or upheaval, and therefore urges hope, courage, and patience as you wait for healing and strive to bring yourself into right relationship with the forces of spirit and nature. A reversed card would indicate a slower process, taking place on a deeper, more unconscious level.

Soul Life

The presence of the Star in any reading, even those pertaining to everyday concerns, indicates that the matter in question is important to your soul life. When this card is reversed, it may signal that in addition to whatever else may be wrong, you are in a state of spiritual "not-rightness." Whether you have consulted the Tarot because of illness or other problems, this card indicates that healing or recovery needs to take place on a spiritual level, that you must strengthen your connection with your deity, as well as your inner being. Depending upon the question and its position in a spread, the reversed Star can point to things that are draining your soul and spirit, such as the stresses of school and work life, or an unhappy home life—among the many other things that can have a soul-numbing effect. If this has resonance for you, it is important to seek out people and activities that nourish and strengthen your soul-spirit.

Spiritual Guidance

In keeping with folkloric traditions that the stars represent the watchful presence of divine beings, this card may indicate that spiritual forces are active in your life, and are assisting you in the matter in question. You can help yourself by paying more attention to personal religious matters, seeking out spiritual wisdom, praying and meditating, strengthening your inner light through positive thinking, listening to your intuition, and making decisions based on what you feel a spiritually evolved person would do. Also, have faith that the information or insights that you need will come to you. The reversed card could point to attitudes that prevent you from fully opening to channels of spiritual energy and wisdom.

XVIII. THE MOON

18 THE MOON

The Moon card deals with the world of instincts, emotions, cycles of nature, incipient life forms, the subconscious mind, and the collective unconscious. (See the glossary for the use of the word "unconscious" and related terms.) Modern illustrations of this card usually feature two dogs or a dog and a wolf who bay at the moon. In the foreground, a crayfish swims in a moat or emerges from a pond; in the background, a winding path runs between two distant towers. The dog and wolf remind us that instincts and emotions can be tamed, yet they always retain their connection to the wild. The water represents the depths of the unconscious, and the crayfish can represent ideas as life forms that take shape there, then gradually emerge into awareness.

These days, the Moon is a more difficult card to interpret, because it is at the center of a cultural debate. In the past, some Tarot readers went along with some dominant trends in thought, which divided the world of nature into a dualistic code that read: the sun = man = good, and the moon = woman = evil. The negative interpretations of the Moon card were furthered by its association with the unconscious; for some this is a dark and scary place where we may confront deception, confusion, and loss of identity. However, some modern Tarot artists and interpreters are questioning these assumptions and renegotiating the meanings, so the unconscious is more often perceived as a source of magic and discovery, and intuitive (feminine) wisdom is valued. Even strict characterizations of the moon as feminine and the sun as masculine break down in the light of cross-cultural comparisons, as there are many mythological systems that portray the sun as feminine and the moon as masculine (for example, seeing the sun's energy as the mother stuff of life, or the moon's measurement of time as a more masculine quality). Thus, although it's a bit tricky, I try to interpret this card more intuitively (though, of course, intuition plays a part in any reading) by trying to sense how comfortable the person I'm reading for is in dealing with things that are below consciousness or in a twilight state where things are mutable and not always what they seem. Following are some of the ways that the Moon's shapeshifting energies could be experienced in your life.

Changeable Conditions

Through the presence of the Moon card, the Tarot is telling you that prediction is difficult because some things are in too early a state of development or other things are in a state of flux. This amorphous state of affairs would indicate that a hoped-for outcome will be slow in developing, and may not materialize at all. Because you may be going through a period of uncertainty where reliable information is not readily available, it is important to make your way as best you can, relying on your intelligence and instincts. If the Moon is surrounded by negative cards, you need to be extra careful and steer clear of potential dangers. The reversed card does not significantly alter these meanings, so it is still important to proceed patiently and cautiously.

Nature

Under some circumstances, the Moon can denote an attraction to the things of the wild, and may point to time spent in nature.

Psychic Activity

The Moon can highlight creative imagination, fantasy, meaningful dreams, premonitions, the surfacing of past-life memories, and so on. If this card is associated with positive cards, it may urge you to trust your intuition; in association with cards that shine light on a situation (such as the Sun or the Hermit), it may predict psychic revelations. The Moon can also indicate that mystical or intuitive people will be influential in your life. The reversed card could imply that you have some latent psychic ability, but need more training.

Romance

The dreamy quality of the Moon hints at heightened emotions, physical attraction, and romantic meetings. However, there is an element of illusion here, and you may be in a susceptible state, where you could be easily influenced by deceivers. If positive cards are present, you may benefit from more protective influences; if the Moon is surrounded by negative cards, it would be a good idea to delay romantic involvement until more clarity can be gained. Similar meanings apply to the reversed card. It could also suggest that illusions are beginning to lift, so any relationship will have to come to terms with more realistic, down-to-earth matters.

Subconscious Motivations

The appearance of the Moon reveals that subconscious factors exert a major influence over your reading. Some things are beginning to stir in the depths of your mind—some old memories or developing ideas and revelations that will penetrate your outer awareness when they take solid form. However, subconscious fears and needs may also be driving the issue in question. Heightened senses make you hypersensitive to cues from your inner and outer environments, and may cause emotional ups and downs. If you've been feeling some anxiety, it may be that your instincts have sensed a developing problem. However, without a clearer understanding, they may also compel you to act in an impulsive and irrational manner. If negative or reversed cards accompany the Moon, you may be dealing with some complexes, which are subconscious facets of the personality that can induce you to act out things you wouldn't normally do. Some readers see the reversed card as indicating a return to clarity, while others think it shows suppression of the subconscious, or the operation of motives at an even deeper level of the unconscious. Look to surrounding cards for further clues as to how this card may operate.

XIX. THE SUN

The Sun card typically portrays a large radiant sun, often with a child or children playing beneath it. Sometimes the children are a boy and a girl or a pair of twins, though the Rider-Waite-Smith versions portray a very young child riding a white horse. Tradition has these children standing (or riding) before a garden wall, an enclosure that suggests protection. This is a card of good news and cheer because it shows you enjoying life, robust health, happiness, and success. People who embody the qualities of the Sun display a positive outlook, exuberance, openness, personal charm, radiance, and a high level of energy. Among the good things this card may promise are luck, growth, freedom, celebrations, gifts, favors, and new life. You may also experience its blessings in some of the following areas.

Affirmative Response

Regarding yes and no questions, especially in response to hoped-for outcomes, the Sun answers "yes." The reversed card would indicate that you have a chance of getting what you want, but it will take some extra work.

Children

Due to the Sun's portrayal of children and childhood joys, it may indicate that children, childbirth, or children's issues are involved in the matter in question. The reversed card could denote worries about children, possibly over a child or children that are troubled or far away.

Influence in Reading

The Sun is held to be such a lucky and powerful card that its meaning is not influenced by any negative cards that surround it. Rather, it has the opposite effect, indicating that something good will come out of whatever problems the reading may reveal. When reversed, the potential for good is still present, but somewhat muted. That means you have to keep thinking positively to activate your luck.

Inner Child

Sometimes the Sun may point to an active "inner child." The inner child is a facet of your personality that expresses your earliest hopes, fears, and experiences. It is present in situations in which you are playful and express yourself freely, when you know that you are in a secure and loving environment. If the Sun is reversed, the inner child may be an unconscious motivator. If surrounded by negative cards, a needy inner child may be acting out or persuading you to cling to childish things.

Popularity

The Sun card's focus can mean that you will get plenty of attention; you will be complimented on your achievements, people will be eager to help you, and things will go your way. People also like to be around you because you radiate warmth and self-assurance. When this card is reversed, it may indicate that you feel uncomfortable about being the center of attention, and may downplay your accomplishments. Although you may not experience great popularity, more perceptive people will recognize your inner light; look to such people for encouragement.

Relationships

The Sun denotes an abundance of love and affection in your life, and bodes well for romance as well as friendship. The reversed card could represent people who are shy about displaying their affection.

Self-Expression

The Sun is concerned with self-expression and development. (This also relates to the Sun's role in astrology.) The appearance of this card implies that you are learning to recognize your personal needs and do the things that allow you to be yourself. As Jungian authority Karen Hamaker-Zondag points out, this self-expression emanates from a personal identity that is secure, adaptable, and accepting, and is therefore able to come to terms with its flaws, and to allow other people their self-expression, too.[37] When reversed, the Sun card may indicate that you are still in the process of developing your sense of Self, and may also need to work out minor problems involving your ego needs. Alternatively, it could indicate that although you may be a strong individualist, you find it necessary to repress some of your desires and opinions in order to get along with other people.

Talent

The Sun promises creative energy and insight, and the ability to find work that you love. It also denotes bright, energetic individuals who can expect to achieve public recognition for their accomplishments. When this card is reversed, it may denote people whose natural talents require more development.

Further Thoughts on the Sun

Chögyam Trungpa Rinpoche, who has some inspiring thoughts on the image of the sun, is quoted by Pema Chödrön as saying, "Hold the sadness and pain of samsara in your heart and at the same time the power and vision of the Great Eastern Sun. Then the warrior can make a proper cup of tea." *Samsara* refers to the repeated cycles of existence, and Chödrön interprets this as meaning that if you can maintain a hopeful, positive vision even while acknowledging the fundamental "sadness of human life," you can carry out the rituals of daily living in a more skillful manner.[38] Although I've never seen a Tarot card that has captured the magnificence of the rising sun, the Sun card can make a good talisman or image for meditation because as a symbol of hope, the image of the Sun can help us to face each new day, even when our troubles seem insurmountable.

XX. JUDGEMENT

The Judgement card usually portrays the angel Gabriel flying overhead as he blows on a bannered trumpet. Below him, the dead are at the moment of awakening. They have been restored to full health and wholeness, and joyously rise from their tombs. Among them are young and old, all naked, symbolizing their rebirth into a new state of innocence. *The Robin Wood Tarot Deck* offers an alternative image of rejuvenation: a woman rises from the cauldron of regeneration, with the aura of the phoenix behind her. In a general sense, Judgement may signal your commitment to personal transformation through self-improvement, virtuous behavior, and elevated thought. In its highest sense, Judgement portrays the realization of great spiritual truths. Different philosophers have described this as the ability to see beyond illusion and know what is eternal, to understand your spiritual nature and your place in the universe, to perceive the soul life in the world around us and the interconnectedness of all things, and to achieve a sense of oneness with your God, and with all of life. Such realizations often accompany life-transforming experiences. Although this card has such a profound spiritual message, it also has meaning for the affairs of daily life. Following are some of its more common implications.

Awareness

Judgement especially applies to changes in consciousness. As mentioned above, this may denote an insight into certain spiritual truths. Whether as the result of your ongoing spiritual development, a major event, or a momentary spark of recognition, you gain some understanding of how the spiritual world interpenetrates our everyday existence. As several authorities have pointed out, this awakening brings the awareness that "happiness doesn't lie outside yourself,"[39] and that you can choose your own reality. There are many ways that this heightened awareness can influence the course of your life and actions. For many young people, this could be a realization of what you want to do with your life. You may, indeed, experience a "calling," that is, the conviction that you have a special mission to fulfill. The reversed card may hint at revelations that are still below consciousness; you may feel some anticipation, like you are just on the brink of a great discovery.

Change

The Judgement card can stand for a major change in personal status that is usually an improvement. For students and workers, this card could pertain to promotions or new positions. The changes indicated may also come about by natural processes, and can include biological transitions, such as adolescence. Sometimes these developments involve "rites of passage," which are transitional states (often periods of preparation and training) followed by formalized ceremonies—as in the case of graduations, bar or bat mitzvahs, weddings, and so on. Judgement can denote many other situations in which you feel you are leaving one way of life behind and moving up into something better. The reversed card could reveal resistance to changes that may not be entirely to your liking (even if they are setting you on a higher path), or changes that are taking place in a slower or less visible manner.

Decisions

You may have to review your life lessons and then exercise your judgement in making decisions that have far-reaching consequences. In her book *Living the Tarot*, Amber Jayanti suggests posing the question, "How important is this in the whole scheme of my life?" She also emphasizes the need for decisions that take the ethical high ground, reminding us, "Doing the right thing always has its rewards . . . but whether they are immediate or come somewhere down the line isn't predictable."[40] The reversed card could represent indecision; perhaps you must look beyond your ego needs in order to make the best judgement.

Judgement, Evaluation, and Rewards

As the title of this card suggests, people in power may be judging you, but this is likely to be favorable, resulting in public recognition of your achievements or change in status, possibly followed by celebrations and rewards—though in some cases (such as with a scholarship or job offer), the judgement and award may make the change in status possible. The reversed card could warn of complications or delays in this process, or that an award may depend on your fulfilling additional conditions. You may also experience some discomfort in dealing with very judgmental people—even if their assessments of you are deserved.

Legal Matters

Related to Judgement's word associations, this card may predict that the law or some other authority will make a favorable decision in a legal matter (especially if Justice is also present), while the reversed card could indicate frustrations and delays.

Renewal

In keeping with the drama of rebirth portrayed in its illustration, Judgement can signify a break with the past, followed by renewed life, energy, faith, and hope. For example, if the zest has gone out of a relationship, it foretells a chance to regain the original passion and sense of newness (unless this is a bad relationship that needs to end). In case of illness, it promises recovery and rehabilitation; it also denotes recovery from "deadening" experiences, such as depression and loss. If you have lost interest in your work, studies, or other pursuits, you may discover new inspiration, enthusiasm, and breakthrough ideas. Even your identity may be affected: life changes or special opportunities enable you to feel like a new person, starting out fresh and with a new sense of self and purpose. You may be impelled to throw off old behaviors and modes of self-presentation that prevent people from seeing the real you. You may even start to "reinvent" yourself. (Your plan of action might include new directions, a new course of education, new relationships, and so on.) This reemergence is likely to involve a reconfiguration of your psychological imagery, which will enable you to deal with the world in a new way. [41] (This is when you know that your transformation has really "taken.") All of these things are likely to accompany a renewed spiritual life. When this card is reversed, it may signify a physical or psychological recovery that proceeds more slowly; healing may be at work on a deeper level, and it may take you some time to effect genuine change in your attitudes and actions.

Social Change

The collective scene that is usually portrayed in this card shows that the reconstruction of Self has positive implications for our social world and future progress. As Luisa Teish has pointed out, the radical changes needed to create a better world and avoid the abuses of past history require that we "imagine ourselves as different beings."[42]

21 The Universe

XXI. THE WORLD

The World card usually portrays a woman who dances within a circle of greenery, which represents the interconnecting spheres of life. Sometimes she holds two wands, which represent the balanced forces that she has mastered. In the Rider-Waite-Smith deck, the card's corners feature the heads of a man, an eagle, a bull, and a lion, to illustrate her synthesis of the elemental and zodiacal powers. (These figures represent Aquarius/Air, Scorpio/Water, Taurus/Earth, and Leo/Fire, respectively.) *The Witches Tarot Deck* has renamed this card "Universe," and the *Crowley Thoth Tarot Deck* calls it "Aeon." As the final numbered card in the Major Arcana, it represents the culmination of the major lessons and experiences that the Tarot has to offer. Consequently, its highest expression shows the individual in an enlightened state of consciousness, enjoying her oneness with the living universe. However, as few of us regularly reach or sustain such an exalted level, this card usually means that you are living well and working toward harmony of mind, body, and spirit. Its common divinatory meanings are rewards, success, happiness, completion, and connection with the wider world. These blessings may be experienced in some of the following areas.

Career

The World card points to a rewarding career that allows you to pursue your best destiny. The reversed card would indicate a need to question whether you are doing (or planning to do) the right work, in the right place, among the right people.

Character

The World card portrays an individual who is in control of his life, expressing his own power and creativity as he manages things smoothly and wisely, with everyone's best interest in mind. Self-development is important to him. He also has an "inclusive" sense of self, which means that he strives to understand a broad range of human concerns, and extends empathy to all beings, including the creatures of nature. The reversed card may denote an individual who is struggling to achieve an enlightened outlook, but is hampered, perhaps because of fear of the outside world.

Completion

This card predicts the successful completion of goals, projects, and courses of study, but it also denotes a state of fulfillment—you are developing the best of your potentials and attaining everything you want. When reversed, it may indicate that you are falling short of achieving your potential, or that something important is lacking in an otherwise fortunate or prosperous situation. Perhaps you need to expand the dimensions and meaning of your life by finding something to share with others, or by becoming more aware of your spiritual nature.

Environment

Because of this card's emphasis on the quality of your surroundings, your home, work, or school environment may have some bearing on the matter in question. Because of this card's concern with interpenetrating spheres of existence, it may also show you in good relationship with the natural environment, and with the forces of the living universe. The reversed card would indicate a need to find surroundings that better promote your growth and awareness.

Life Path

This card is about following a good destiny as you understand and celebrate your place in the universe, so it would indicate that the decisions you are making are putting you on the right path. The reversed card may indicate that you have a sense of what your ideal life should be, but your attitudes or actions may be preventing you from going after it.

Manifestation

This card relates to the ability to manifest good things in your life through positive thoughts and actions. If reversed, it may indicate that you have problems manifesting your desires, either because your goals and actions aren't in harmony with your inner being, or because you need to set your mind on nobler things.

Relationships

As an expression of this card's sense of celebration, unity, and wholeness, it can predict a happy marriage or other fulfilling relationships. If reversed, it may indicate that your existing relationships don't allow the most rounded expression of who you are.

World Community

The World card may indicate that your connection with a larger world or greater cultural concerns is important to the matter in question. This could be expressed in many ways; for example, travel is a traditional meaning of this card, but it could also refer to being part of a global network or enterprise. In a general sense, it may denote your ability to get along in a diverse community, having meaningful connections with many other people. Alternatively, it could pertain to finding your own people, a community of choice that is supportive of your individuality. Since you are a person who is reading a book on Tarot, you might have some affinity for the people that the poet Gary Snyder calls "the Great Subculture," a "Tribe" without ethnic, religious, or historical boundaries that is dedicated to peace, creativity, the preservation of nature, the transmission of ancient wisdom, and the exploration of mind and spirit. He says that these people do not necessarily recognize each other "by beards, long hair, bare feet, or beads," but rather, "the signal is a bright and tender look; calmness and gentleness, freshness and ease of manner."[43] When this card is reversed, it may indicate that you want to be a part of a larger world, but have not yet linked up with the right opportunities.

7

THE WANDS

The suit most commonly known as Wands has gone by many different titles, including Scepters, Batons, Rods, Clubs, and Staves. The Rider-Waite-Smith deck portrays its wands made from long, straight branches with leaves growing out of the ends in order to emphasize the idea of life and growth; they are incorporated into illustrations that often feature people engaged in active competition and commerce. Some older decks portray simple wooden clubs or groupings of decorative scepters or polished rods. Wands are most commonly identified with elemental Fire. We can relate this to the lore of magic, in which wands are used to direct vital energy and to make things happen. Also, Wands are usually made of wood, and some ancient people believed that the reason wood could burn was because it contained heat (elemental Fire) within it.

The qualities that the Wands cards represent are active in our inner lives when we are working on self-confidence and identity development, and when we are expressing our personal ideals. They also concern the way we express ourselves in the outer world, through projects, enterprises and achievements, recreational activities, and social interactions. Wands-type intuition is at work when we are able to sense the creative possibilities of a situation, to act quickly to solve budding problems, or to get in on something new. Because energetic, self-confident people tend to radiate charisma, it is when we are expressing Wands qualities that other people are likely to find us most attractive. We may experience some of the more negative aspects of the Wands suit when we have to deal with stress brought on by too much activity or competition.

The Wands cards are similar to the Pentacles in that they both have a lot to do with job and business-related activities. However, the Wands are interested in the innovative, entrepreneurial, communicative aspects of doing business, while the

Pentacles are more concerned with the production of goods, management, and the financial side of business. Some of the Wands cards portray struggles and challenges to overcome. However, unless accompanied by negative cards, the Wands point to eventual success, because individuals who are able to summon the Wands' high level of energy usually go farther and earn more money than others who were born into similar circumstances, but are less energetic. Energy level combined with a "can do" attitude can make the difference between the haves and the have-nots, so learning how to generate the inner fire that the Wands represent can alter a person's fate.

Teens and young adults can experience Wands' energies through a broad range of activities, plans, and interactions. They experience the visionary, goal-oriented qualities of the Wands cards in the course of career planning, communicating ideals, creative work, and school and family projects. The Wands' active, competitive qualities are experienced through various extracurricular activities, including games, athletics and outdoor adventuring, different types of competition, and small-scale enterprises. Interactions with the public (as with different types of jobs or service clubs) and outings with friends or larger groups of peers activate the Wands' outgoing, social qualities. Most young people are learning to explore and express their personal identities—trying out different styles and modes of behavior in the process—and this also involves Wands' concerns with self-presentation and development.

Wands-type people (or people going through Wands-type phases) tend to be self-starters who are also good at leading and motivating other people. They are exciting to be with, and they encourage their friends to express their own talents. They enjoy acting upon the world through their relationships, and through their creative role in society. In fact, many see their outer-world accomplishments as an essential expression of personal potency. Wands people can become overstressed when they are overprogrammed, trying to participate in too many activities. People who exhibit negative Wands traits can be superficial, self-centered, and egotistical, and they sometimes repress other peoples' self-expression by trying to outshine them.

When Wands cards appear in a reading, different situations may come up very quickly, often bringing opportunities and the chance for adventure. Interesting people may suddenly appear in your life, and those around you will be more energized and enthusiastic, eager to deal in the exchange of ideas and activities.

THE ACE OF WANDS

The Ace of Wands signifies an increase of activity in your life. You may find yourself acting quickly to take advantage of opportunities for creative expression and personal growth. Things will be happening, and new energies and ideas will be making themselves felt. You and the people around you are probably experiencing some strong inspirations and desires, and are likely to act on them. This card often portrays a hand coming out of a cloud, holding a stout wooden club or wand, or it may simply feature a single wand from which green leaflets are sprouting. Following are some areas where its intense energies may be felt.

Energy Levels

In a reading, the Ace of Wands is an indicator of your energy level. This is important because your success in the matter in question may depend on how much energy you have. If the Ace of Wands is upright, especially if accompanied by positive cards, it shows you in a position of strength. While younger people tend to have more energy than their elders, some clinicians have become concerned because many high-school students and others are experiencing problems with sleepiness and sluggishness. A certain amount of this is due to modern living and working conditions that reprogram the metabolism and body rhythms, such as activities that keep you up late, or long hours spent staring at video screens. The bodily demands of adolescence and continued growth can also sap your strength. Consequently, a reversed Ace of Wands, showing lowered

energy, may be a warning to alter your lifestyle. Think about getting more rest, as well as some fresh air and exercise.

Enthusiasm

The Ace of Wands signals a burst of inspiration for getting started on new projects or stirring up the motivation that you need to get something else done. It predicts success in new adventures or other activities, because you have enthusiasm for doing new things, strong ideals, and a sense of "possibility." The enterprising spirit usually also leads to wealth and possible fame. The reversed card can indicate that attitudes or other circumstances may be blocking your ability to fully summon your energy and enthusiasm. You may need greater clarity about your motivations and goals in order to carry out a certain project successfully.

Health

For people with health problems, this card is a good sign because it predicts a return of the vitality that is so necessary for recovery. When this card is reversed, recovery may proceed more slowly because the energy you desire is not always "on tap."

Influence

The presence of this card reveals high energy and strong motivations, so it can amplify the meaning of surrounding cards—especially cards of action and purpose. However, if it is followed by cards of inertia, such as the Four of Cups or Eight of Swords, it may denote frustrated energies that have no outlet. If reversed, it may indicate that the power of the other cards isn't experienced consistently, but in sporadic outbursts.

Newness

The Ace of Wands is always concerned with the new, so new people, projects, goals, ideas, or technologies may somehow figure into your reading—perhaps launching you on a bold adventure.

Romance

Because this card stands for exciting new energies and experiences coming into your life, it may promise a new love, or the infusion of more passion into an existing relationship. Also, when you are embodying the fiery qualities of the Ace of Wands, you project charisma and qualities of leadership, which is something that other people find attractive. The reversed card could signify an uneven expression of passion, possibly because one or both partners have too many distractions. It could also denote people who keep their love secret.

Timing

The Ace of Wands points to situations or desires that will materialize very quickly. If accompanied by favorable cards, the reversed Ace could indicate some progress after a slower start.

Two of Spears

Bedivere & Kay

Two of Wands

BASTONI BATONS   2   WANDS BASTOS

STÄBE   STAVEN

THE TWO OF WANDS

The Two of Wands typically portrays a man looking toward the sea as he stands on the battlements of a castle; he wears a heavy cape and a fancy hat and holds an orb or world globe in his hands—images that suggest wealth and power. Many versions show him looking toward the left, which indicates an orientation to the past. He grasps a staff in his left hand, while another stands fixed in place behind him. Following are some Two of Wands–type issues.

Choices

The Twos often involve choices, and the Two of Wands may especially point to the need to decide between two equally attractive opportunities—possibly between two invitations, projects, colleges, jobs, places of residence, or ways of living. In a layout, the cards on either side of the Two of Wands could provide some clues as to what sort of things you are being compelled to choose between. In the Rider-Waite-Smith deck and others where the man pictured in the card faces toward the left, the card to the left of it may indicate the more favored choice. It could also indicate a desire to go with whichever choice is more familiar, that which is "tried and true." The reversed card could denote indecision or irrational motives in choicemaking.

Lifestyle

Sometimes the Two of Wands indicates that a person's lifestyle makes it necessary to divide her energies two ways. This could apply to many things, such as going to school and working at the same time, having a very demanding sport or extracurricular activity, having two jobs, and so on. Under some circumstances, it could apply to personal commitments, such as having two very different sets of friends, or dividing your time between two families. The reversed card could predict a stressful period which might make it necessary to simplify your life; you may have to give something up in order to enjoy greater freedom.

Relationships

The Twos often pertain to different kinds of relationships, and the Two of Wands may especially denote a friendship, or even a business or project partnership, based on a shared creative vision. If you are wondering whether love is about to enter your life, this card can also point to romantic partnerships; you might meet a new love through a common interest. Whatever the case, you may also have to modify some of your plans in order to work around your partner's needs. Issues of Self and Other might figure into a romantic relationship, meaning that the two people in question may have to discover the extent to which each needs to assert his or her individuality while respecting the other's individuality, and yet also learning how to function harmoniously as a "couple." If this card is reversed, it may indicate that the partners' energies don't mesh well; perhaps they have differing visions of what the goals should be, or they want to go off in different directions. The reversed card could also warn of friction due to an inequality in the relationship, which could be the case if one partner has more power, charisma, energy, ideas, or enthusiasm—or maybe more ego. If this is a problem for you, it may be possible to maintain mutual respect but find a way to get the other person to contribute more by suggesting other talents or resources he or she can bring to the partnership.

Success

Because the Rider-Waite-Smith version of this card portrays a rich, lordly looking figure, popular interpretations of this card suggest prosperity and power. Your success can best be achieved by cooperating with others, seeking help from influential people, and getting feedback on your ideas. The reversed card could point to a success that is farther off in the future; perhaps more time is needed for the right elements to come together.

THREE OF SPEARS

THE HORSE FAIR

THREE OF WANDS

BASTONI BATONS   3   WANDS BASTOS

STÄBE   STAVEN

THE THREE OF WANDS

The Three of Wands signifies the creative energy that promotes the circulation of new ideas. In the most popular illustrations of the Three of Wands, a man with his back turned to the viewer stands on a high cliff by a river or bay, observing three ships; the curve of their sails indicates that they are all headed outward. Two staffs are planted in the ground behind him, but he holds onto a third staff with his right hand, suggesting an orientation to the future. An alternative image is provided by *The Witches Tarot Deck*, which shows three women of different ages using their wands to form a triangle, suggesting an orientation to a creative community. Following are some of the ways that Three of Wands energies may express themselves in your life.

Business

Conventional meanings of this card are primarily concerned with business and commercial activity. Gray suggests that it may denote "practical help from a successful merchant."[1] In a daily reading, it could denote a shopping trip or a business interaction. It could also indicate an enterprise shared with a few friends. A reversed card could signify an individual who is just beginning to develop or learn about a business; problems could result from her lack of experience.

Communication

The combination of the Threes' easy energy flow and the Wands' urge for self-expression predicts success in things that involve communicating with others, and may even point to a communications-related career, such as advertising, journalism, work on the Internet, writing, or teaching. You might find yourself speaking in front of the public, or as part of a committee. You might also send out an important personal communication, and you can expect to get something in return. Some type of discovery might be involved. If reversed, you may have a desire to communicate, but more practice is needed in order to do so more effectively. There may also be a reason why you are hesitant to tell someone something that needs to be said.

Creative Expression

If you do creative work, you will be enjoying greater productivity and gaining some recognition for your talent. The reversed card could indicate creative block; keeping company with creative or stimulating people could be the remedy.

Planning

The seaward looking figure often portrayed in this card seems to be assessing what is out there, thinking about the area ahead and beyond. This indicates a widening of interests and new perspectives that encourage you to think about your future career and other opportunities. Because the graphics also convey the image of a merchant who is sending his ships out to sail, this card may be telling you that society offers many opportunities, but you have to make an effort to seek them out. If reversed, it may be that you need more direction or more information about the outside world. Try to learn from other peoples' experience.

Relationships

You could become involved with someone who is very dynamic (possibly someone you meet on the Internet, or through your network of friends), or your existing relationships may take on a more lively and productive quality. This card may come up in relation to matters involving a trio of friends or coworkers. The reversed card could warn of love triangles, a relationship that is threatened by an overactive social life, or problems within a small group of friends.

Work and Study

In addition to its association with the creative or communicative work mentioned above, the Three of Wands can denote good job contacts, an exciting job opportunity, or increased activity in your existing work or study routine, and rewarding interactions with friends, coworkers, or classmates. Your job or studies may also enable you to travel or interact with interesting people. If reversed, you may have to go farther or be more aggressive about discovering new contacts and opportunities.

THE FOUR OF WANDS

Many illustrations of the Four of Wands depict a scene of celebration: four tall poles stand in the foreground with floral garlands strung between them, while people in the background appear to be dancing, feasting, and parading; the outline of a castle or walled city rises in the distance behind them. In *The Celtic Dragon Tarot*, the castle is especially emphasized, while *The Robin Wood Tarot Deck* focuses on the celebrational elements, featuring a man and woman dancing beneath a square canopy. Generally, this card predicts the coming of happiness and the ability to lead a good life in a safe space. Because it combines the energy of the Wands with the materiality of the Fours, it shows you obtaining the things you want. Following are some of the ways that these things could manifest in your life.

FOUR OF WANDS

Celebration

Because the Four of Wands often portrays a festive scene and can denote a desire to formalize social status and relationships, it can predict marriages, adoptions, christenings, bar and bat mitzvahs, graduation or awards ceremonies, promotions, and other ritualized occasions. You may also be celebrating the completion of a goal or project. A reversed card may indicate a celebration or ceremony that is still in the planning process, such as an engagement or wedding preparations.

House and Home

When this card comes up, the focus of your reading may be on your home life. Your family may be buying

a new home or making improvements, or you may be experiencing improved family relations and good times at home. This card could also point to your ability to get a place of your own, or your future plans for a dream house. The time you spend at home is likely to be very productive. In some cases, this card could represent a home business. When the Four of Wands is reversed, it can indicate that although you may have a home place, it does not feel like a haven of refuge for you. Perhaps disruptive forces like frequent moves, family quarrels, too many people coming and going, or other types of problems prevent you from enjoying your time at home. Also, many young people do not experience a sense of shared "ownership" because they do not have much of a say about their surroundings. If this is the case for you, you might want to talk to your parents about finding ways that you can claim some space where you can express yourself.

Self-Esteem

Gail Fairfield, the author of *Choice Centered Tarot*, emphasizes the role of Wands in identity development and interprets the Four of Wands as "manifesting a new identity."[2] This can tie in with the way we express ourselves through our things and through our accomplishments, and how these things also improve our self-esteem. The reversed card may point to problems with trying to base identity and self-esteem on something that's not solid enough: a person needs real accomplishments to prove to himself that he is capable of managing challenges.

Success

Your goal-setting, hard work, and accomplishments pay off with greater security and improved finances, and possibly also some local prestige. At this stage you can slow down and relax a bit because the main work has been done. You will be able to have and enjoy nice things. The reversed card may indicate that you need to build your life on a more solid foundation before you can get everything you want.

THE FIVE OF WANDS

The Five of Wands represents changing conditions that introduce you to new ideas and experiences. This can happen when either outside forces or your own discontent may force you to become actively involved in challenging contacts with other people, as well as in different types of competition and conflict. Depending on how adaptable and outgoing you are, this can be disruptive, stressful, or stimulating. Attitude is important to the interpretation of this card. It can be bad news for shy people, but good news for people who are looking for variety and excitement. The ambivalent nature of this card is portrayed in the graphic image used in the Rider-Waite-Smith deck: a group of youths appear to be engaged in armed conflict, battling with staves or quarterstaffs. Upon closer inspection, however, no one seems to be getting hurt, and their melee could be a sporting event. Following are some common situations to which this card's different meanings may apply.

FIVE OF WANDS

Breaking Away

The Five cards can signal the desire, need, or act of breaking away, and with the Five of Wands, this is likely to denote restless individuals who want to break away from ordinary routines, both at home and in the workplace, to go in search of more action and get out among the crowds. If this card is reversed, it may indicate that you are making some attempts at getting away from what you view as a boring way of life, but don't quite have the ability to get to where the action is.

Competition

This card can represent the many competitive forces to which young people and others in our society are subjected when trying to do well in studies, participating in clubs or sports, or vying for social popularity, for example. There are also many forces within our larger culture that promote competitive actions and attitudes, and judge individuals' value by how well they succeed in certain narrow, culturally celebrated activities. Therefore, this card may denote the likelihood of getting pulled into competitive activities, possibly as part of the process of change in your life. This can be a good thing if you're feeling up to the challenge, because competitive situations push you to do your best, enabling you to improve your skills, communications, and creative talents. However, if you find that the nature of the competition forces you to go against your values, or if it is too stressful or too big a drain on your energy, you might think about how you can back out of it or make it more manageable. If reversed, the Five of Wands can indicate that you are experiencing stress as a result of a covert competition; that is, you and others, perhaps people you consider your friends, could be competing with each other without being fully aware of it.

Conflict

Another traditional interpretation of this card is conflict. This may be a problem if the Five of Wands is surrounded by other cards of strife. Conflict is especially likely to break out when peoples' egos clash due to disagreements about ways of doing things. It can also denote personality types who stir up arguments because they like the adrenalin rush, or who go running to every conflict to see what's going on and possibly to get involved. If reversed, this card could signal conflict that is unexpressed—it may seem that a group of people are getting along okay, but inside they are seething with resentments.

Group Influences

Because it can stand for group activities, the Five of Wands can also denote the influence of peer groups, crowds, and other types of mass associations. On the positive side, this card may mean that you will enjoy stimulating activities with a larger group of people. However, because it denotes a break from the stable and industrious way of life pictured in the previous card, the Four of Wands, the Five of Wands can also signal the dangers of mob behavior. This card could therefore stand as a warning to avoid being sucked into stupid or dangerous things because you want to go along with the crowd. When this card is reversed, it may indicate that while you are attracted to certain groups, they have less influence over you; you may have some difficulty finding a group with whom you completely fit in.

Other People

The Five of Wands doesn't always stand for competition and conflict—its association with novelty, change, stimulation, the circulation of ideas, and groups of people can also denote social contacts where there is a diversity of people and opinions. You may find yourself interacting with people who are different from you, and giving each person a chance to be heard. The reversed Five of Wands could indicate a situation in which you may be unhappy about dealing with other peoples' beliefs and ways of doing things.

SIX OF SPEARS

THE RETURN OF AMBROSIUS

SIX OF WANDS

THE SIX OF WANDS

The Sixes represent a state of harmony and periods of time when it's easy to accomplish goals because there is a dynamic balance between active forces and stabilizing influences. At such times a natural flow of energy carries progress forward. When combined with the active, ambitious Wands cards in the Six of Wands, the qualities represented are confidence, empowerment, and success, which is why this card is often labeled "victory" and portrays a man riding in a triumphal procession. We can assume that he is a person who meets challenges quickly and efficiently because he knows how to channel his competitive instincts; at the same time, he has the wisdom not to value competition over cooperation, and so inspires the loyalty of people around him. Following are some common areas of life where the Six of Wands' easy energy may be experienced.

Competence

The Six of Wands is about achieving the stage in personal development when you can deal with both routine and challenging situations confidently and skillfully. There is an implication that you have already overcome some challenges and can be counted on to step forward, take responsibility, and handle any situation that comes up. You have also gained a sense of perspective: you know what is important and what is not, and you don't overreact to minor crises. You deal with new matters with clarity and efficiency. When the Six of Wands is reversed, it may indicate that you lack confidence or haven't had the opportunity to demonstrate your skill and competence in leadership positions or other areas of accomplishment. Sometimes this card can refer to your "positive" shadow (other people may see greatness in you before you realize it yourself).

Cooperation

The success predicted by the Six of Wands is likely to come from your ability to gain cooperation from other people. It may even evolve out of a creative partnership (6 = 2 x 3, with Twos standing for relationships and Threes for creative energies). It has been said that behind every successful person is another person who is supporting her dreams. If this card is reversed, it may indicate that you have the potential to be successful, but you need to do some more work to bring other people into harmony with your goals.

Flow

This card can denote conditions or periods of time in which everything and everyone is working smoothly together, and tasks are accomplished effortlessly. Sometimes this denotes "peak experiences" or the state of "being in flow"; you are performing expertly and everything is working so well that it's almost magical. If reversed, things are going forward, but there may be disruptions or some uncertainty about your goals, which prevent things from going as smoothly as possible.

Popularity

The Six of Wands can signify social success, related to the pleasurable, sociable qualities of the Sixes. This card signifies the ability to feel at ease in a crowd, to interact with lots of people, to know the right things to say, and to have a sense of what other people want. When the Six of Wands comes up for you, it also indicates that because of these qualities, people will have confidence in you, praise your achievements, and look to you for leadership. Chances are that you will find yourself in positions of high visibility. Luckily for you, the people you are dealing with are also likely to be friendly, cooperative, and well organized. If this card is reversed, it can indicate that you are becoming more active socially, but are still a bit shy and don't yet feel comfortable about speaking, performing, or doing other sorts of things in public.

Success

The Six of Wands is good news in any Tarot reading: it predicts that you will achieve success—academic, athletic, social, career, or other—as a result of your confidence and skill. What's more, the sort of accomplishments denoted by this card are ongoing: love of action and pride in mastery spur you on to greater accomplishments. If reversed, this card indicates that success is within your reach, but you probably need more practice and experience in order to perform at the level for which you strive.

THE SEVEN OF WANDS

The challenging situations represented by the Sevens are illustrated in the Seven of Wands, which often portrays a young man who stands on a hilltop, defensively wielding a long wand like a quarterstaff, while six other wands appear to be coming at him, possibly thrust toward him by unseen opponents below the picture space. In an alternative interpretation of this illustration, my father sees the young man as making a giant step forward in order to unsettle and reposition the wands, illustrating the need for new ideas and viewpoints. (It's good to get other peoples' impressions of the card illustrations, because they often see new things in them.) *The Witches Tarot Deck* offers a new rendition of this card—it portrays a painter working at his easel, which emphasizes creative vision. Generally, this card stands for vision, imagination, inventiveness, courage, and problem-solving. Following are some of the ways the tests of this card may be experienced in your life.

Challenges

The Seven of Wands most commonly denotes the need to overcome obstacles and opposition, which will require you to be a good tactician—this means you will need to be alert and able to move quickly to deal with problems that come up. It shows you rising to meet some challenges, possibly taking a stand in defense of your ideas and ideals. Among other things, people may challenge your plans for a future career or lifestyle, or possibly your religious or political beliefs. You may be working on a project, invention, or creative inspiration

that's ahead of its time. This card could also denote people engaged in athletics or other competitive activities. Much energy and endurance will be needed. The reversed card shows some problems with meeting challenges, perhaps because you have some doubts about your mission, or you need to develop a clearer vision of what you want to accomplish and how to proceed.

Individualism

The problems of going it alone are typically associated with the Sevens. You may have a strong desire to get out and prove yourself in a larger, tougher world. You might also feel compelled to go against social convention in order to follow a highly personal ideal. When you are at odds with what "society" or an influential peer group expects and thinks is good for you, you can anticipate a long lonely struggle. Some risks are involved, and you can't expect much help or understanding. However, unless the Seven of Wands is accompanied by negative cards, the implication is that you will be able to make a go of it. The reversed card may point to situations in which rugged individualism is not enough to succeed; you may need to reach out to a wider community for help.

Positioning

This card can make a statement about the need to position yourself well, to stand your ground, and to take the ethical high ground, while the reversed card could mean that you will have to give some ground, possibly in order to get along with others. Sometimes it's necessary to give up on pressing a point or being judgmental in order to preserve harmony.

Success

This card tends to indicate long-term, hard-won success because Wands people usually have the energy to carry out their visions—unless they get distracted and find new causes. Therefore, greater success is assured if this card is accompanied by cards of will and focus, less if surrounded by cards that show depletion of energy or interest.

Timing

Because of the futuristic orientation of the Sevens, as well as the challenges associated with the Seven of Wands, this card would indicate that your desires will
materialize later rather than sooner, after encountering some obstacles, unexpected turns of events, and changes in plans. The reversed card would indicate
even more uncertainty.

Some Thoughts on Social Outsiders

Because the Seven of Wands often shows an embattled loner and also stands for
the assertion of individualistic ideals, this card can hold special meanings for
young people who have been excluded as a result of being labeled "geeks,"
"freaks," "nerds," "Goths," or "queers," for being artistic or intellectual, for being
interested in mysticism or unconventional religions, for being in a lower social
class or different ethnic group, for simply being unfashionable, or for the myriad
other reasons that the people who are in the majority discriminate against the
people who are "different." However, take heart, because in keeping with the
visionary powers of the Sevens, it is the outcasts who usually make the greatest
cultural contributions. As Jon Katz has explained in his book *Geeks,* these
are/were young people who "rose above a suffocatingly unimaginative educational system, where they were surrounded by obnoxious social values and hostile
peers, to build the freest and most inventive culture on the planet: the Internet
and the World Wide Web."[3] (Incidentally, the Internet can be a Wands concern,
and many different types of outsiders find it a necessary means of connecting with
kindred spirits.) Similarly, young people who pursue philosophies that promote
inquisitiveness, imagination, creativity, respect for the earth, tolerance, and other
humanistic values are also transforming our culture and contributing to the quality of the "noosphere" (mind sphere), which can be described as this planet's
evolving "brain," generated by human ideals and intelligence.

Wands relate to identity development, too, and Katz has pointed out how, in a
type of "language inversion," geeks and nerds (as well as gays and others) are now
claiming the labels that were originally intended to dehumanize them as a source
of pride and empowerment by emphasizing their positive qualities. He also says,
"In this culture, I figure people have the right to name themselves; if you feel like
a geek, you are one."[4] The Seven of Wands can well apply to acts of self-naming;

for groups of individuals, it can bring up issues of self-representation—that is, whether members of a group are able to represent themselves as they want to be seen, or whether other, more powerful social groups determine what their public image shall be.

One of the problems with the outsiders' mystique is that their intense individualism prevents some of them from taking organized social action to stop the abuses. Thus, for example, bullies continue not merely to be tolerated but celebrated because people aren't willing to confront this problem. (Imagine how much better life could be for future generations if parents of outsiders and outsider parents were louder in demanding that school districts put an end to harassment.) The reversed Seven of Wands could therefore point to situations in which the inability to join with others works against real progress.

THE EIGHT OF WANDS

The Eight of Wands stands for the organization of energies, ideas, activities, plans, and people. It is often represented by a tight grouping of wands that fly like arrows over a countryscape; their downward slant shows them hurtling toward an unknown destination. When this card comes up in a reading, things are coming together for you, so it's a good time to take action and get things done. Following are some of the ways that Eight of Wands energies may be operating in your life.

Group Strength

This card reveals that people can accomplish awesome things when they unite and work together in an orderly and efficient manner. Therefore, the Eight of Wands shows goals completed as a result of cooperation, and it may even signify organized action to bring about social change. The reversed card may indicate that a group needs a realignment in order to function more efficiently, or possibly that a group is reassembling in another direction or formation.

Habits

The Eights represent organized patterns of thought and action; thus, the Eight of Wands shows how habits can be used effectively. When you work at instilling good habits until they become second nature, your worries are far fewer. (One secret is to incorporate good habits into the things you enjoy doing; for example, exercise or floss your teeth while you watch television.) Bad habits may be indicated by the reversed Eight of Wands or the presence of negative cards.

Romance

A. E. Waite has suggested that this card can signify "the arrows of love," while the reverse denotes "arrows of jealousy."[5]

Success

The Eight of Wands shows you in a position of strength because you have gathered and focused all of your energies. Plans are put into action, loose ends are tied up, and projects are completed. The end is in sight, and success is likely. When this card is reversed, there could be problems with scattered energies, oversights, or things coming apart, so it is important to make sure that all phases of a plan or project are well thought out and coordinated. Pay extra attention to paperwork or other details that are involved. You may have to oversee these things personally—don't expect that they will get done by themselves.

Timing

This card is sometimes labeled "Swiftness," and when it appears in a reading, some new events will unfold very quickly, or you will see the conclusion of something that you've been waiting for. The reversed card is commonly seen as plans or other matters that are still "up in the air." Obstacles, delays, changes in plans, disagreements, quarrels, or a reevaluation of priorities may be part of the reason that nothing is getting done. It could also be that more time is needed for the necessary elements to come together.

Trends

This card can denote your ability to take advantage of trends—or to get carried away by trends, depending on what kind of cards accompany it. Social trends may have some bearing on the matter in question. The reversed card could point to a type of retromovement.

Travel

The Eight of Wands has a traditional association with movement and travel; it may especially denote travel by air. The reversed card could indicate delays and other problems in travel.

THE NINE OF WANDS

Because Nine is the number of multiplicity (in numerology, it is the self-replicating number), the Nine of Wands represents the multiplication of the things that the Wands stand for—including energy, activity, enthusiasm, and opportunities. However, a person must develop the experience and discipline to handle this diversity of energies. Such knowledge is often gained the hard way, which may be why popular illustrations of this card commonly feature a man whose bandaged head and defensive stance suggest that his experience has taught him to be selective and watchful. He also leans upon a long pole as he stands before a line of eight similar poles. Following are some ways that this card could apply to your life.

Activity

The Nine of Wands can signify your ability to generate energy and integrate multiple activities into your lifestyle. In an ideal situation, it suggests peak performance. The potential problem here is that of being overprogrammed—having too much going on, too much to do—a situation that may be indicated by the reversed card. The common illustration suggests a solution: the man in the picture seems to have selected one particular wand out of his group of nine. This implies that he's chosen one activity or opportunity that he has a feeling for, that he senses is the most favorable. This could mean that after trying out a number of different things, you will make your choice and then work with that choice to take your capability and creativity to a higher level. Among the ways that this

might apply to young adults is as a suggestion to try a variety of things and get lots of experience, so you can then make educational and career choices based on knowledge, self-confidence, and your ability to take on challenges.

Advocacy

Related to the defensive stance portrayed in the Nine of Wands, this card can point to situations in which you need to be your own advocate. (An advocate is someone who looks out for your rights and works hard to promote your personal advancement.) Your life will go better if you don't assume that other people and institutions will go out of their way to help you or inform you of everything you need to know, because they're all too busy and they can't stay on top of everything. Rather, you need to be on the lookout, not only for violations of your rights, but also for certain rights, perks, and privileges to which you may be entitled, but which no one has bothered to tell you about. The reversed card may warn that you could do a better job of looking out for your own interests. Perhaps you are overlooking an opportunity or ignoring a developing problem.

Force Multipliers

This card's image of a defensive man combined with the multiplicity of the Nines suggests the concept of force multipliers—a term that the military uses to describe methods and technologies that make it possible to get greater power and efficiency out of a fighting force and its weapons. When this card comes up in a reading, it may suggest ways that we can apply this concept to daily life to increase our own effectiveness. One of the big things that comes to mind is the Internet; among other things, it allows ordinary people to spread their ideas, it enables job hunters to seek out more opportunities while circulating their resumés to more potential employers, and it enables very specialized businesses to reach the right customers.

Protection

Depending upon the context, this card could depict someone who is overly suspicious or defensive, or it could denote a need for caution. Because they are concerned with ideas and enterprises, Wands cards don't normally denote physical threats. However, because of the graphic symbolism in this card, which commonly portrays a wary man with a head wound, it would be a good idea to watch out for potential dangers. The reversed card could indicate carelessness, possibly as a result of having too many distractions.

Strength

Strength is the most common interpretation of this card—the *Crowley Thoth Tarot Deck* labels it "Strength," while others say it stands for "strength in reserve" or "strength in opposition." A person who has all of his energies aligned has the strength needed to go up against obstacles. With the reversed card, the potential for strength is there, but more self-discipline may be needed.

Thoughts on Self-Advocacy and Opportunity

As mentioned earlier, the Nine of Wands can stand for the multiplication of opportunities. However, you need to be your own advocate by being alert to where the possibilities are. For example, consider careers—most people aren't even aware of the myriad of interesting careers that are available. Because our educational system does a poor job of counseling young people about careers or inspiring students' imaginations by discussing different occupations, it is up to you to go out and investigate these things. Even when you do get out into the job or career world, it is necessary to continue looking and listening for new opportunities, because you can't assume that you will automatically receive the recognition or promotions that you deserve merely by being a good worker (whether or not you want to remain on one career track or jump to another).

Of course, the Nine of Wands would suggest not merely going after career opportunities, but seeking out a variety of interesting experiences so you can become an interesting person. As a school volunteer, I have overseen teenagers on essay writing and essay tests; unfortunately, some teens had nothing to write about because they had never done anything interesting. (It is easier to write well when you have something memorable to write about.) If they had gone on travels, camping trips, or field trips, they hadn't thought about their experiences deeply enough to find philosophical meaning in them. However, you can meet the challenges of the Nine of Wands (and of the Wands cards in general) by finding clever ways to create your own experiences, and by uncovering meaning through questioning and probing. You can also ask the Tarot to help reveal the meaning in your experiences.

TEN OF SPEARS

THE GREEN KNIGHT

TEN OF WANDS

BASTONI BATONS 10 WANDS BASTOS

STÄBE STAVEN

THE TEN OF WANDS

The common illustration of the Ten of Wands shows a man bearing ten long wands or staves as he trudges toward a city. Although he is bent over with the weight he carries, his destination is not far off. However, in some versions the man's bundle of staves blocks or partially blocks his view, making the statement that too much expansion of a person's activities or other matters can cause her to lose sight of a meaningful purpose. While this illustration emphasizes oppressive burdens, *The Witches Tarot Deck* features a person looking at a house built according to the design which he or she holds, illustrating the idea of building toward goals—especially by keeping an objective in sight. Tens also represent completion and cycles, so interpretation of this card is especially dependent on context. Following are some of the ways that its trends toward accumulation and conclusions could manifest in your life.

Burdens

Related to the image of the man carrying a heavy load, this card can denote many different types of burdens. For young people, recognition of your increasing maturity and capability may bring increased responsibilities at home, school, or work. It could also mean taking on multiple responsibilities, having to manage all phases of a project, taking on special family responsibilities (as the Tens often apply to family matters), having to "carry" other people who aren't pulling their own weight, being imposed upon in some way, or bearing another kind of metaphorical load. Your burden may seem very oppressive (see the following section about oppression) and require your full commitment, but at the same time, the Tarot implies that you have the strength—the right stuff to do the job. In a positive context, the reversed card may indicate a lightening of your burden. However, if accompanied by negative cards, you may question whether all of the work is worth it.

Conclusions and Cycles

In keeping with the Tens' concern for endings and new beginnings, and the common image of the man in sight of his goal, this card may indicate that your burden will soon be lifted, or a problem will be resolved. However, it can also represent a change of whatever you've been carrying for a new load. (People of proven reliability tend to attract responsibilities, and workaholics always get into new projects.) In some cases, it could signal a change of careers—which is something to think about in regard to long-range predictions, since people growing up today can expect to make several career changes in the course of their lives. For students, this could denote the transition into your first job or career; it is likely that you will be able to carry some of your current skills and experience into your new line of work. A reversed Ten of Wands could indicate that you've been preparing for some changes on an unconscious level, but you may not yet be ready to commit to a new course of action.

Consequences

The Ten of Wands can stand for those times when we have to bear the consequences of our actions—whether good, bad, or neutral—with adjoining cards possibly indicating the original actions and the consequences. Perhaps you made a decision or commitment to something, only to discover that there's more to it than you expected, so it demands more work or something else from you. The reversed card may indicate lighter consequences than expected, especially if accompanied by cards of happiness.

Oppression

The most negative potentials of this card are emphasized in the decks that label it "Oppression." While the things that the Wands denote—such as activities, projects, ideas, responsibilities, and opportunities—are normally considered good things, the accumulation of these things can be very oppressive. (For example, I know people who have so many hobbies, interests, and other commitments that their lives are a mess; they are always overstressed, and they neglect the things that are most important because they have too much going on.) Many people start piling on these kinds of commitments while they are still young, but you can avoid that by heeding the words of Henry David Thoreau, who said, "Our life is frittered away by detail . . . let your affairs be as two or three, and not a hundred or a thousand. . . . Simplify, simplify."[6] If the Ten of Wands is accompanied by more negative cards, the feeling of oppression could be especially heavy, or it could be coming from outside sources. Consistent with the Tens' association with a wider world, it could reveal that social or political oppression have some bearing on the matter in question. (Stop to think about forces in your larger culture that could be making your life more difficult.) The reversed card might indicate a person who is starting to throw off or detach from the things that are oppressing him.

Success

The Ten of Wands is also a card of success, indicating that through hard work, you will reach your goals, prosper, and gain recognition for your accomplishments. However, note that the most successful people often accumulate the greatest cares, which include all of the efforts needed to keep up their social status. The reversed card could represent backsliding or obstacles on the road to success. Alternately, it could represent a decision to "downscale," as may be the case with people who choose to earn less money in preference for a more enjoyable job or a less stressful lifestyle.

Time Element

This card implies that a long period of hard work will be needed to achieve your goals, but once you've reached "critical mass," meaning you've built things up to a certain point, things will fall into place more quickly.

8   THE CUPS

Because cups are containers, they are symbols of receptivity, evoking images of nurturing and fulfillment. Illustrations of the Cups suit often feature beautifully decorated, long-stemmed goblets. The scenes portrayed in these cards can be somewhat dreamy and hint at different kinds of moods. Associated with elemental Water, the Cups suit relates to emotions and feelings.[1] We use our feelings to evaluate our likes and dislikes, and they have a major influence on how we make sense of our experiences, including our memories and the information of our five senses. The Cups cards reflect events and processes by which we become aware of our emotions, as well as different ways that we accept, repress, or act on our feelings. The Cups also bring up issues from the unconscious, and they reveal matters of importance to our inner lives of soul and spirit. When a reading highlights their special gifts, the Cups cards portend many blessings, including happiness, abundance, healing, fertility, creativity, and celebration.

Because they symbolize the things that nourish the spirit, the Cups cards and the Water element also have creative associations, so we sometimes discuss them in terms of the fertility of the mind. Clarissa Pinkola Estes beautifully describes the metaphorical connection between water and the creative life when she says, "The creative force flows over the terrain of our psyches looking for the natural hollows, the arroyos, the channels that exist in us." (Notice how hollows, arroyos, and channels can be cuplike forms—enclosing empty spaces that can be filled with substance.) She also describes the nurturing power of creativity: "Whatever is touched by it, whoever hears it, sees it, senses it, knows it, is fed. . . . A single creative act has the potential to feed a continent."[2]

In everyday life, we experience the positive things pictured in the Cups cards when we are able to enjoy emotional comforts, social pleasures, and little favors.

However, they can also represent those very special experiences that touch our souls, those sensations that enable us to feel most human, and those moments of time when we are able to drink from the deep sources of spiritual and emotional nourishment. This suit is also the one most especially concerned with relationships: through the types of heart-to-heart interactions portrayed in the Cups cards, we are able to connect with other people on the most intimate and meaningful levels. The negative experiences denoted by Cups cards often involve mood changes, dissatisfaction, or relationship problems. They can also portray the crises people sometimes go through when they feel that their lives are empty of meaning.

Teenagers and young adults most commonly experience the sort of situations denoted by the Cups cards when they are exploring their emotions, learning to express feelings and manage relationships, and daydreaming about love and romance. Young people embody the Cups' social values when they are spending quality time with friends, family members, pets, and others, or when they are comforting and caring for anyone who is sick or in pain, or when performing other acts of compassion. They are also engaging Cups-related concerns when they are praying or performing other acts of religious devotion, or exploring spiritual, psychological, or mystical insights.

People who model the positive qualities of the Cups suit, or who are going through Cups-type phases, tend to be sensitive, kindhearted, spiritual, and emotionally intuitive. They value peace and harmony, and may take an interest in social welfare issues. People who are acting out the negative Cups qualities can be emotionally demanding due to deep insecurities, and their own emotions can also be manipulated. Also, they can have a hard time structuring their lives, so they may engage in too much wishful thinking, and they can be easily distracted.

When Cups cards come up in a reading, the emphasis is likely to be on awakened emotions, moods, relationships, expressions of love, home and family issues, or things that have spiritual significance. Cups cards can reveal that unconscious motivations are influencing the matter in question; as these subconscious issues start to surface, they may become more visible, even manifesting in outer-world events. Generally, these are times to explore your emotional responses, develop your skills and sense of identity as a feeling person, and satisfy your soul needs.

THE ACE OF CUPS

The Ace of Cups, usually depicted as an elegant chalice, represents an inner life that is both deep and overflowing with emotional and spiritual force. When this card appears in a reading, you experience the qualities of elemental Water in a very personal way, and these qualities pervade many areas of your life. This is a lucky card, as it signals the awakening of new emotions; its expression of inner-world values promotes love, happiness, harmony, and well-being. You get a better appreciation of what it means to be a feeling person, and you can find joy and pleasure in your life, work, and the people around you. Ace of Cups experiences may manifest in a number of ways, including the following.

Emotional Issues

New emotional experiences boost your self-esteem, and expressing your feelings becomes important to your sense of identity. The reversed interpretation could point to a number of things: you may have mixed emotions and don't understand your response to a situation in question. Mood swings are likely. Alternatively, it could be that you are affected on a deep, unconscious level, but hold back your feelings or don't fully experience your emotions for other reasons. You may also be acting out some behaviors that are delayed reactions to past events.

Fertility

The Ace of Cups and its Water element symbolize fertility and can predict pregnancy and childbirth. This card may also denote the mental and material fertility that produces creativity and abundance. The reversed card could indicate that the potential for fertility is present but not consistent.

Health

This card is traditionally a promise of healing. Since physical illness is often aggravated by emotional frustration, wellness may best be achieved by an inflow of nurturing energy. For depressed people, this card indicates a change of emotional state, a lifting of fog and shadow that enables people to see things in a new way, with a better frame of mind. The reversed card warns of the danger of running out of the emotional energy needed for physical resilience.

Influence on Reading

When the Ace of Cups is associated with positive cards, it promises the free flow of their blessings. When it comes up in a reading that otherwise looks bad, it assures you that some good things will come out of the experience. Any bad things that may happen are significant to your spiritual growth, and even an emotional wounding will leave you with a deepened understanding—wisdom that will be a resource to share with others. When this card is reversed, it tells you that to change the nature of your experience or to get the most out of it, you need to reframe your outlook—to look for the positive in the situation.

Love

The Ace of Cups represents a quality of love that is true, pure, overflowing, and unconditional. It indicates your ability to open your heart, to give and receive love. For these reasons, it often signals a new love entering your life; however, it can also represent the deepening of an existing love, greater intimacy, and stronger demonstrations of affection. In some cases, it predicts a marriage proposal. A reversed Ace of Cups would indicate restraints on the expression of love, as might be the case with people who find it difficult to be openly affectionate or those who are unable to make commitments.

Motivations

This card denotes people who are acting upon their feelings and modeling sincere feeling values (often influenced by religious principles). When reversed, this card indicates that strong but confused and unconscious motivations make the situation difficult to understand and predict.

Relationships

In addition to the potential love relationships indicated previously, the Ace of Cups denotes all sorts of positive interactions with other people. Your sincerity and heightened sense of empathy promotes mutual care and trust. Other people respond by being friendly and helpful, and may present you with gifts, favors, and other forms of help. Relations with parents and others close to you become easier and more satisfying. You can help the good energy of this card along by being more openly affectionate, more giving of yourself, more nurturing of other peoples' good feelings.

Spirituality

This card's association with richness of the inner life implies that the issues and events denoted in your reading have spiritual significance. Your faith brings you satisfaction, and you may experience a state of "grace," which is the sense of being supported by divine powers. The reversed card may indicate that you are aware of spiritual forces, but circumstances are making it difficult for you to connect with your spiritual nature.

THE TWO OF CUPS

Two of Cups

Tristram & Isolt

The Two of Cups deals with relationships in which there is an emotional connection between the partners; this can refer to relationships between friends, lovers, business partners, and others, as well as situations where one-on-one interactions are important. This card's presence affirms that the quality of your relationships is important to you, and is also likely to be important to any special person in your life. Following are some of its other meanings.

Choices

Two of Cups

Twos often deal with the need to make choices. The Two of Cups indicates that you may have to change some of your plans in order to meet the needs of another person. (Two of Cups behavior is about trying to please, basing decisions on the needs of the other.) However, this is probably someone that you care about, so you are willing to put up with the inconvenience. The reversed card could indicate some hesitance in deciding.

Cooperation

You can expect help or cooperation from friends—particularly a special friend or partner—as well as from other people. If it is reversed, this card may indicate that certain people may be unwilling to help you, or unable to get along with you, because they don't understand your feelings on a matter in question (and you probably aren't taking their feelings into consideration either). Therefore, it's important to cultivate "sympathetic imagination," which is the ability to imagine yourself in other peoples' emotional situations, in order to better relate to them.

Relationships

This card reveals that two individuals support each other's needs, understand each other's feelings, and engage in a healthy give-and-take. When this card is reversed, it indicates that two people may be drifting apart, or they may be going through a period of adjustment. They probably have different understandings of the nature of their relationship, and they want different things out of it. Certain inequalities may make the relationship awkward. On the other hand, differences in emotional expression may be the problem: perhaps one partner is more giving, more demonstrative, while the other holds back and doesn't express feelings. (You will have to come to terms with this, either by accepting the other person for what she is, working to nurture the expression of feelings in the other person, or seeking a partner who is a better match.) The reversed Two of Cups may also indicate that a situation will affect the members of a partnership differently. It is possible that what is good for one partner may not be so good for the other partner (for example, one partner may be offered a scholarship or job in another state).

Romance

Because the Two of Cups often represents love relationships, it may speak of romance entering your life. It could simply mean a date, but in some cases it could be a prediction of marriage. The same qualities indicated in the paragraph on relationships (above) would also apply.

Position in Reading

When the Two of Cups is in a central position, that is, between two or more cards, the things pictured in the cards to either side may represent different qualities or resources that the two individuals bring to the relationship. If the Two of Cups is reversed, the cards to either side may give clues as to what sort of issues are dividing the two people. For example, if the reversed Two of Cups is accompanied by one of the Aces, one or both of the partners may be unwilling to compromise his goals and activities in interest of the relationship; in association with one of the

Threes, it may indicate that a relationship is strained by one or both of the partners' outside friendships or activities; if accompanied by a Four, complacency (that is, comfort with a certain way of life, such as living with one's parents) may make one or both of the partners unwilling to put everything into the relationship; if accompanied by one of the Fives, restlessness and the desire for change are likely to be problems.

Reconciliation

If there has been bitterness or estrangement between two individuals or parties, this card predicts a reconciliation. If the card is reversed, it may indicate that the parties are interested in reconciliation, but don't know how to approach each other to make up.

A Note on Reading Technique

If you want more information about a pair of friends, lovers, or other partners, ask your question, shuffle the cards, and then thumb through the deck until you find the Two of Cups. Look to the cards on either side of it to learn more about each person's role in the relationship. (In the Rider-Waite-Smith deck, the male is to the right and the female to the left.) For inquiries about friends of the same sex, you will need to use your intuition and prior knowledge about the people to determine which side of the Two of Cups card pertains to which person.

THE THREE OF CUPS

The Three of Cups stands for creative energy, celebration, and social pleasures, and many renditions of this card picture three dancing maidens who resemble the Three Graces of classical mythology.[3] According to *Book of Goddesses,* by Patricia Monaghan, their names were Thaleia (abundant, overflowing, flowering), Aglaia (radiance, splendor), and Euphrosyne (joy, merriment, delight).[4] Their cult was already very old in classical times, and the Greeks took the Graces very seriously, for as Alexander Murray has noted in his book *Who's Who in Mythology,* many temples were dedicated to them, they were honored with annual festivals, and the goddess of wisdom, Athene, "called in their aid in the serious business of life over which she presided, because without gracefulness all labour was in vain."[5] The Three of Cups card also stands for the blessings of the Graces, including the ability to find joy and beauty in life through festivities, friendship, and good times shared. Following are some of this card's common meanings.

THREE OF CUPS

Celebration

You may be attending social events such as parties, recreational outings, family and neighborhood gatherings, or seasonal festivals. You may also have something important to celebrate, perhaps a victory or other success (possibly achieved through a cooperative effort). If this card is reversed, you may not be able to fully enjoy a celebration, perhaps because other people aren't very appreciative. Unfortunately, many of us forget how important it is to recognize and express sympathetic joy in our friends' good fortune.

Communication

Communication is a concern of the Threes, and, indeed, the god Hermes (Mercury) relied on the Graces for his gift of speech. The Three of Cups shows you using your communication skills to spread good feelings and connect with your community. This card may also predict that you will receive pleasurable communications such as compliments, congratulations, or invitations. If reversed, communications may be delayed or offer less than you expected.

Community

One of the paradigms (socially influential ideas) of the current era is the idea of "making community." As part of the desire to make community, many people are doing more to create meaningful connections to the people around them (whether they be local, ethnic, professional, or other types of communities), or they are seeking out "communities of choice" so they can spend more time with people who share their interests. If you are lonely because you can't find any kindred spirits, this card promises that things will get better. Many young people feel frustrated because they aren't able to meet more people. This can be at its worst in junior high school, though as people move up through high school and into college and the work force, they increasingly encounter a larger, yet more select, group of people who are more focused on special interests. Also, the formation of cyber-communities on the Internet has enabled many people to find like-minded friends.

Creativity

Good relations with friends and coworkers stimulates your creative life, leading to a very fertile, successful period. If reversed, creative block may be due to an inability to find stimulating company.

Friends

The Three of Cups often stands for the bonds that unite a circle of friends; it can especially apply to questions pertaining to a trio of friends. This card may also pertain to your relationships with brothers, sisters, and cousins. It tends to indicate that these relationships are important to you, and that they are involved in the matter in question. When this card is reversed, something may be interfering with your social life and causing your circle of friends to drift apart. The cards to either side of the reversed Three of Cups may reveal the type of forces that are at work here. When the Three of Cups card is surrounded by negative cards, it may indicate that your friends will support you through times of trouble, but if it is also reversed, it may instead imply that your friends are unreliable. In such cases, it helps to remember one of the teachings of the Buddha, who stressed the need to associate with wise people who uplift you spiritually; he called this "friendship with the lovely."

Healing

Eden Gray and A. E. Waite suggested that the Three of Cups portends a healing.[6] Considering the creative, energetic nature of the Threes, playfully expressed in the Cups suit, both physical and psychological healing are most likely to be achieved by discovering a zest for life. (But be careful of overindulgence in food, drink, or celebration, because that, too, is a potential of this card.)

Romance

This card hints at celebrations of relationships, including marriages. It may also come up if you and your significant other have successfully worked out some differences. On the other hand, if you are still looking for romance, this card may advise that you have a good chance of meeting someone at a celebrational event or through your circle of friends. The reversed card may indicate that a romance is strained by one of the partners' need to spend more time hanging out with friends. In some cases it could warn of a love triangle.

THE FOUR OF CUPS

The Four of Cups provides an example of how different artists and authors focus on different aspects of a Tarot card's meanings. Cups represent the inner life and the number four stands for stability and materiality, so the Four of Cups denotes emotional security, often based on one's material well-being. This may be why the *Crowley Thoth Tarot Deck* labels this card "Luxury," and Angeles Arrien, a modern interpreter of the Thoth deck, says that the Four of Cups "represents the experience of feeling emotionally satisfied internally."[7] However, periods of stability are also often periods of stasis, that is, times when nothing seems to be happening; this can lead to boredom and discontent, since humans crave novelty, excitement, and change. Keying in to this problem, Pamela Coleman Smith portrayed a young man whose expression "is one of discontent with his environment."[8] Since the Rider-Waite-Smith deck has been so influential, many of the newer decks also emphasize this interpretation, such as *The Sacred Circle Tarot*, which has no human figure in the illustration, but labels it "Discontent." *The New Golden Dawn Ritual Tarot* bridges the positive and negative interpretations by labeling it "Blended Pleasure"; in their manual for this deck, Chic and Sandra Cicero state, "It is too passive a symbol to represent perfectly complete happiness."[9] When this card comes up in one of your own readings, you can take your cues from the deck that you have, or you can consider whether the stable condition that the Four of Cups indicates is reassuring or disappointing, depending upon your own desires. Following are some situations in which Four of Cups influences may manifest.

Behavior

This card may denote a period of time when you are not ready to make decisions or take action, possibly because you need a better understanding of the obstacles that keep you where you are, which include your own motivations. You may be so settled into your job, relationships, or way of living that it's hard to change, even if your life lacks variety, challenge, or excitement. You probably have a strong sense of responsibility, and you may also be experiencing pressure to conform to social expectations. When this card is reversed, it can indicate an event, which can include a psychological development, the demands of an authority figure, or the appearance of new information, that provokes you to think about change and go after new opportunities. The reversed Four of Cups could also indicate that you are a person who is motivated by something deeper than material values and pleasures.

Contemplation

Because of the Fours' powers of manifestation, the Four of Cups applies to those times when our unconscious needs become solid and "visible" to us. However, in some versions of this card, a spirit hand protrudes from a cloud, offering the fourth cup to a person who is so focused on the other three that he does not see it. Therefore, Tarot readers often suggest that there is something you are overlooking, and urge the need for greater awareness because the solutions to your problem are at hand. Pay more attention to the good things in your life, because at times when life doesn't seem to be going anywhere, you can lapse into a depressive state that distorts your ability to see things as they really are. This card also hints at finding the spiritual meanings in everyday life.

Emotional Ties

If there have been tensions between your family members, friends, coworkers, or others, this predicts that things will go more smoothly, although some of you may be repressing emotions in order to protect your feelings as well as to preserve order. When surrounded by negative cards, it may indicate a person who clings to things that are not good for her, or even stays in bad relationships due to emotional insecurity. When this card is reversed, it may indicate that your emotional life is opening up, so new relationships may be predicted. However, when reversed and surrounded by negative cards, it can mean that emotional immaturity makes it difficult for the people close to you to get along, even though you all have a sincere desire for peace and harmony.

Also, because of this card's numerical relationship to the Emperor, your father or another authority figure may be exerting a heavy influence upon your life.

Health

Because the Four of Cups applies to the outer-world manifestation of emotional states, it can point to depression and psychosomatic illnesses. This would be more likely to apply to people who are already dealing with a lot of stress, or who have a history of emotional disappointment.

Home Life

The Fours often pertain to the home environment, so you may be required to spend more time at home, where the atmosphere can make you apathetic, though it can also provide comfort and security. Surrounded by various other cards, it could denote moving, renovating, roommates or visitors coming, or other things pertaining to house and home. If reversed, it may indicate the desire to get out on your own. Surrounded by negative cards, it can warn of a troubled family. There may also be influences that threaten to disrupt your home, but are not yet visible.

Personalities

This card may represent an introverted person who is afraid of vulnerability or failure. Alternatively, it may denote a time in a person's life when he needs regenerative solitude, even at the cost of being isolated and misunderstood by other people. When reversed, it can indicate that the individual is now feeling ready to come out of his shell. This may coincide with invitations and the appearance of new people in his life.

Romance

When surrounded by positive cards, you can feel more comfortably settled into an existing relationship. The presence of negative cards could indicate boredom with a relationship and the failure to appreciate the love of someone who is close to you. The reversed Four of Cups may indicate a feeling that something is wrong in a relationship. Young couples often experience tensions when one or both of the partners wonder if they have committed themselves too soon, and if someone more exciting could come along.

Five of Cups

Lancelot & Elaine

Five of Cups

THE FIVE OF CUPS

The Five of Cups represents the energies of change at work in the inner life. This can be good when it brings stimulation and excitement, but we often fear the conflict, instability, and loss that may accompany change—even change for the better—when it affects us emotionally. This card commonly features a cloaked person with head bowed low in an attitude of shame or sorrow, standing near five cups, three of which lie overturned, their contents spilled out. The *Crowley Thoth Tarot Deck, The New Golden Dawn,* and *The Sacred Circle Tarot* do not use human figures in their illustrations, but respectively label the Five of Cups as "Disappointment," "Loss in Pleasure," and "Regret." The relationship between this card and the previous one, the Four of Cups, which often portrays a person suffering from discontent, almost tells a little story: a person who found his life dissatisfying has reacted impulsively, due to a craving for change, and now he has cause for regret. However, although this card often foretells problems brought on by one's own actions, it can also indicate destabilized conditions brought about by outside forces. Following are some of the ways that the Five of Cups may be experienced.

Activity

Because the Fives signify activity, this card may denote several things that are going on in your emotional life, drawing you out into the wider world. On the positive side, you may experience surprises, excitement, adventures, variety, creative energy, new opportunities, and the quest for greater knowledge. However, challenges—

including challenging contacts with other people—may also arise and pull you into conflict. The potentially negative implications of this card are impulsive words and actions, the inability to stick to tasks, and risk-taking behavior. When reversed, the activity and energy associated with this card may be slower and more restrained (low key), and, therefore, possibly more manageable.

Loss and Regret

It can be difficult to take risks and make changes without hurting people or having to give something up, which is a reason why most interpretations of this card focus on loss and regret. In some cases, the damage represented by this card may result from stimulation-seeking behavior or rebellion against limitations. When the pursuit of new pleasures isn't all it promised to be, you may be left disappointed, disoriented, confused, and insecure. Unexpected situations and events may also bring on emotional hardship. With this card, Tarot readers typically advise the need to learn from your mistakes and get on with your life (represented by the two cups that are left standing). This process of making sense out of change and crisis may be indicated by the reversed Five of Cups.

Relationships

You have to adjust to changed relationships with your friends and family members. Sometimes you aren't sure where you stand with these people. In the way that major disruptions in your life are reflected in those around you, they may have their own problems to deal with, and are not able to be very supportive at this time. Old friends may be changing or leaving, but new people are also likely to show up. Some events may alter your family dynamics, possibly due to someone leaving or a new person joining your household. The reversed card may denote resistance to these changes; in some cases it may indicate a person who wants to return home or to another secure emotional situation; Eden Gray has seen it as foretelling the "return of an old friend."[10]

Romantic Relationships

In addition to the changed dynamics indicated previously, the Five of Cups may denote a crisis that destabilizes an existing romantic relationship and may result in a breakup. Exciting new romances may also be predicted, but they are likely to be impulsive and short-lived. Reversed, this card may denote the desire to go back to an old relationship, possibly after having been disappointed by a new person who seemed more alluring. If you want to revive an old relationship, you may have to work hard to rebuild a sense of trust or security.

Survival Issues

Because Fives can represent unstable conditions in which people have been cut loose emotionally and are often overwhelmed by conflicting feelings, people may feel that they're in a survival situation. When this card depicts people who are coping with emotional trauma, it calls for our compassion and understanding. However, there is a darker side to this card: when people feel that they're "in survival," they often neglect their ordinary responsibilities, and they may rationalize a need to lie, cheat, steal, and even betray their closest friends. Therefore, the card is a warning to preserve your personal integrity, and to hold your loved ones to ethical standards, even while you try to understand their anxieties. Reversed, this card may denote a person who is experiencing a series of transformations as he attempts to grow out of a victim identity.

THE SIX OF CUPS

The Six of Cups denotes a relaxed and fairly prosperous interval, often a time when you are beginning to enjoy some success following a period of insecurity. You have achieved a sense of self-esteem by living in harmony with your inner values and gaining confidence from dealing with emotional challenges. Now you know that you are a person who can manage problems and make relationships work. Because the Six of Cups also represents those points in the cycles of life when peoples' thoughts turn toward an idealized past, this card often depicts two children playing in the garden of a castle. Following are some of the ways you may experience Six of Cups intervals in your life.

Children

As this card commonly portrays two children, your reading may emphasize things relating to children. (In *The Barbara Walker Tarot Deck*, this card is labeled "Childhood.") Among other things, it could predict children in your future or refer to children that you know or are concerned about, or it could bear upon issues surrounding your own childhood, depending upon the matter in question. If surrounded by very negative cards, it could indicate a bad situation for children. The reversed card may apply to issues involving your "inner child" and its need to play, to feel secure, and to feel special.

Gift Exchanges

As the number Six expresses an exchange of creative energies (2 x 3), this card may signify gift-giving, favors,

205

and other types of exchanges, either between two people or small groups of people. Under some circumstances, the reversed card could predict an inheritance or a gift resulting from a past relationship.

Past Memories and Pleasures

Most readers emphasize this card's focus on the past. Perhaps an event has revived memories or triggered issues from the past. In some cases, people in question may be clinging to a belief that wishing will make the past come back. The reversed card, in particular, may denote attempts to return to the past.

Note: When the cards next to it portray figures who are either gesturing toward the Six of Cups, walking or riding toward it, or, in the case of the Hermit, holding a lamp toward it, the Tarot may be telling you that the answer to your question lies in the past, or that someone is returning to something from the past.

Recreation and Social Pleasures

You may be in for a peaceful, pleasurable interlude, such as a vacation or a time out from the pressures of work or school, when you can enjoy recreational activities and social events. This may involve a chance to make new friends and to reunite with old ones. In some cases, this card may denote a get-together between two families or two groups of friends. When reversed, this card may indicate that minor disagreements between groups of people or other worries may cast a shadow on a social or recreational occasion, but unless it is also surrounded by negative cards, things are likely to be okay.

Relationships

This is a card about feeling loved and protected in your relationships, and related to its numerical association with The Lovers, it can also imply a romance. It especially betokens harmonious relationships in which partners are "in sync" with each other's feelings and support each other's dreams. The reversed Six of Cups may tell of a desire to return to an old relationship, or the appearance of an old friend or an old love.

THE SEVEN OF CUPS

THE QUESTING BEAST

In the Seven of Cups, the powers of the visionary number Seven combine personal desires with a rich imaginative life. Because dreams of the ideal life can take many forms, and because some are also more realistic, romantic, adventurous, or eccentric than others, this card often depicts an individual gazing at seven cups that float in the air and bubble over with wonders. This card can be especially significant for young people, many of whom are at a point when they have to make plans for the future. Unfortunately, many people occupy different ends of the spectrum when it comes to dreams—some have none at all, while others don't have realistic strategies for working toward their dreams. Reflection on how the Seven of Cups applies to your life can help provide inspiration and test reality.

SEVEN OF CUPS

Choices

The Seven of Cups usually indicates that you can visualize the future life that you desire, but are uncertain about how to achieve it. You may be confused by too many choices, and are scattering your energies by trying too many things. Reversed, it could signify a narrowing of your options, perhaps as a result of gaining some clarity and focusing on what would be manageable as well as fulfilling. You may also be going through a process of change, and the dreams that mean so much to you now may not seem as important later.

Daydreams

Because our active, no-nonsense society views daydreaming suspiciously, the Seven of Cups is often described as a negative card, portraying a person who overindulges in escapist fantasies (in other words, a "loser"). However, it is important to have a guiding vision, for as Eleanor Roosevelt has said, "The future belongs to those who believe in the beauty of their dreams." Actually, a person needs to find balance so she can be both a dreamer and a doer. Note whether the Seven of Cups is accompanied by cards of success—this may determine whether a person has the energy and know-how to work toward a goal. Most Tarot readers see the reversed Seven of Cups in a positive light, denoting will power, determination, and projects completed, perhaps because an individual has internalized a vision that is practical enough to carry through.

Imagination

Dealing with artistic inventiveness, this card encourages people in creative work or those exploring the magic of active visualization (which is the ability to manifest desires by visualizing them, as well as by acting them out symbolically).

Illusion

This card may warn that things are not as they seem, so it is advisable to be cautious and put off decisions until you have more information. The reversed card can signal moments of slippage, when the masks fall and you can see beyond the illusion.

Individualism

Sevens have an individualistic bent, so this card may reveal the areas where your dreams and desires put you out of sync with society, and possibly out of sync with your own friends. Reversed, it may apply to the act of suppressing some of your ideals in order to adapt to other peoples' expectations.

Outcomes

Although there is a potential for some progress as well as some lucky breaks (what A. E. Waite referred to as "Fairy Favours"),[11] the Seven of Cups tends to indicate that the final outcome of a reading is indeterminate because things are "up in the air." There are too many variables, and the people in question have confused ideas about how things should be. When reversed, it can mean that a more decisive situation is starting to take shape, though the direction it takes may be different from what is envisioned.

Romance

Because the Cups cards concern the emotions, this card may represent a person with romantic fantasies. This is a person who can bring charm and excitement into a relationship, but his unreasonable expectations could eventually be a problem. Reversed, it can indicate that partners' illusions about each other are lifting.

Additional Thoughts

In her book *Goddesses in Every Woman*, Jean Shinoda Bolen states, "To make a dream come true, one must have a dream, believe in it, and work toward it. Often it is essential that another significant person believe that the dream is possible: that person is a vision carrier . . ." With this in mind, think about how you and your friends can carry visions for each other—this applies to males as well as females. (Bolen believes that there are fewer influential women because, although women have traditionally carried men's dreams, men "haven't nurtured the dream very well for the women in their lives.")[12]

THE EIGHT OF CUPS

EIGHT OF CUPS
CHAPEL PERILOUS

EIGHT OF CUPS

The number Eight represents the balance of solid matters (as 2 x 4), so it deals with order and organization. With the Eight of Cups, we see the different ways that people experience an ordered and organized emotional life, depending on their attitudes and conditions. The positive aspect of this card is described in Ellen Cannon Reed's manual for *The Witches Tarot Deck* as, "Emotion with thought—common sense and logic prevails. Mind and heart are in accord."[13] However, human emotions rebel against too much imposed order, so people feel stifled when they experience Eight of Cups' influences negatively. Some of the popular depictions of this card play up these tensions by showing a person who seems to be walking away from a life of luxury and security, possibly because she is bored with her way of life. Following are different ways that the Eight of Cups may be experienced.

Abandonment

In keeping with the common illustration for this card, most readers interpret it as a person who is walking away from the situation in question. (When people feel locked into place by habits, obligations, and other attachments, they sometimes feel that the only solution is to pick up and move to a new situation entirely.) The reversed card could mean many things, including a short getaway vacation or a return to a more stable but less challenging way of life. It can also indicate that a person is staying with a situation, but has lost interest in it.

210

Whether upright or reversed, make note of what sort of situation the person is walking away from and where he is heading, as indicated by the adjoining cards.

Behavior Patterns

Due to the fixity of the Eights, this card tends to indicate habits and repetitive emotional response patterns. You might see a "figure 8" pattern in a person's behavior, moving between one thing and another, but always returning to the same place. With the reversed card, the process may be more internal.

Equanimity

The most positive expression of the emotional balance represented by the Eight of Cups is the state of equanimity, which is the ability to see things for what they are and to deal with them skillfully, without stress or strain. When you achieve equanimity, you don't get overly excited by things, but you also don't get disappointed. You recognize that it is the nature of things to come and go, so you can enjoy them without clinging to them. When you have equanimity, you have a better sense of how to deal with people and situations. You don't take things personally because you understand why people say the things they say and do the things they do. You know which relationships and activities to get involved in, and which to walk away from. You know which people need your sympathy, and on whom the expenditure of kindness and compassion would be stupid. Reversed, this card may indicate a person who recognizes the need for equanimity, but isn't quite able to achieve that state of mind.

Households

Because the number Four can represent a home space and household, and 8 = 2 x 4, the Eight of Cups could pertain to relationships between two households, as might be the case when second marriages produce combined families, or when children are in shared custody situations, or when adult children return to live with their parents (or the other way around). Reversed, this card could point to tensions in such an arrangement. If other cards are positive, the people in question are handling these complications well; if negative, the effect of being bounced around between households may be stressful.

Philosophical Aspects

This card may denote a person who is looking back over his life to make sense of it all and find patterns of meaning. This may result in the desire to spend more time alone, or to seek more meaningful work and relationships.

Relationships

When the Eight of Cups comes up in a question about relationships, if accompanied by positive cards, it probably indicates that both partners have settled into a harmonious and long-standing emotional situation, even though they may pursue separate interests and have very self-contained inner lives. If negative influences are indicated, relationships may have become too programmed and routine; they may also feel oppressive because they've become so heavily weighted with obligations. The reversed card may indicate people who stay in a relationship, but are detached from it emotionally, or who are unable to make a wholehearted commitment.

Also, this card may reveal that a person has a strong support network of friends and family, even though she may feel overwhelmed by her social entanglements.

THE NINE OF CUPS

The Nine of Cups is the card of blessings multiplied, so it promises many good things. As 3 x 3, the number Nine expands the creative potentials that are the emotional riches of the Cups suit, and as the last single digit in the number sequence, Nine represents the completion of a goal (before the start of a new cycle, represented by the number Ten). The common illustration of the Nine of Cups portrays a fat man who appears to be a jolly host, showing off his abundance, although *The Witches Tarot Deck* highlights the more mystical aspects of this card by portraying a fortuneteller.

Fulfillment

The Nine of Cups points to a satisfying and rewarding style of life. Because of the abundance of cups and the corpulence of the man often pictured in the illustration, many readers emphasize physical goods, including the attainment of wealth and robust health. However, as a Cups card, fulfillment is also experienced on an emotional and spiritual level, resulting in a richly textured soul life. (Meaningful dreams and intuitive knowledge are also implied.) Sometimes the reversed card may contain warnings about having too much of a good thing, which could lead to overindulgence, selfishness, or a lack of appreciation. It can also signal disappointments, especially if accompanied by negative cards.

Future Contentment

Tradition has it that this card predicts that a person's happiness is assured. (This relates to Nine's powers as a self-replicating number: by adding the digits in any of its products, you get Nine again; thus, 8 x 9 = 54, and 5 + 4 = 9). Because joys increase when they are shared, be generous with others to make this a self-fulfilling prophecy. The reversed card does not negate this potential, but advises that it will take some work on your part to set the right energies in motion; find creative ways to achieve inner and outer harmony.

Gestation

Because of the number Nine's association with pregnancy, it could predict motherhood. It could also indicate that the things to which you look forward will come about through a nine-month process.

Relationships

Blessings come through your relationships with other people, and your interactions are or will be numerous. Your ability to receive and provide emotional support also points to a satisfying romantic relationship. The reversed card may indicate a person who is content with a more introverted lifestyle and prefers just a few close relationships with special friends.

Wishes

Vicki Noble has pointed out that the Nine of Cups is called the "wishing card,"[14] and Anthony Louis has stated that, "When the Nine of cups appears, especially as an outcome card, you will get what you desire."[15] Indeed, whereas Seven is the mystical number in Judeo-Christian tradition, in the old Celtic and Teutonic cultures, as well as in various African traditions, the most magical number was Nine, and astrological systems associate it with the mystical planet Neptune. As such, the Nine of Cups would also be a good card to use as a charm, carried in your wallet or affixed to your wall, and Nine figures as a charm in a number of folk beliefs (for example, girls used to make "charm strings" with 999 buttons or "charm quilts" with 999 squares, with the belief that when completed, a wish would be granted). The reversed card may indicate that you'll get your wish, but it will take some time and some extra work to make it happen. You may also find that, once you've achieved it, it no longer means as much to you.

THE TEN OF CUPS

CORBENIC

The Ten of Cups represents a state of wholeness that comprises happiness, well-being, success, and the ability to lead a purposeful, meaningful life. Because the Cups cards place so much value on emotional relationships, this card's promise of fulfillment especially applies to family happiness, which is why many renditions of this card portray a mother, father, and two children. They celebrate their unity beneath a wondrous rainbow that represents this card's summation of all of the positive qualities of the Cups suit, as well as its connection with the spiritual world. Following are some of the situations to which this card may apply.

TEN OF CUPS

Emotional Maturity

The Ten of Cups denotes success on many levels, and it is achieved by your experience in establishing human connections (often with people of different ages, and from different walks of life), and your competence in dealing with emotional matters. In this state, you are able to be yourself, rely on your intuition, and experience life to the fullest because you know that even when you encounter problems, your positive outlook enables you to deal with them and then move beyond them. At the core of your happiness is your ability to live according to your spiritual principles. When reversed, this card may suggest that if you want to achieve happiness, you need to open to a wider world of feeling and relatedness by committing to things higher than yourself.

Family Matters

The Ten of Cups often points to good relationships within your family. You may soon be participating in family celebrations, vacations, and other types of events. Your family members are supportive, as well as understanding and forgiving, so you can count on them for help with a matter in question. When reversed, this card could apply to physical or emotional divisions that impair a family's sense of wholeness. If reversed and surrounded by negative cards, it could denote a dysfunctional family. However, do not settle on this interpretation unless you have other reasons to believe this is true, because it could point to many other types of private family sorrows.

Friendship and Families of Choice

The mobility of modern society has enabled many individuals to seek out the company of other people who energize them spiritually and emotionally, sometimes constructing new and close-knit "families of choice."[16] As Clarissa Pinkola Estes has noted in her discussion of "finding the people you belong to," when a person "is surrounded by psychic acknowledgment and acceptance, that person feels life and power as never before."[17] The Ten of Cups epitomizes this state of belongingness and empowerment, and is therefore very good news for anyone currently suffering from loneliness and alienation. Because of this card's concern with larger world contacts, it can also denote your sense of membership in a clan or tribe of people who share special interests, rather than confining social and ethnic distinctions. (Your first recognition that you are part of a "tribe" can be a very heady experience.) When reversed, this card may indicate that the people around you are kind and well meaning (unless surrounded by very negative cards), but they may not be a perfect spiritual and emotional match for you.

Outcome

The Ten of Cups indicates that everything will turn out well, and to the benefit of all people concerned. If cards representing another person are also present, she may influence this happy outcome—as A. E. Waite has noted, it can portray "a person who is taking charge of the Querent's interests."[18] The reversed card may indicate that many interpersonal obstacles have to be overcome; your best strategy is to think inclusively, and to open your heart to your fellow beings.

Romance

Some readers emphasize the idyllic romantic nature of this card, predicting love and passion. Palladini's *Aquarian Tarot Deck* and the *Morgan Greer Tarot Deck* focus on this aspect of the card, the one showing two lovers facing each other (reminiscent of the Two of Cups), and the other showing a man and woman's interlocked arms holding up a goblet. In keeping with the Tens' concern with the start of new cycles, this card could also predict marriage and the formation of a new family. Reversed, it may point to something unsatisfactory in an otherwise good relationship.

Further Thoughts on Family Relationships

Because the Ten of Cups so commonly refers to family life, Virginia Satir's insights into family relationships can help you understand some of the issues that this card may raise. In her book *Peoplemaking*, Satir poses the questions, "Does it feel good to you to live in your family right now?" and "Do you feel you are living with friends, people you like and trust, and who like and trust you?" Satir declares that, "Yes, there really are families in which the members find home one of the most interesting and rewarding places they can be." However, people who answer "no" to these questions are probably dealing with "troubled" families. As Satir relates, "Traditionally, we have looked upon the family as the place where we could find love and understanding and support, even when all else failed; the place where we could be refreshed and 'recharged' to cope more effectively with the world outside. But for millions of troubled families, this is a myth."[19] If you believe that your own family is troubled, it is important to develop healthy coping skills and to become aware of the ways in which negative behavior patterns repeat in families, so you can avoid problems in the future.

9 THE SWORDS

The mentally oriented Swords suit is commonly associated with elemental Air, which is why the backgrounds of the Swords cards often show skyscapes and clouds—with the sky color revealing the cards' moods. Swords situations often force you to get involved in causes and conflicts, which is why the card illustrations often feature scenes of worry, frustration, and strife. Consistent with the way the swords in these cards are depicted, their energy is experienced as sharp and cutting. This isn't necessarily a bad thing, because Swords' energies can promote clearer thinking, especially when it is needed to detach from confusing emotions. They also encourage us to take necessary actions and to stand up for our rights.

It is helpful to understand the Swords suit by comparing it to the Wands suit. Like the Wands, the Swords deal with ideas; however, Swords are often concerned with the ideas at the center of religious, political, and philosophical struggles, while Wands are more interested in inspirational and creative ideas, and in the possibility of turning ideas into enterprises. Like the Wands, the Swords are also concerned with communication, but the Wands use communication to promote social and business relations, while the Swords can use communication to assert power. In Swords situations, words can be used as weapons, and when accompanied by negative cards, they may involve gossip, criticism, and argument.

The Swords cards also have a lot to do with the workings of Power. Swords issues often center around who has power and who doesn't, and the main concern of Power is the control of people. When people are subjected to police or military force, this is called power "from the top down." However, Power only seldom comes from the top down—it is mostly diffused in the world around us, influencing us from all directions. It works through institutions like school and church, through mass entities like the media or peer groups, and through smaller groups like families and friends, but most of it is not easily traced to any source. Power is most effective (and invisible) when it works through "ideologies," which are beliefs about the way things should be. Unfortunately, great wars have been fought over belief systems, and conflicting beliefs about how people should live provoke conflicts between ordinary people in everyday life. Of course, Power is not always bad, because both its diffuse and top-down forms can help protect lives and encourage people to treat each other decently. However, we see some of the negative effects of Power when young people are pressured into doing harmful things in order to be cool, when ordinary people are made to feel bad about their bodies, when workers are induced to work under unsafe conditions, or when anyone who is "different" is viewed with suspicion.

People identified with the Swords suit are known for their aggressiveness, intellectual thoroughness, and hardened, realistic outlook. They can exemplify qualities of courage and self-discipline, but they can also become preoccupied with power struggles and develop an ends-justifies-the-means outlook, making enemies in the process.

Young adults are most likely to experience Swords situations when they are defending their personal space, trying to solve problems, coping with heartaches, worrying about what other people think, getting into disagreements about lifestyles, ethics, behaviors, and goals, and dealing with competitive or aggressive people.

With the appearance of Swords cards in a reading, the Tarot is calling upon you to use your powers of discernment. Where are you expending your mental energy? You need to step back from your problems so you can sort out illusions and identify areas where your own habits and mental patterns might be making things worse. Also, think about what the power relationships are (who is holding the power?), and which agencies of Power have affected your thinking on the issue in question. To transform Swords-type conflicts, try to work for the kind of solutions that benefit everyone, taking account of other peoples' needs and feelings. A good model for handling Swords energies is found in Robert Moore and Douglas Gillette's ideal of the warrior: a person who uses aggressiveness to energize, motivate, and tackle problems; whose aggressiveness is moderated by clear thinking; who assesses situations realistically and recognizes limitations; who is flexible enough to shift strategies; whose training unites body and mind in a single purpose; whose commitment is transpersonal (that is, to something greater than personal needs or interests); and who "destroys only what needs to be destroyed."[1]

THE ACE OF SWORDS

SWORD OF STRANGE HANGINGS

The Ace of Swords points to a situation or event that triggers some intense energies in your life; its qualities will be expressed in your beliefs, your activities, your environment, and your interactions with people. Philosophical, political, and intellectual issues are especially emphasized, and people around you are ready to take action on these issues. There is a chance that some things may be carried to extremes. Pictorial versions of this card often feature a hand that emerges from a cloud, holding a sword upright. The sword may be circled by a crown to emphasize the Swords' connection with mental activity and the realm of ideas and ideologies. (Ideologies are peoples' beliefs about what is natural, how people should behave, and how the world should be; all of us have them, but our own ideologies seem like "common sense" to us.) Ace of Swords energies work in many different ways, but following are some common areas of life where you may experience them.

ACE OF SWORDS

Conflict

This card can signify entry into a period of conflict, but at the same time it denotes the urge to get involved in this struggle and the will to cut through it. This conflict may challenge your sense of identity and force you to stand up for your right to express your own ideas and defend your personal "space." If this card is reversed, it could mean that you would prefer to avoid confrontation or other types of stress, even if it's necessary to suppress some very strong feelings. However, you are likely to experience frustration and tension.

Enemies

Arthur Edward Waite observed that the Ace of Swords indicates "the excessive degree in everything."[2] Because people are easily antagonized when others carry something to excess, and the Ace of Swords' intensity unfortunately provokes people into acting out their worst sides, there is a potential for making enemies. When this card is reversed, it could indicate people who are secretly brooding over real or imagined wrongs.

Intensity

When the Ace of Swords comes up in a reading, it signals the most intense expression of the other cards with which it is associated. For example, associated with the Justice card, it assures you that the agents of justice have a deep commitment to ideals, as well as the will to carry out the law. On the other hand, if associated with the Devil, it may emphasize the potential for danger. Furthermore, in considering how the intensity of this card may apply to you, think about whether an intense focus is desirable or undesirable in the context of your reading. For example, if you are an athlete wondering how you'll do at the next track meet, the Ace of Swords suggests that you'll be able to summon the combination of mental and physical concentration needed to do well. On the other hand, if your question pertains to a relationship with a friend, this card may warn of an obsession that is inappropriate for a simple friendship. When this card is reversed, it indicates that other forces may be having a restraining effect.

Love

If the Ace of Swords comes up in response to a question about love, it can reveal great passion, though it is likely to be complicated by conflicting emotions and would not make for a very harmonious relationship. When it is reversed, it could indicate a passion that is being kept secret or repressed.

Motivations

The Ace of Swords indicates that you (and probably the people with whom you are dealing) are very clear about what you want, and what you think needs to be done, and are willing to go after it. These desires and actions are likely to be influenced by personal ideologies and ideals. They may also grow out of a strong desire for independence. If this card is reversed, it may indicate that you feel driven to take action and become involved in a major event or conflict, but you may feel frustrated because you don't fully understand your motivations and haven't clearly articulated your beliefs. You may also feel that external forces are preventing you from getting out on your own.

Personal Reactions

This card may appear at times when your sense of Self seems to be under attack. This problem may be accompanied by narcissistic behavior (selfishness), because, as Robert Jay Lifton has noted, "extreme self-absorption is a way of struggling with what are perceived as extreme threats to the self."[3] The reversed card may denote a tendency to turn anger inward, often with intense self-criticism.

Problem-solving

This card can represent an insight into the nature of a problem; when it is reversed, you may grasp the nature of a problem or situation, but may be struggling to achieve a clear understanding—perhaps more information is needed.

Success

Because the Ace of Swords denotes your ability to summon great force and focus, your projects or enterprises are likely to be successful (provided that you control impulsive behavior and pay attention to the warning about making enemies, mentioned previously). When this card is reversed, you may make a good start, but your success could be hampered by your running out of energy or interest, or getting bogged down in disagreements with other people.

THE KNIGHT OF
TWO SWORDS

TWO OF SWORDS

THE TWO OF SWORDS

The Two of Swords represents a balance of opposing forces that either halts progress or demands cooperation, adjustment, or decisions. However, the Swords cards' pointed energies do not allow an easy balance of forces, so there may be much underlying tension. This card often portrays a woman who sits, holding up two crossed swords. She is blindfolded in order to show her desire to weigh matters impartially. When you are the querent, this is a card that has to be interpreted in the context of the question and the situation as you know it to determine whether you are one of a pair of opposing parties, or whether you are someone who is caught in the middle. Following are some of the ways the Two of Swords may be experienced.

Beliefs

This card may signal confrontations with another person's beliefs (ideologies). As mentioned previously, our own beliefs always seem natural to us, so beliefs that are different can seem unnatural. Therefore, your success in handling Two of Swords situations may be determined by your tolerance. If the card is reversed, it would be a good idea to search your heart to ensure that you are not harboring a bias toward someone.

Indecision

The Twos often indicate that a person is faced with choosing between two equally compelling options, although in the case of the Two of Swords, the choices may be equally uncomfortable and unsatisfactory. It may be that whatever choice you make, something is going to be lost or some-one is going to be disappointed. However, once your decision is made (an action that may be denoted by the reversed card), events can go forward again and you may gain a sense of relief. In their book *Spiritual Tarot,* Signe Echols, Robert Mueller, and Sandra Thompson suggest that the solution is to use intuition rather than logic to decide, because weighing your options intellectually just leads to stalemate.[4]

Legal Issues

Laws, rules of order, red tape, and other bureaucratic complications may be a part of the matter in question. The reversed card may warn of some rule-breaking.

Negotiation

This card can denote the need to negotiate a problem. If it is surrounded by very positive cards, it shows that people are willing to talk, and it may be possible to achieve a win-win situation, possibly by convincing both parties that they share the same goals. However, compromises usually require both parties to give some-thing up, so they must believe that peace and harmony are more important than anything else. (With Swords cards, it is especially necessary to give up the need to be "the winner.") If this card is reversed, it may indicate that people are unable to come together to negotiate because of strongly held beliefs, an inability to achieve a meeting of the minds, or the perception that they'll come out at too great a dis-advantage. If they do make an agreement, it may not be long before someone attempts some kind of maneuver to get around it. Alternatively, the reversed card could indicate that changed circumstances have removed either the source of dis-agreement or the need to compromise.

Protection

The blockage that this card portrays also has protective implications. It can denote the act of defining your boundaries—deciding how much you are willing to put up with and where to draw the line. If reversed, it may indicate that you allow other people to take advantage of you.

Relationships

This card tends to indicate that there have been disagreements and other types of problems between two or more individuals, but that they are able to reach a compromise or reconciliation. Indeed, the ability to negotiate conflict is characteristic of rational people in healthy relationships. But, due to the uneasy nature of this card, there may be some fundamental inequalities or incompatibilities in the relationship—especially if it is surrounded by problematic cards. Within important relationships, such as between family members and other individuals with whom we have to get along for everyone's greater good, it is important to make the sacrifices needed for compromise. However, if you are thinking about pursuing a romantic relationship in which there are such differences, it may be better to give it up, because the underlying differences could resurface and create too much trouble in the future. The reversed card may indicate that two people would like to reconcile, but don't know how to approach each other, or each is waiting for the other person to make the first move.

Taking Sides

One of the most painful aspects of the Two of Swords is experienced when friends, family, or social groups expect you to take sides with one against the other. Assuming that everyone is equally to blame in a dispute, this is inherently unfair and unreasonable. The reversed card could signify your decision to walk away from such a conflict.

Time Element

This card usually predicts delays, due to a stalemated situation and the need to work out problems. When reversed, it may warn of unforeseen problems, possibly at an unconscious level.

THE THREE OF SWORDS

PALOMIDES

In the Three of Swords, the natural creativity and fertility of the Threes have a tendency to generate trouble and worry when combined with the mental conflicts of the Swords. Its usual illustration features a heart pierced by three swords, suggesting the problems, conflicts, and heartaches that are likely to emerge from peoples' *reactions* to conflict, and this card answers most hopeful questions with a definite "no." Therefore, the theme of suffering may have some bearing on the matter in question, and may be experienced in some of the following areas.

THREE OF SWORDS

Communication

Because of the Threes' concern with communications, this card could predict bad news, rumors, and other disturbing messages. However, the Threes' expressive qualities may also enable you to identify and confront the source of your problem, and to express your personal sorrows, making them known to others. In keeping with the Threes' creative affinities, you may find it helpful to pour your feelings into a form of artistic expression, such as painting or poetry. The reversed card may denote attempts to hide bad news.

Health

Due to the mental qualities of the Swords, this card usually concerns injuries to the emotions or ego. However, there are some circumstances under which it may warn of danger to your health, possibly foretelling injuries, heart trouble (related to the common graphic illustration of a pierced heart), or surgery. Such predictions are uncommon, however, and only likely to apply when a person in question is particularly susceptible. The reversed card could point to health problems in an early stage of development, denoting the importance of managing stress and taking care of your body.

Human Suffering

In reading other peoples' cards, I've encountered some situations in which the sorrow predicted by the Three of Swords didn't turn out to be a disaster for the person in question, but the need to deal with the stress and sadness of other people, or in the person's line of work or general environment. Unfortunately, suffering is all around us, and the troubles of other people—especially the people we love—can affect us deeply because we are all interconnected. So when the Three of Swords comes up, be sympathetic to others and give help when you can, but also prepare yourself to deal with it philosophically. If this card is reversed, it could indicate that a person near you is suffering, but you may not be fully aware of the extent of her problems. Also, it may indicate that sorrow has become such a presence in your life (or that of someone you know) that it is no longer spoken of.

Mental Aspects

The Three of Swords often represents the types of problems that we make for ourselves when we get things worked up in our minds. There is something stimulating about the flow of energy in the Three cards, and emotional pain, too, can be a mental stimulant. Thus, some people get energized by rehashing memories of old injuries. This is one of the reasons we like to hear gossip or negative things in the news. Also, this card could denote someone whose view of reality has been distorted by depression, indicating a need to change his perceptions. The reversed card may indicate efforts to repress or control negative thoughts, possibly through therapy or mood management techniques.

Relationships

The Three of Swords may warn of problems within relationships, and may point to major incompatibilities, arguments, abusive behaviors, jealousy, unfaithfulness, and separation. This card has a traditional association with love triangles and other situations that can pull a couple apart. There may be a tendency of one of the partners to keep bad company. P. Scott Hollander says that it warns you to "protect your interests" in a breakup, because you can't count on your partner to behave reasonably.[5] When reversed and surrounded by positive cards, it may show attempts to improve a relationship or to leave it and move on to something better. On the other hand, if accompanied by other unfortunate cards, the reversed card could show a person in denial, trying to stay in a relationship from which no good can come.

Troublemakers

The Threes can sometimes denote the influences of "third parties," so this card could warn you about people who bring trouble to your doorstep, either by passing along gossip, picking arguments, or trying to involve you in their own problems—possibly pressuring you to take sides against other people. Also, if you've been concerned about certain people who always seem to be upset about something, ask yourself whether they are attracting trouble to themselves or thriving on the problems of others.

FOUR OF SWORDS

THE FOUR OF SWORDS

In the Four of Swords, the Fours' qualities of stability, security, and enclosure apply to the need for self-protection, withdrawal from conflict, and recovery. To illustrate this card's concern for safe spaces, the Rider-Waite-Smith card depicts the stone funeral effigy of a knight within a medieval chapel, but this image can be misleading because the card is really about necessary seclusion for the living. If you have been dealing with a problem, this card's promises of peace may be achieved in some of the following ways.

Health

Some Tarot books say that this card denotes convalescence and time needed for recovery from illness. If you are contending with health problems, or if you just have a very heavy stress load, the appearance of this card *gives you permission* to claim the time and space you need to regenerate yourself. You may especially want to back out of activities that are demanding too much of you, or limit time spent with people who drain your energy. If surrounded by more troublesome cards, it could warn of the need for enforced recovery, as in the case of hospitalization, so it is important to look after your health in the hope of avoiding this. Reversed, this card may indicate either that stressors are wearing down your health, or that your health is improving and you will want to become more active—depending upon the cards that accompany it.

Home Life

The Fours often pertain to home life, and they are also cards of peace, stability, and enclosure, so if you have been worried about your home environment, perhaps due to disagreements with family members, this card would tend to predict that things will be more calm, if not exactly comfortable. Alternately, it can indicate that you will have a reason to spend more time at home or in a secluded environment. The reversed Four of Swords may indicate concerns about your home life. Perhaps you don't feel "at home" due to tensions between family members.

Protection

Protection is a major theme of this card, and decks like *The Barbara Walker Tarot Deck,* whose Four of Swords shows a warriorlike woman performing magic with swords driven into the ground marking the quarters, and *The Witches Tarot Deck,* whose card shows a man laying daggers out in a magical square, emphasize the need for self-defensive measures—including watchful awareness. In practical, everyday terms, this may urge you to define your personal boundaries, that is, to let other people know what is okay with you and what is not, and be willing to stand up for your rights. A reversed card may denote a person who is trying, but hasn't satisfactorily learned, how to say "no" to other people.

Relationships

If this card comes up in response to questions about relationships, it would tend to indicate an individual who is seeking seclusion rather than relationship, but might be responsive to relationships that offer a strong protective quality. The reversed card could indicate a desire to open up to other people, especially if accompanied by cards that have expansive qualities.

Safe Spaces

The Four of Swords can represent a "safe space," which, in addition to a physical place such as your home, may be a place of retreat inside your head, within a social circle, or among friends and family who respect your right to your own life and beliefs and won't put you down for any reason. Thus, this card may predict that you will come into an emotional, social, and intellectual environment in which you can let down your guard and be yourself (although it also implies that fear is an underlying motivation in your reading). You can help this card's protective powers along by letting other people know that they are in a safe space with you, because you will honor their individual differences and keep their confidence. If this card is reversed, it can warn of a violation of your physical, social, or emotional space.

Time Element

In response to general questions, this card would suggest that a matter needs time to develop (or wounds need time to heal), so don't expect rapid progress or success. If there have been delays, the reversed card could mean that things are going to start moving again—but slowly.

THE FIVE OF SWORDS

The Fives represent forces of change, and in the Five of Swords, these can be expressed through disruptive events or stimulation-seeking behavior that brings you into challenging contacts with other people. Because the restless energies and conflict often associated with this have the potential to destabilize a secure condition, some decks have labeled this card "Defeat," and the Rider-Waite-Smith illustration shows a man who disdainfully clutches three swords, while two additional swords lie at his feet; he looks over his shoulder toward two figures who are bent over in an attitude of dejection. However, if softened by the presence of luckier cards, the Five of Swords could point to contests of ideas that bring you mental stimulation, excitement, and the opportunity to test yourself. Following are some areas where this card's energies may be experienced.

Change

Because the Fives represent forces of change, this card may represent actions and events that make an abrupt break with the past and require painful adjustments in your way of life. When reversed, it may denote fear and resistance to change, which may include denial that change has occurred.

Character

When accompanied by positive cards, the Five of Swords can indicate a character that is assertive, adventurous, and willing to take on challenges and go after opportunities. However, the presence of negative cards

may have more sinister implications: when changing times bring about crises, people can take on a "survivor" mentality, breaking with traditional standards and making their own rules. Those who deal with these people are at a disadvantage because they don't know what the rules are, and they can be changed in the middle of the game. Unfortunately, when people act badly, we sometimes excuse them by saying that hard times forced them to go against their character. In actuality, it is during times of crisis that a person's true character is tested and revealed. Therefore, to assure that you're one of the good guys, deal with your situation by reaching out to make mutually supportive connections with other people, rather than by taking a view that any means are justified for survival. However, do be cautious because other people may not be ethical or consistent. The reversed card may especially warn of complex motivations and unpredictable actions, so don't expect to find easy solutions to the problem in question.

Competition

This card can indicate active and energetic competition with other people. Swords' cards usually deal with ideological competition, but if you are an athlete or a person engaged in competitive activity, this card foretells a lively contest. Because conditions are so changeable, it is difficult to predict who will come out on top, which is why it is often unclear whether the triumphant figure in the popular versions of this card represents the questioner or her rivals. Unfortunately, if some cherished ideas and beliefs are at stake, this card can warn of highly motivated enemies. Also, there is a potential for larger groups of people to be pulled into these conflicts. When difficulty keeping up with change or competition results in a sense of defeat, a person may feel that things are falling apart; she can lose her sense of Self as well as her connection to others; there is likely to be a crisis of faith and questioning of ideals. When this card is reversed, it may indicate a person who is trying to pull away from a competitive lifestyle, perhaps trying to return to more cooperative values and more peaceful surroundings.

Conflict

The Five of Swords can denote involvement with people who are attracted to conflict, or even overstimulated by it. It can also point to situations in which you have to learn to manage conflict. If these things are factors in your life, you need to decide how much competition and conflict you're able to handle. A reversed card could indicate unconscious conflicts.

Groups

Related to the Fives' concern with social groups, and the graphic elements in the Rider-Waite-Smith card, the Five of Swords may point to issues of inclusion and exclusion involving cliques or other groups of people. In a positive framework, it could be about making the team, while in the negative, it could make a statement about the cruelty often practiced by insider groups. The reversed card could indicate someone who is beginning to detach from a larger group.

Relationships

This card could warn of power struggles within a relationship. If reversed, the competitive urges may be more unconscious.

The Eachtra

Six of Swords

THE SIX OF SWORDS

Sixes represent a state of harmony and balance, often a peaceful interlude or phase in a cycle, between periods of challenge. Because of the tension inherent in the Swords cards, the type of peace denoted by the Six of Swords has been achieved by bringing strong forces into agreement. This card commonly depicts people crossing a tranquil stretch of water in a small boat; the other shore is in sight. The man who stands and steers the boat may be the ferryman, although, because the two seated, huddled figures in the Rider-Waite-Smith version appear to be a woman and child, this could also be a family group. (Like so many of the Minor Arcana illustrations, this picture could tell a number of different stories.) They carry six swords along with them, which indicates that they carry reminders of old conflicts. Generally, this card is positive, denoting an easing of problems and a turning point that enables you to move in new directions. Following are some of the ways it might apply to your life.

Cooperation

The combination of Swords with the sociable Sixes reveals opportunities for cooperative efforts. This is a good time to ask for favors or get people to work together, because they are less stressed, more open to new ideas, and eager to get things done. Solutions to conflict are likely to arise when two different parties bring their creative insights to a matter (6 = 2 sides x 3, which is the number of creative energy). Reversed, this card may warn that solutions to problems are not obvious to you, your friends, family, or coworkers, possibly because of different ideas and beliefs. You or other people may complain about having to go along with things that you disagree with in order to preserve harmony.

Diplomacy

The desire for peace associated with this card sometimes leads to diplomatic missions. According to some traditions, you may send someone somewhere to speak on your behalf (or you may go to speak for someone else). This could involve personal matters or social groups (such as school political factions). The reversed card would indicate that greater communication skills are needed to persuade other people to listen.

Future Directions

The common graphic design of this card suggests movement from one situation to another, probably also involving a transitional state with movement toward the future and better times. This is often a time of hope and expectation, tinged with uncertainty. For young people, this could point to many things, including the transitional phases between junior high and high school, or between high school and higher education or work, or a change of jobs. If reversed, it could denote a longer period of transition, or it could even reveal a return to the past; for example, returning to an old boyfriend or girlfriend. If the reversed Six of Swords is accompanied by negative cards, it could warn of not learning from past mistakes.

Radical Dislocation

Under some circumstances, the Six of Swords may denote the experience of "radical dislocation," which can occur when we are yanked out of our familiar surroundings, often as a result of travel or some type of psychological event. After a temporary sense of disorientation, we may be able to achieve a new sense of equilibrium, as well as gain perspectives on personal issues. Then we can come back to our daily routines with renewed energy and clarity, and a strategy for dealing with problems both large and small. (Sometimes radical dislocation promotes life-changing revelations; many famous thinkers have gone to strange places in order to provoke this kind of experience.)

Reconciliation

This card predicts relief for troubled relationships. You may be able to work your differences out with another person or other people. If there have been some tensions, you will find that your environment at home, school, or work will become more pleasant. This doesn't mean that everyone will get over all of their differences; however, they are willing to find areas of agreement because they recognize the need to start over. When reversed, this card warns that conflicts may go unhealed unless the people involved work harder to suppress resentments.

Stress

If you have been dealing with a lot of stress, this card can indicate a return to more stability (as well as a vacation or a time out). However, if the Six of Swords comes up frequently in your readings, it may indicate that stress is a consistent factor in your life—part of a regular cycle—though you manage it fairly well. If this card is reversed, it may be that stress is so much a part of your lifestyle that you must make a decision to either change your way of living, or else find ways to adapt. This could be the case for young adults who have too many extracurricular activities, or who have friends who pull them into problems of their own making.

Travel

In keeping with the graphic symbolism of this card, you may be able to go on a vacation or a trip, possibly by boat or near water. This trip may signal a new sense of harmony within your family, although under some circumstances (possibly indicated by neighboring cards) it could be undertaken to promote peace or reconciliation, or to get away from some problems. If accompanied by Fours or other cards that can pertain to house and home, it could signal a move. If reversed, your travel plans could meet with minor delays or complications, or your trip may not be as relaxing as it could be, possibly because you're not really getting away from it all. You may be taking aggravations along with you—like people who take their beepers or cell phones along on vacation. On the other hand, the reversed card could simply denote a shorter trip or a return trip.

THE SEVEN OF SWORDS

The popular illustration of the Seven of Swords depicts a man who appears to be sneaking away from a military encampment. He carries five swords and leaves two others stuck in the ground behind him. He moves quickly, looking back over his shoulder, and goes unnoticed by a small group of people in the distant background. This illustration highlights the cunning that can be associated with this card, although it can also stand for planning, problem-solving, and ingenuity. Following are some situations in which Seven of Swords influences may be involved.

Anticipating Problems

Both the Swords and the Sevens deal with vision and with mental challenges, so the appearance of this card can encourage you to make plans, gather information, and use your inventiveness to prevent problems. If you have some motivated rivals, you may have to think of ways to stay ahead of your competition. However, because of the risks and the element of the unexpected associated with Sevens-style experimentation, be flexible enough to have some alternate plans and accept the possibility of not getting everything you want, or even taking some losses. The reversed card may especially warn of several different turns in a situation. People might change their minds and take new directions, especially if things that were formerly important to them suddenly become less important. The reversed card could also indicate an inability to think of everything, or it may represent a decision to stop controlling things and to let things take their own course.

Dishonesty

Related to the common illustration of this card, it could warn of theft or other hurtful acts, especially if accompanied by negative cards. Someone may be trying to get away with something, so it is important to be watchful. But don't allow yourself to develop a suspicious imagination. Confucius had the right idea when he said, "Is not he a sage who neither anticipates deceit nor suspects bad faith in others, yet is prompt to detect them when they appear?"[6] The reversed card could indicate that people are acting from confused or delusional motives, possibly driven by personal insecurities, real or imagined insults, or wishful thinking. There is a danger that you may also be coming under these influences, so it's a good habit of mind to question your own actions and motivations.

Note: There is an interesting connection between the idealism associated with Sevens and the dishonesty sometimes implied in the Seven of Swords. I have noticed that some (though not most) idealistic people occasionally get in trouble because they can be disorganized and fail to take care of practical matters. Because they get into tight situations, some end up lying, cheating, stealing from their friends, or doing other unethical things, but then they rationalize their acts as necessary to preserve their idealistic lifestyle. Also, people who are con artists often think their cleverness makes them heroic—they don't think about how their actions hurt other people.

Individualism

The Sevens have an individualistic bent, and the idea of going it alone is graphically depicted in this card's illustration. It may especially represent the problems and frustrations of people who get little understanding, and fear that they can't express their desires or pursue their interests openly. Nevertheless, isolation and lack of feedback from others can lead to impulsive and ineffective actions—as Rachel Pollack points out, the man's "schemes and actions . . . do not solve anything."[7] This is probably one of the reasons some readers interpret the reversed Seven of Swords as turning to others for advice and information.

Graphic Elements

Because this card commonly depicts two swords being left behind, it may be necessary to set priorities, make compromises, and be willing to give some things up in order to achieve your goals. In an article about this card, Mary K. Greer suggests other graphic associations, including the desire to avoid confrontation, the act of collecting ideas, the redistribution of materials, or experimenting with creative design arrangements.[8]

Positive Qualities

Although some Tarot readers focus on the more negative aspects of this card, others emphasize positive qualities related to its combination of mental focus and inventiveness. Thus, Gail Fairfield labels it "Mental Flexibility" and describes it as involving experimentation with lifestyles and beliefs,[9] while *The Witches Tarot Deck* links it to creative activities and illustrates the card with a group of musicians.

GUENEVERE
AT THE STAKE

THE EIGHT OF SWORDS

Due to the mental nature of the Swords cards, the problems they depict often result from peoples' habits of thought. Because the Eights denote tight systems of organization, the Eight of Swords can denote mental organization, but it can also apply to rigid thinking, as well as an inability to take action when our personal circumstances have locked us in to a holding pattern. The illustration of this card often features a blindfolded woman who stands with her arms bound, amidst a cluster of swords that are driven into the ground around her. In most traditions, this card warns of obstacles, frustrations, and difficult situations. Depending upon the nature of your question, the Eight of Swords may have some of the following applications.

Attitude

The Eight of Swords can represent the ability to focus all of your thoughts on something you want to accomplish. However, it can also reveal the different ways in which peoples' attitudes get them enmeshed in problems and prevent them from seeing a way out. Negative attitudinal factors can include (1) being caught between competing issues, ideas, and choices, all of which seem to carry equal weight; (2) feeling too attached to things that unnecessarily tie you down; (3) the feeling that you don't have "permission" to be yourself and act independently; (4) the belief (often stemming from cultural or familial conditioning) that you are a "lesser" human being and therefore deserving of second-class treatment (or even victimization); (5) learned helplessness, which is avoiding responsibility by failing to develop personal

242

skills; and (6) perfectionism paralysis, which occurs when a person becomes depressed and loses the will to do anything as a result of trying to please everyone and do everything perfectly. If you feel that these or other limiting patterns of thought may apply to you, analyze the ways your thoughts and actions have kept you tied up. If you take a close look at the Rider-Waite-Smith illustration of the Eight of Swords, you will notice that the blindfolded woman is not totally bound, because her feet are free, and there appears to be no one guarding her. This suggests that a possible way out of the predicament is by taking small, careful steps, while also working to loosen the bonds. The reversed card may indicate that you have recognized the need to make changes, and are starting to make some progress.

Circumstances

Most people have to make choices to work within certain limitations or live within certain confining circumstances in order to get their education, get their jobs done, support themselves and their families, and so on. Life also presents some limitations that we can't do much about. Therefore, this card may simply point to the types of restrictions that are a part of your own life at this time. Because many young people experience a sense of imprisonment while they are going through school or depending on parents, this card may especially denote those kinds of frustrations—but fortunately, they're only temporary. If, however, you consider imposed limitations unreasonable, it would be good to start sorting out your issues. Perhaps you can negotiate an alternative set of responsibilities with those in power over you. (They might be more receptive to negotiation if you can show that you are organized and have a well-reasoned plan.) If this card is reversed, it could denote the easing or lifting of some restrictive circumstances.

Imprisonment

Because it can sometimes denote imprisonment and other legal complications, this card is a warning to anyone who is likely to get into trouble with the law. The reversed card may predict liberation after imprisonment.

Oppression

Under some circumstances, the Eight of Swords could stand for oppressive conditions imposed by outside forces. (The castle pictured on a peak in the background of some versions could symbolize power from above, and the line of swords for power diffused in the world around us—see the discussion of Power at the beginning of this chapter.) Although most of the young people reading this book are unlikely to suffer the overt forms of oppression that exist in other societies, the appearance of this card can remind us to reflect on the meaning of human rights.

Other People

Because 8 = 2 x 4, with Two representing our responsibilities to other people and Four representing materiality, that is, "things," the Eights can sometimes represent other peoples' things. In the case of the Eight of Swords, the things in question can be other peoples' problems. (In some cases, these problems may involve trouble between two households.) Some of us never feel more helpless and hopeless than when we're dealing with other peoples' problems, because so often the solutions are obvious to us, but not to the other people, who have all kinds of excuses as to why something can't be done. If you are being pressured to get involved in someone else's problems, offer sympathy, but try to keep your "equanimity," which is the ability to stay clear-headed and emotionally detached.

Vision

Sometimes this card may warn that there's something you're not seeing—a literal response to the woman's blindfold. It is possible that you are paying such close attention to organizing certain details that you have overlooked something else. The reversed card would indicate an opening awareness of outside factors.

THE NINE OF SWORDS

The number Nine is the product of 3 x 3; as Three is the number of creative energy, 3 x 3 multiplies the creative possibilities of a situation. However, because the Swords deal with mental energies that are often focused on conflict, the Nine of Swords can signify multiplied anxieties. Usually the problems or other situations associated with this card have been building up over time, getting to the point where they're self-regenerating (that is, continually producing new problems or situations). As a result, the people affected by these problems often have a personal history of hardship, and they feel worn-out and depressed. The Nine of Swords' association with worry and sorrow is reflected in its common illustration, which shows a woman sitting in bed, her hands over her face in a gesture of grief.

Anxiety

This card may indicate that you worry too much. When the same worries keep going around in your head, getting magnified in the process, this is called a "cybernetic loop." It is this kind of looping that often keeps people sitting up at night, unable to sleep. When this card is reversed, it can point to anxiety at a more unconscious level, giving you the feeling that something is wrong, but not being able to explain it or pinpoint where it is coming from. In either case, try to put off your worries until you are in a clearer frame of mind. It is a good idea to seek a positive distraction, like watching a good movie. If the Nine of Swords is accompanied by negative cards, or if you find your worries are preventing you from functioning normally,

you might want to find someone—possibly a counselor or another professional—with whom you can talk them over.

Conflict

Because it warns of the multiplication of problems, it would be a good idea to avoid conflicts of all sorts. Chances are that they will drag on indefinitely and lead to many complications. The reversed card may reveal conflicts of a lesser nature; if accompanied by positive cards, it may be that some problems are beginning to clear up.

Other People

Related to the popular illustration that is suggestive of a woman who sits up at night worrying about her loved ones, this card can signify time spent worrying about others. Sasha Fenton has found that this card often denotes "problems with regard to females in the family and also to 'female' health problems."[10] Also, many families have an empathic "caretaker" (often female) who seems to take on everybody else's problems as her own, and this card could be a significator for such a person. If this card is reversed, it could denote someone who is suppressing her problems, not wishing to be a burden to others.

Worst Case Planning

Although the problems represented by the Nine of Swords are usually due to anxieties that we build up in our minds, when this card comes up, it is a good idea to think about the worst things that could happen in relation to the question you are asking, as well as the worst things that are actually likely to happen. When you seriously study your "worst case scenarios," you will realize that the worst things that could happen are not the same as the worst things that are likely to happen, and that most of these potential problems are manageable. When you have a realistic idea about the problems that might come up, you are also able to gather information and make plans to counteract them. When reversed, it may indicate that problems are more in the nature of minor worries and anxieties, but information gathering and planning can still help you get a grip on them.

Thoughts on the Sadness of Life

The Nine of Swords reminds us that we should be sensitive to the deep and genuine sorrows that all people experience. It may be true that at higher levels of spiritual development we will discover that all suffering is an illusion, but most of us have to find meaning in our suffering here and now. While it is important to focus on the positive and look for solutions to problems, it is also necessary to "validate" our own and other peoples' experiences, which includes acknowledging and respecting the pain they have endured or are enduring.

Americans have a problem with this, because we have a certain expectation that life should always be happy. Because we view suffering as something that disrupts the natural order, we differ from people in many other cultures, whose traditions are built around the belief that sadness is a part of the natural order. By being aware of this, you may be able to deal with Nine of Swords issues more philosophically, reminding the people for whom you read that this card tells them what they already know—that certain losses just have to be grieved.

THE TEN OF SWORDS

CAMLANN

TEN OF SWORDS

One of the lessons of the Tens is that history repeats itself: things go around in cycles, and people come back to the same places they were before, though usually with greater understanding. The Ten of Swords stands for cyclic patterns of conflict, as well as the maturity to face them. When we learn from experience, we can avoid repeating negative patterns. However, if we are too easily attracted to conflict, we can be sucked into new problems, the psychological burden of which is symbolically portrayed in versions of the Ten of Swords, which depict a man lying on the ground with ten swords piercing his back. If this card is accompanied by Major Arcana cards, they may indicate that repeating patterns are the expression of a greater archetypal theme that you need to come to terms with. Following are some of the ways that this card's warnings may affect your life.

Conditions of Life

The Ten's concern with cycles of life tells us that everyone can expect to deal with problems and suffer some personal disappointments and setbacks as part of the natural rhythms of life. As Ernest Hemingway has said, "The world breaks everyone and afterward many are strong at the broken places."[11] Part of maturity is accepting this fact in the knowledge that you will learn to deal with whatever mistakes you make, and manage whatever crises may arise. This idea is reflected in *The Witches Tarot Deck*'s illustration of this card, which shows a warriorlike man and woman who face outward, ready to take on the next problem. The reversed card may reflect Terry Gorski's saying: "Growth is moving from one set of problems to a better set of problems."[12]

Enemies

As you may gather from the common depiction of this card, the Tarot may speak of enemies and warn you to "watch your back." When our behavior draws us into repeated conflicts, we can accumulate enemies. If you choose a career or life path that requires your participation in conflict, this is a reality that you will have to adjust to. However, if you are the kind of person who doesn't care what other people think, you may be immune to some of the worst potentials of this card. The reversed card may warn of individuals with secret resentments; they may not even be aware of their bad feelings.

Family Matters

Unlike the common illustrations for the Ten of Cups and the Ten of Pentacles, the Ten of Swords does not depict a family scene. However, because of the Tens' concern with cyclic patterns and intergenerational matters, the Ten of Swords may point to family feuds or inherited problems, or to problems that are perpetuated by family-instilled behavior patterns, so it is important to study the ways your family gets pulled into conflict if you want to break the cycle. If reversed, family problems may be working on you on an unconscious level.

Health

Due to the graphic nature of the Rider-Waite-Smith deck's illustration of this card, some readers consider it a warning to look after your health (although it is not, traditionally, a card of death). The reversed card many indicate that health problems are under control, but still need attention. In either case, outside stress is likely to be a major factor.

Recurring Problems

When this card appears in a reading, there is a possibility that you may be dealing with some major problems; these could be long-standing problems that you may have thought were resolved, or they could be very similar to problems you've dealt with in the past. Think about the ways that your problems may be part of a repeating pattern, and whether self-defeating attitudes are involved. On the other hand, the reversed card may show that you are starting to adopt attitudes or actions necessary to break these patterns.

World Problems

Tens can represent times when the life cycles of an individual or an individual family interact with the cycles of history and of the world at large. Consequently, this card may indicate conditions in which major social issues have some impact on you and your family (for example, international conflicts or changing economies). On the other hand, this card could indicate that world problems weigh very heavily on your mind. Reversed, this card may hint that world problems are having an indirect or delayed influence on your personal condition.

Some Philosophical Thoughts on Defeat

There are times in peoples' lives when they may come to have such an accumulation and repetition of troubles and sorrows that they feel like giving up. While people should never give up on their necessary responsibilities toward their loved ones, or on their own survival, there are times when admitting defeat can free a person from certain impossible or artificial standards—such as worrying about what other people think, setting goals that are too far out of reach, or trying to do everything on one's own. I am reminded of a humorous sign I once saw in an office, which said something like, "Now that I've given up, I feel a lot better." Furthermore, at the point of giving up on such things, the point of release, we open a space for the higher powers to enter. We may achieve a state of grace when we admit that certain problems are bigger than we can handle and turn to spiritual sources for guidance. Here, genuine transformation is possible, allowing us to step into new and more positive phases of life.

10 THE PENTACLES

The suit of Pentacles is associated with elemental Earth, and deals with money, material goods, resources, social status, work, security issues, and worldly values. In older decks, this is the suit of Coins, and sometimes it is known as Disks. A. E. Waite introduced the use of Pentacles in modern Tarot decks. A pentacle is a tool used by magicians to connect with elemental Earth. In his discussion of magical ritual methods, William G. Gray states that a pentacle is essentially a surface, and that "it can be any type or shape of surface, but for convenience and artistry [it] is frequently circular . . ."[1] Tarot decks that use Pentacles almost always portray them as round and inscribed with pentagrams. The roundness symbolizes the Earth, and the pentagram stands for human striving for self-improvement and unity with the world of nature and the cosmos.

Interpreters have linked the Pentacles suit and the Earth element with what the psychologist Carl Jung described as the "sensing" function, which is a mode of awareness that is focused on concrete facts, practical details, and matters in "the here and now," as well as with the "thinking" function, which refers to a way of processing information through objective and impersonal criteria. By the way, when we cite Jung's functions of consciousness, the qualities of different Tarot suits, or the four elements of ancient lore, this is our way of dividing reality into categories so we can talk about it, and translating it into different metaphors so we can sense it on deeper, symbolic levels. This is something we do for our own convenience, but in real life these associations are never pure, and their categories sometimes overlap. This is why it is possible for one Tarot scholar to look at the Pentacles and see them as representing sensing qualities, while others focus on their thinking qualities (or why some interpreters associate the Wands with Air and the Swords with Fire).

We are experiencing things represented by the Pentacles cards when we are concerned with practical, "real world" matters, which usually means carrying out our jobs and chores, looking after our physical needs, fulfilling our responsibilities to other people, preparing for the future, and making a place for ourselves in society. Young adults and teenagers are likely to deal with Pentacles-related issues when they are focusing on their studies, negotiating family obligations, developing job skills, entering the work world, or setting practical goals for their future. Of course, Pentacles-related concerns are very much on young peoples' minds when they are thinking about money—earning it, spending it, or worrying about it—as well as their other possessions, or things they would like to acquire. Young people may engage some Pentacles-related conflicts when they encounter materialism and snobbery, and must decide which of these they are willing (or pressured) to go along with.

Pentacles-type people (or people who are going through phases denoted by the Pentacles cards) are likely to take pride in solid accomplishments and the knowledge that they can analyze and manage any problems that come up. They like to deal with hard facts or things that they can see and touch. Some of them activate their earth connection by becoming involved with crafts or other hand work, while others surround themselves with beautiful things. They often identify with traditional values, though these days they are more likely to pick and choose which traditions they will uphold. (For example, a New Age herbalist may very much identify with his eighteenth-century ancestors, even if he seems odd by the standards of modern middle-class society.) When people are acting out some of the negative traits associated with the Pentacles, they may become too rigid in their thinking, or judgmental of people who have fewer material goods, or they may be unable to see value in anything besides material accumulation. They also tend to make fun of any interest in futurism, sentiment, or mysticism.

The appearance of Pentacles in a reading may point to situations in which we must learn through hands-on experience, often involving trial and error. We may find ourselves having to take better care of our own things, and maybe other peoples' things as well. We can express the Pentacles' higher qualities when we see our goods and skills as means rather than ends, especially when using them to transmit meaningful values or care for the needs of others.

THE ACE
OF PENTACLES

The Ace of Pentacles usually depicts a single pentacle, coin, or disk. It signifies material world concerns, such as money and other types of goods, as well as the ability to work toward goals. Because Aces represent new beginnings, the Ace of Pentacles can signify new goods (such as gifts, money, and other material things), new jobs or responsibilities, new projects, new objectives, and, in keeping with the Pentacles' Earth symbolism, possibly a new way of connecting with nature. When this card comes up in a Tarot reading, it lets you know that a number of things in your life will focus on money and material things, as well as issues relating to work, security, and well-being. Opportunities to improve these aspects of your life can appear in many forms. Following are some of the common types of situations to which this card may apply.

Goals

This card signals a good time to work for solid goals and material self-betterment. This would be especially true for people who have been experiencing loss or instability in their lives. In keeping with the earthy nature of the Pentacles cards, goals with very concrete objects stand the best chance of success. If the Ace of Pentacles card is reversed, there may be a problem with staying focused on goals. If this is true for you, it might be easier to work for small rewards on a step-by-step basis, so you can have something tangible—things that you can see and touch—to reassure you. Surround yourself with pictures and other types of images of what you want to achieve, so you can keep a guiding vision of success in front of you.

Jobs

This card can denote a successful job hunt, a promotion at work, or a new line of work. If you don't have a job, you may experience some pressure to get one because of the pull to take on responsibilities, as well as the desire to be able to buy nice things. The reversed card may indicate that employment or promotion is almost within your reach, but you have to work a little harder to get employers to notice you.

Money and Material Aid

The Ace of Pentacles is very welcome because it can predict that money or other good things are or will be coming into your life—especially if it is surrounded by very positive cards. The things toward which you have been working will start to pay off. Someone may bring you a gift, give you money, or offer financial aid; perhaps you will win a contest or earn a scholarship. Channels of abundance are opening for you. At the very least, this card lets you know that the resources you need are available to you, though to manifest these things most fully, you may need to set some worthwhile objective on which to focus. You may also have to spend some money, though the implication is that you will have the money to spend, and will make good decisions (unless negative cards are present). A shopping trip may turn out to be a central event for you. If the Ace of Pentacles is reversed, the Tarot may predict difficulty in getting all of the help you need. It seems that the money or resources are there for you, but your access to them is sporadic and unpredictable, or perhaps for some reason they are being withheld or delayed. (Think about whether there is anything in your attitude or environment that could be causing this blockage.)

Opportunities

The Ace of Pentacles can stand for new projects and other types of opportunities coming your way. If you get involved, you will enjoy solid gains as a result of the experience. If reversed, you may be in danger of missing a good opportunity, or perhaps it will take more work to find out where the opportunities are.

Values and Personal Identity

The people around you may be preoccupied with material things and material values, maybe showing off what they have, or judging you by what you have. Your own sense of identity could be affected by your financial status, so think about whether you are basing your self-esteem on the appearances of wealth, or on your ability to work toward solid goals. If this card is reversed, you may have some confusion about defining your values and deciding where your duties and your priorities lie. Meditation on the set of Pentacles cards can help you find pride and pleasure in a down-to-earth identity based on competence, hard work, thrift, and concern for the well-being of others.

Two of Shields

Castle Pendragon

Two of Pentacles

THE TWO
OF PENTACLES

The Two of Pentacles, which commonly portrays a person balancing two disks (with some difficulty), indicates the need to balance different responsibilities, make choices, and negotiate relationships. Following are some of the ways that this card might apply to your life.

Activities and Lifestyles

This card may indicate that the act of devoting yourself to two different aspects of your life, such as school and work, or school and friends, could turn out to be something of a strain for you. The outlook usually tends to be good, though, indicating that you take pride in your ability to handle many things at once, and you will continue to manage things competently, as this balancing act is a reality of most peoples' lives, and one to which most of us must adapt at an early age. Think about the types of adjustments and adaptations that you have already had to make in your life, and how your experience with managing these things has given you confidence. However, if the Two of Pentacles is reversed or surrounded by negative cards, it could warn against taking on more responsibilities than you can handle.

Choices

Since Twos often deal with the need to make choices, the appearance of the Two of Pentacles can mean that you must decide how to divide your attention between two or more competing matters—matters that weigh heavily upon you. If this card is reversed, you may be uneasy about making decisions. Perhaps you feel that you're not ready, that you need more time, money, or information. It may be good to alleviate some of this pressure by asking for help or postponing tough choices until you have gained more experience or maturity.

Relationships

The Twos often deal with relationships and the way that relationships affect our plans. If you have been hoping to develop a relationship or partnership, this card predicts that it will come to pass, and that you will be making commitments to another person. This could mean that a lover, a friend, or a partner will come into your life; this is likely to be someone with whom you will share important projects (such as a project buddy or business partner). If this card is reversed, it indicates that you and your partner are likely to be pulled in different directions. You may not be a good partner to someone else at this time, perhaps because you are disorganized or afraid of intimacy. Or perhaps you will feel a very strong pull between your duty to the other person, and what you consider your duty toward yourself. You might consider whether you need to develop better cooperative skills, or whether you are the type of person who needs to work alone. Dissatisfaction could also result from inequalities in a relationship. Perhaps you are embarrassed because one of you is conspicuously wealthier than the other, or because one of you has to work harder. Think about how you can work out a more balanced sense of give and take in the relationship.

Relationships and Responsibilities

Taking the needs of another person into consideration may delay some of your own plans and inhibit your freedom to do what you want. This is not a bad thing, this is just something fundamental to preserving good human relationships. When this card is reversed, it may make a statement about being unreliable in your duties toward others. Even if you mean well, it's distressing to your loved ones when you let them down. If preserving good relationships is important to you, you might think about adjusting your activity schedule so you can better fulfill your responsibilities, even if you are a very busy person.

Values

You may find yourself in a situation that pulls you between competing value systems, possibly between the more materialistic values of our culture, and those that stress human values. If reversed, this card may indicate that things could get so confused that it might be difficult for you to sort out your priorities.

THE THREE OF PENTACLES

The Three of Pentacles is a card about applying your creativity to useful projects that express your values, contribute to community pride, and produce things of beauty. The common illustration of this card, which portrays an artisan conferring with others regarding a building project, depicts how important cooperation and creative inspiration are to real world objectives. This emphasis on creativity contributes to the energy and quality of your life everywhere—at home, at work, and out with your friends. Following are some of this card's potential applications.

THREE OF PENTACLES

Creative Life

Because Threes stand for creative expression and Pentacles represent material things, the Three of Pentacles is lucky for people who aspire to become artists, and others who like to express themselves by making things or otherwise working with their hands. It promises inspiration and the ability to make creative connections, to see the hidden potentials within the raw materials you use. It suggests that your creative success flows when you do something that you love, concentrating on the process as well as the final product. If this card is reversed, it may indicate that you have trouble sustaining the inspiration or obtaining the materials you need, which frustrates your desire to express yourself.

Money

Related to this card's association with communications and creative work to come, it bodes well for your ability to earn money. If reversed, it may indicate that you will have to work harder, to gain more recognition, before you are well compensated for your work.

Work

This is a card that traditionally predicts work to come, as well as a good quality of work life. The reversed Three of Pentacles can point to people who have a bad attitude, and are trying to get by with a minimum commitment and expenditure of energy. Because careless work equals poor compensation or lack of promotion, you might think about whether there is a need to improve your skills and put your heart and mind into what you do. Also, it helps to take the attitude that you are in the employment of the Higher Powers (to activate one of this card's traditional associations with the occult), and trust that your work is meaningful and necessary, even if in ways that you can't yet understand.

Work and Community Recognition

Threes highlight community interactions, so you may have a chance to display your creative skills in a club or community project, or perhaps through a job or special program, and you will achieve some local recognition as a result. This may lead to bigger things, such as promotions, new assignments, commissions, and other types of opportunities. It also can stand for the enjoyment of productive, creative activities with your friends, extended family, and coworkers with whom you have a lot in common, and the ability to make new friends and gain popularity through your creative work. If reversed, there could be problems with carrying out a project due to creative differences or an inability to translate concepts into a working product. Alternatively, you may not get the recognition you deserve because your local community doesn't value the product that you have to offer.

THE FOUR
OF PENTACLES

Four of Shields

KING MARK

Both the number Four and the Pentacle cards represent matter and materiality, so the Four of Pentacles represents the most solid manifestation of these qualities. Consequently, when this card comes up, issues tend to focus on material accumulation, the desire to build things, and the social power that comes with affluence. It indicates that you and probably the people around you are motivated by a need for security and status, and will be concerned with practical, tangible things. Following are some of this card's most common applications.

Actions, Behavior, Decisions

The Four of Pentacles may indicate that your decisions and life choices are based on security issues, which means acting conservatively and avoiding risks. This is a good thing if you need to settle down, get focused, work hard, stay closer to home, take care of your things, and avoid immature, risk-taking behavior. On the other hand, it may indicate a lack of progress if you have the opposite problem—if you are so security conscious or so tied down to your things or to a certain sedentary way of life that you are afraid to become more active, to get out more, to try new things, to change your line of work, or to make other types of change. When reversed, this card may indicate that you are concerned about your security and well-being and are making some tentative steps toward laying down foundations, but you still need to get better organized and make more practical plans.

FOUR OF PENTACLES

DENARI
DENIERS

4

PENTACLES
OROS

MÜNZEN

MUNTEN

Home Life

Because of the Fours' associations with stability, security, and home life, and the Pentacles concern with materiality, this card has a lot to do with houses, living spaces, and life at home, especially the material quality of life at home. I particularly like the *Motherpeace Tarot Deck's* rendition of this card, because it shows a woman enjoying the security of a home that she has decorated with disks containing spiritual symbols. Therefore, this card may indicate that a secure and comfortable home life is on your mind, and indicates that you are able to enjoy your time at home. It may relate to the idea of having "a room of one's own," and it may even denote the desire and ability to have a place of your own (if you do not yet have one). If reversed, this card may warn that lack of privacy or materially poor conditions at home could be on your mind, or create problems for you.

Money and Material Goods

The Four of Pentacles signifies material comfort and indicates that you can expect to build a secure financial base over time. If the Four of Pentacles is reversed, it may warn of the possible loss of some of the resources you have been counting on. Perhaps you have not been saving your money or taking good care of your things.

Status Quo

This card may indicate that you or the people you are dealing with like things the way they are, or are afraid to change them, feeling that it's better to be content with your work, your relationships, your social status, and the belief systems with which you were brought up. The reversed card indicates some nagging dissatisfaction with the status quo, but you may be afraid to let go of your personal attachments.

Values

This card may indicate that you and the people around you will be very concerned with hanging on to material possessions, because there are a lot of security issues involved. (Therefore, other people in question will be unlikely to loan you money or help you out with other problems.) Despite the fact that some Tarot artists depict this concept negatively, illustrating this card with a picture of a miserly person clutching his coins or pentacles, this is not necessarily a bad thing, because there are times when it is important to take care of the things we have. Also, when we are materially well off, we can create a more secure environment to comfort and nurture others. However, you may want to examine your material values and attitudes toward money. Ask yourself, *When is it appropriate to be materialistic, and when not?* Do you want to let the desire for material gain get in the way of love, friendship, or your sense of honor? Reversed, this card may represent a values shift, in which material things become less important to you.

FIVE OF SHIELDS

THE WASTELAND

FIVE OF PENTACLES

THE FIVE
OF PENTACLES

The Five of Pentacles represents the fears—but also the challenges—that arise when a seemingly settled and secure situation is subjected to the forces of change. Because changes that destabilize the foundations of daily life result in times of stress, this card often depicts a pair of injured and impoverished people who are wandering in the cold, and the card is usually interpreted as denoting risk, loss, worry, and hardship. However, bear in mind that change isn't always bad. Change itself is neutral. Whether it's a good or bad experience for you depends on how you deal with it. The best advice is to roll with it, and look for where the advantages and opportunities may lie. Five of Pentacles–type of changes may be experienced in a number of ways, but following are some of the most common areas of life that are likely to be affected.

Financial and Material Insecurity

This card could warn of a change in your material conditions that might make you feel needy or like you've been cut loose from the things you've been depending on. When the Five of Pentacles is reversed, financial worries are likely to be present, but changes may proceed in fits and starts and major misfortunes may not affect you in the most direct and immediate way. (For example, anxiety about a wave of layoffs may force your family to economize and prepare for the worst, but whether the worst will actually happen is not yet certain.)

Health

Sick and wounded people are often foregrounded in illustrations of this card, so it can serve as a warning to take care of your health. This includes learning to deal with stress and worry, because they can lead to accidents and illness. Due to the more restrained nature of reversed cards, when this one is reversed it may indicate not so much a threat, but a strain on your health.

Home Life

This card may represent a disruption in your home life—possibly a move or another major change in your way of living. For many of us, such changes can be traumatic, and moving is high on the list of stressful experiences, even when it's something to which you've been looking forward. Alternatively, the Five of Pentacles could denote a home life that is normally unsettled or unstable. For many young people, this card could reflect their worries about not being able to feel comfortable at home due to many moves, the parents' economic circumstances, or unusual living arrangements. It could also point to a problem with needy family members. When this card is reversed, it indicates that the impact of change may not affect the home life directly, but is nevertheless a cause of worry.

Lifestyles

The Fives are cards about breaking away from conventional values, so the Five of Pentacles can represent a disregard for the living standards and social position that are represented in the previous card, the Four of Pentacles. For people who want to break out of what they consider to be a physically or socially confining situation, this card predicts that they'll get their wish. The ragged figures often portrayed in the card's illustration stand as a warning that being different can require a great capacity for endurance. However, some people prefer to live without material luxuries or social status. As Mary K. Greer has noted in her book *Tarot for Your Self,* this card can represent the "unconventional life situations" sometimes necessary for living according to one's inner values.[2] This card may also denote situations in which people live in a voluntary state of hardship in order to accomplish something special, like trying to start a business or studying toward a degree. The reversed card could indicate more moderate living circumstances, or lifestyle changes that are being made in a quiet, inward way.

Relationships

Processes of change may alter your relationships, though they could also lead to new ones. Also, hardship and fear of change may be expressed in the people around you, and divisiveness may threaten your relationships, possibly resulting from jealousy or disagreements about how to deal with money, material things, and changing financial conditions. The reversed card could point to relationships that are motivated by emotional neediness.

Risky Behavior

The Five cards represent a desire for change that can lead to risks involving the management of money and things, career planning, the people with whom you associate, and other areas where your safety and security is affected. The reversed card would indicate smaller-scale risk, or the potential for risk.

Social Order and Authority

When this card comes up, it can indicate the unsettling forces that encourage people to engage in antisocial behavior. When reversed, it may indicate circumstances in which people are more lawful, but their resentments are eroding their respect for authority.

Social Position

This card may signal a change in social status that affects your popularity. For many young people in today's society, such changes are most likely to be related to their parents' prosperity or the amount of prestige held by the groups or cliques of people they associate with, though personal accomplishments as well as risks can also bring about such changes. To determine whether this means changes for the better or worse, you would need to examine surrounding cards and consider the context of the question. If this card is reversed, it may denote a situation in which your social status is in such a state of flux that you aren't sure where you stand; alternatively, it can denote worries about the possibility of losing status.

THE SIX OF PENTACLES

The Six of Pentacles represents those peaceful interludes when life is easier and relatively problem-free. You can expect a secure and prosperous period when you can enjoy prestige and indulge the impulse to be generous. Illustrations for this card often depict a richly dressed man who is handing out coins. This person can afford to be generous to others because he has confidence in his own ability to get through cycles of hardship and plenty. Some Tarot decks have labeled the Six of Pentacles "Success." Its position in the Pentacles suit teaches that success comes from being able to find your balance despite life's ups and downs, finding creative ways to cooperate with others, and sharing what you have as a way of circulating psychic energy. Following are some of the most common expressions of this card.

SIX OF PENTACLES

Generosity

You may find yourself sharing your money or whatever resources you may have, and your generosity will boost your popularity. The reversed card may indicate that you waver between the desire to share freely and the expectation of getting something back in return, due to a philosophical tension between the open spirit of the Sixes and the Pentacles' concern for material gain.

Money

Graphic renditions of this card often emphasize the act of distributing money, and this implies that you have or will have money to spend. If you are worried about

money problems, this is very reassuring, so have faith that the next cycle will bring you more prosperity. This card can also represent occasions for which you spend money, so perhaps a trip to the mall, a major purchase, or another event involving the exchange of cash is indicated in your reading. Reversed, this card can mean that you are not able to spend as freely as you wish.

Peace and Harmony

In the state of balance that the Six of Pentacles denotes, people cooperate with each other and things run smoothly. If you have been undergoing a period of change and stress, this card, therefore, predicts that things will eventually get back to normal—maybe even better than normal. When this card is reversed, it tends to indicate that a state of harmony is achievable, but may take more time or extra effort from you and the people in your life.

Relationships

The good times denoted by the Sixes are often the product of creative partnerships (because 2 x 3 = 6, and Two stands for mutuality while Three is for creative energies). Sixes also have a symbolic correspondence with "The Lovers" card. Therefore, the Six of Pentacles indicates that your relationships are or will be harmonious and productive, and may even involve an exchange of favors, gifts, and other goods. Generally, contacts with other people will go well, because they are in a mood to cooperate. If this card is reversed, it could indicate that your relationships have the potential to go very well, but you need to work a few things out. In this situation, you have a good chance to win over the other person by giving in to a certain point, or by presenting a nice gift.

Social Life

The "social Sixes" can represent the enjoyment of good times with friends and other pleasant people. The material well-being indicated by the Six of Pentacles especially makes this possible because it's always easier to get out and find entertainment when you have money to spend. Reversed, this card may indicate a somewhat less active social life—perhaps you will need to find cheaper amusements or spend time with a smaller circle of friends.

Social Responsibility

The sociability of the Sixes combined with the Pentacles' sense of duty highlights concern for the well-being of other people. Therefore, this card may indicate that any matters in question are influenced by your social conscience. You may be actively involved in things like service clubs, or perhaps you pay attention to the problems of people around you, helping out when you can. You are probably also more aware of what is going on in the world. Reversed, this card may indicate that you mean well, but your acts of kindness are sporadic. Perhaps you are preoccupied with too many other things, or maybe you haven't made a genuine empathic connection to other people.

SEVEN OF SHIELDS

CASTLE OF WONDERS

SEVEN OF PENTACLES

THE SEVEN
OF PENTACLES

The Sevens are cards about vision and imagination, and in the Seven of Pentacles, we learn how to apply imagination to the physical world. In some versions of this card, the Pentacles are depicted as a farmer's crop, and a young man stands daydreaming among them. This card emphasizes the necessity of doing the ground work—and also being able to bide the time needed—to make your dreams manifest as solid objects. Following are some of the more common ways that its meanings are experienced in the lives of young people.

Career Choices and Visualization

The visionary but practical Seven of Pentacles represents the ability to imagine yourself with a good career, as well as the need to go through all the training and other types of unglamorous, real-world experiences necessary to reach your goal. The Seven of Pentacles' emphasis on knowing, visualizing, and taking the right steps has an important message for many people in our society: one of the reasons why women, minorities, and children of the poor have been slow to move into certain occupations, even though society for some years now has allowed them entry, is because they haven't received childhood exposure to the *idea* that these are jobs that are attainable; they can't imagine themselves performing certain jobs or going through all the other steps required to qualify for them. Regardless of your sex, ethnicity, and financial condition, if none of the people you know are able to convey to you a good mental image of what it takes to succeed in different careers, then you will stand a much greater chance of success if you can seek out other role models.

When you can visualize yourself performing a certain role, pathways start opening in what occultists sometimes refer to as "the ether" (channels for magical energy to flow through). But as the Pentacles emphasize, it is not enough to imagine yourself enjoying the prestige, salary, or other benefits of a particular career—you also have to picture the grunt work involved. For example, if you want to be a veterinarian, picture yourself enjoying the gratitude of small furry animals and their owners, but also visualize yourself giving up your social life so you can slog through the long, hard years of grad school, and imagine the unglamorous aspects of the job. I don't wish to discourage you, but rather to make the point that when you can visualize yourself performing the hard, dirty work, and performing it cheerfully, the work actually will become easier to do, and your goals will also be magically supported. When reversed, this card may warn that you have unrealistic ideas about your career path. Gathering the right information and finding a role model become all the more important.

Failure

While many Tarot systems see this card as denoting growth, development, and long-term planning, the *Crowley Thoth Tarot Deck* labels it "Failure." Perhaps this more negative interpretation reflects the tension between the Pentacles suit, which emphasizes the cautious management of money and resources, and the symbolism of "Seven," which advocates risk as a necessary part of innovation, invention, and discovery. However, a capitalistic system depends upon money and resources put at risk in the hopes of big payoffs. The deciding factors are effort and endurance. Don't risk your money or goods unless you are willing to keep working hard to make up for your losses if things go bad. A competent person needs to be able to tolerate some losses. I'm reminded of an old Native American Indian saying for planting corn that went something like, "One for the squirrel, one for the crow, one for the worm, and one for me." This is not negative thinking—it gives you the flexibility to deal with natural cycles of gain and loss. Bear in mind, also, that failure is a part of the process of discovery, and that the people who have enjoyed the greatest successes have also experienced the greatest failures. Therefore, do not be dismayed if the Seven of Pentacles predicts some setbacks, because with the right attitude and some hard work, you will gain in the end. When this card is reversed, the likelihood of failure is greater.

Perhaps you are impatient, losing the will to continue, or are looking for short-cuts to success because you're not willing to put in the time and effort.

Future Planning

The Seven of Pentacles makes a statement about the importance of planning for the future, even though there may be forces in your environment, as well as voices in your peer group and in the popular culture, that make fun of the desire to plan and save, and urge you to live for nothing but the moment. Future planning implies the ability to plan sequentially, knowing what you have to do next, and what must be done after that, but it also requires you to allow for experimentation and uncertainty. When surrounded by positive cards, this card tends to indicate that you are or will become clear about what you want to do, visualizing what you want out of life and how to work to achieve it. When this card is reversed, it indicates problems with being unclear about your goals.

Personalities

In this card, the visionary idealism of the Sevens and the practical, hard-working nature of the Pentacles translates into self-reliant individualism. When this card applies to people, it denotes individuals who are able to go against the mainstream and persevere in the struggle to achieve goals and stand up for personal values. Therefore, it is a good indication of a reliable and, eventually, successful person. When reversed, it can indicate a person who has a sense of what needs to be achieved, but may need to cultivate more self-reliance and practicality.

Time Element

The Seven of Pentacles indicates that much time may pass before you are able to get something that you've been hoping for (such as love, money, or any number of things). However, unless it is surrounded by negative cards, success is the likely eventual outcome. The situation in question involves some variables, that is, different factors that could cause things to go in different directions or lead to some unexpected turns of events. When reversed, the time element becomes all the more uncertain. The indication is that you need to gather more information and do a lot of work.

THE EIGHT
OF PENTACLES

The Eights are cards of order and organization, and the Pentacles are concerned with material things, so when the Eight of Pentacles comes up in a Tarot reading, issues may revolve around the act of organizing and caring for your things, or getting involved in other types of detailed work. This card portrays work as part of the necessary rhythm and balance of life. It provides a suggestion for dealing with the previous card, which is about waiting for your dreams to materialize, because one of the best ways to bide time and deal with uncertainty is to shift focus to the present while you concentrate on all the little details that need attention. Its emphasis on training and care is reflected in some of the popular depictions of this card, which portray an apprentice who is crafting and arranging a set of pentacles. Following are some of this card's potential applications. As always, to determine which application is most likely to fit you, you have to consider the nature of your question and the context of your situation.

EIGHT OF PENTACLES

Career Training and Employment

This is a good time to focus on your job or planning your career. If you are looking for a job, the Eight of Pentacles is a good sign because it predicts that you will soon be busy. If reversed, it could indicate the need to get more training as well as better organized for your job hunt, or in order to hold on to the job you have.

Craftsmanship

Like the Three of Pentacles, the Eight of Pentacles is concerned with craftsmanship and the ability to bring a professional attitude to the work you do. However, here the focus is on the detail work that goes into making a fine product. If this card is reversed, it may indicate frustration when the amount of extra work that goes into a project doesn't pay off as well as you would like.

Health

Because the Pentacles can deal with the needs of your body, this card may denote an organized program of diet, exercise, and other health-maintenance activities. Since many young people aren't often concerned with these things unless there is a more urgent need, it could warn of potential problems with your health (if associated with negative cards). If this card is reversed, it can point to problems with a lack of vitality and a health regimen that is unbalanced.

Organization

This card may indicate that you will be spending more time organizing and caring for your things, but is positive in affirming that you have or will have belongings to care for—possibly a special collection. If reversed, it may denote a need to go back and reorganize something that has gotten mixed up or wasn't done properly the first time. It could also mean that you may get tired of having to take care of things, feeling that there must be more to life.

Other People's Stuff

The Eight of Pentacles' numerical symbolism of 2 x 4 relates partnerships (Twos) to possessions (Fours), so you may find yourself caring for someone else's property as well as your own. This may simply mean being responsible for other people's things, but in some cases it could indicate that you will inherit or be gifted with property, or double your wealth through marriage or partnership. If this card is reversed, it warns of problems with the management of shared goods—so if other people want to borrow something from you, you might want to think twice about letting them have it; if you are borrowing something from someone else, make a point of taking extra special care of it.

Ways of Doing Things

If you are wondering about other peoples' motives or whether they will go along with your plans, the Eight of Pentacles may indicate that they have their own ways of doing things. Often, people who have worked out their own system are unwilling to do things differently, and they get annoyed with people who want them to try something new. The reversed card may indicate someone who is still trying to get organized, and may appreciate some help.

NINE OF SHIELDS

RAGNELL

NINE OF PENTACLES

THE NINE
OF PENTACLES

The Nine of Pentacles represents the multiplied blessings of the Earth powers because Nine is a numerologically self-replicating number (in what J. E. Circlot refers to as "mystic addition");[3] by adding the digits in any of its products, you get nine again. (For example, 9 x 13 = 117, and 1 + 1 + 7 = 9.) Popular renditions of this card often feature a lone woman enjoying what appears to be a self-contained life; she walks in the garden of a country manor, often accompanied by a pet. Following are some of this card's expressions.

Abundance

This card may promise financial independence and material abundance continued into the future. Perhaps you will make some good investments or take other actions that will enable you to be self-sufficient. Reversed cards indicate that a card's potential is present but its expression is restrained, so this could mean different things: it may be that you will be able to get along okay, but that it will take some time to reach your goals. At any rate, it's a good idea to activate this card's potential by working and investing wisely to make its best meanings come true.

Character

The Nine of Pentacles can represent the independent-minded type of person who is cautious, introspective, disciplined, skillful, resourceful, hard-working, committed to self-improvement, and focused on solid accomplishments. Because she has some absorbing interests, she is content to spend time by herself. Because of her careful management, she is likely to accumulate savings and property, and can expect to enjoy the rewards of her diligence. The reversed card may indicate a person who finds it difficult to get focused.

Creativity

Because the number Nine is Three times Three (the number of creative energy), the Nine of Pentacles predicts disciplined creative production, so it is good news for people hoping to make it in the arts or other inventive enterprises. However, the reversed card may warn that living the creative life will require some years of struggle, or that it will be hard to get started.

Pets

Because many artistic renditions of this card picture a woman with a bird, it can sometimes represent relationships with pets (this is also consistent with its astrological association with Venus in Virgo, the sign that rules small companion animals). Therefore, if a cherished pet is on your mind, the Tarot may be speaking to this concern; look to the surrounding cards for more information. The reversed card may point to concerns about the health or loss of a pet.

Quality of Life

The Nine of Pentacles can represent different ideas about "the beautiful life." For some, this may mean the ability to surround themselves with beautiful things; for others, this could amount to country living (as hinted by the garden surroundings in some versions of this card). When this card is reversed, it may indicate a need to live modestly and take pleasure in simple things.

Romance

The level of independence that this card implies can put a person in a good position either to enjoy dating or to wait until he meets someone very special. However, such a person may debate whether the benefits of marriage and other relationships are worth the compromises, such as the loss of personal time and closet space. When reversed, it may denote a person who is willing to give up some of his independence to become involved in a relationship.

Solitude

Because the lone figure of the woman suggests solitude, readers often emphasize this aspect of the card. It can make the statement that to achieve independence and security, you need to apply yourself, even if it means sacrificing some of your social life. It can also denote the value of time alone to gain self-knowledge and spiritual reflection (related to this card's numerological association with the Hermit card). When reversed, you may be feeling some frustration about getting enough time to yourself.

Women's Concerns

Some readers feel that this card has a message of encouragement for women who wonder whether they will be able to make it on their own. Under some circumstances, it may indicate that the matter in question involves a woman on her own; if this doesn't describe you, it could pertain to a maiden aunt, widowed grandmother, or another single woman who is concerned about you. When this card is reversed, it may indicate a person who is having problems with dependency.

THE TEN
OF PENTACLES

The Tens denote new cycles of growth and expansion in the qualities of a given suit, so the Ten of Pentacles stands for success, abundance, the accumulation of tangible goods, and the acceptance of new responsibilities. It also concerns the way that these things generate more goods and create a link between past and future generations. As an Earth card, the Ten of Pentacles is concerned with values, but they don't have to be specifically "materialistic" values; they can represent a commitment to living in harmony with the earth and contributing something meaningful to society. Because of this card's concern with things passed down, it is especially applied to family matters, which is why it often depicts several generations of a family gathered in a manorial house or castle. The Ten of Pentacles could also apply to the concerns that follow.

TEN OF PENTACLES

Career

The Ten of Pentacles may denote a job with good benefits, security, and a chance for promotion, possibly within a large corporation (where you will also be expected to participate in the "corporate culture"). Due to this card's concern with cycles of expansion, it can also signify being promoted and taking on new responsibilities. Alternatively, it could show you either becoming involved in or starting a family business. If reversed, corporate downsizing and restructuring may initiate a new cycle in your work life, possibly requiring you to start over in a new place, maybe even doing a different type of work.

Family Heritage

Your family history may have some bearing on the matter in question, perhaps because of a past problem or a responsibility that has to be carried forward. You could also find yourself involved in family celebrations, traditions, and ceremonies, or activities related to your larger ethnic or cultural heritage.

Family Relationships

This card may denote the "nurturing families" described by therapist Virginia Satir—especially when surrounded by positive cards. She claims that in such families "self-worth is high; communication is direct, clear, specific, and honest; rules are flexible, human, appropriate, and subject to change; and the linking to society is open and hopeful." On the other hand, when this card is reversed or surrounded by negative cards, it could indicate the kind of "troubled" families that Satir has worked with, in which "self-worth was low; communication was indirect, vague, and not really honest; rules were rigid, inhuman, nonnegotiable, and everlasting; and the linking to society was fearful, placating, and blaming."[4] However, do not assume that a family is troubled unless you have other evidence, because the reversed Ten of Pentacles could point to other situations, such as the shrinking of a household when the children move away.

Family Responsibility

This card could signify a need to take on more responsibilities. Family responsibility is integral to living a beautiful life because it enables you to be a genuine, active, and valued participant in the life of your household, and in the cycles of life in general (rather than someone who just takes up space). However, different levels of responsibility are appropriate for different times in life. The cause and effect of your responsibilities may be determined by the context of the reading, or by the nature of the surrounding cards. If this card is reversed, it may indicate that you are trying to pull away from some responsibilities.

Family Wealth

This card usually indicates that someone is looking after you and thinking about your security. In questions pertaining to parents' motivations, it could indicate that they are cautious people who are worried about your future. They probably have the resources if you need help; however, they may insist that you fulfill a number of conditions, so the help you need might come later rather than sooner. This card can also predict a future inheritance. The reversed card may warn of the dissipation of a family's substance. Alternatively, it may denote a family that is suffering present hardships, but the long-range prospects are good (unless surrounded by negative card indications) if they are willing to work, save, and set goals.

Generations

A situation in question may involve a multigenerational issue, or many of your family members may be concerned. Among other things, it could pertain to your grandparents—such as having a grandparent come to live with you.

Romance

Matters involving family traditions and wealth (or alternatively, your responsibilities to your company and corporate culture) may have some bearing on your relationships. You may be advised to date or marry someone from your own background, or else be willing to accommodate your partner's family and heritage. However, this card bodes well for a secure, successful, well-connected, and long-lasting union, with children and grandchildren in the future. If reversed, a relationship may be stressed by the different families' ways of doing things; you will have to be diplomatic about finding areas that you can all agree upon.

Success

This card encourages you to "think big," and predicts success and continued growth in your work, business, finances, or whatever goals you focus upon. You will also be able to enjoy social status and a good reputation. The reversed card may warn that your capacity for success is limited by your inability to handle certain major responsibilities, or your desire for a simpler life. You may have to think about more manageable goals.

11   THE COURT CARDS

Most Tarot decks include a royal court of sixteen cards, consisting of a Page, Knight, Queen, and King for each of the Minor Arcana suits. As noted in chapter 1, these figures correspond to those in ordinary playing card decks (though they have four royal characters instead of three), and some Tarot designers have renamed them (for example, referring to the Pages as "Princesses" or the Kings as "Shamans").

The court cards can represent different personalities or roles that you or other people are acting out. Although most of us probably think of ourselves as having a basic, core personality or character, we also take on different roles and personalities under different circumstances. For example, you may display a different personality when you are at home or at work than when you are with your friends. With court cards, cards that come up often or that are especially meaningful to you may denote your basic personality, while other cards may represent personalities that you take on in response to different situations.

Following is a brief rundown on the four types of Tarot royalty cards.

Pages are learners, people who are getting involved in new things, opening to the sort of experiences associated with their suit. Pages can represent special talents under development. They are people who may be learning a discipline, but have not yet achieved full expression and mastery of their creative powers. Pages can be at something of a disadvantage because they don't have much personal power, and a lot of other people have power over them. They are trying to make sense out of their world, but they can sometimes be clueless, especially since they are often required to carry out tasks without having a sense of the "big picture." Page cards have traditionally been used to represent children as well as young women, but modern Tarot readers have broadened the interpretations to include people who are in a "childlike" state in terms of being new to something, or who are acting out their "inner child," which is an unconscious facet of the personality that may be activated at certain times. When Page cards do not seem to apply to actual people, they may instead denote different types of communications.

The Knights of the Tarot are empowered in a way that the Pages are not, because they have achieved greater competence and skill in the interest areas of their suits. The Knights have traditionally represented young men, but in an era where more women and girls can enjoy greater self-determination and mobility, more Tarot interpreters have also come to allow the possibility that a Knight may represent females—as well as people of all ages who are participating in the world in a "knightly" sort of way. The appearance of a knight is a call to action. You know that people are going to be on the move, and things are going to be happening. Knights can predict arrivals, especially the arrival of new and passionate people who get you involved in major affairs and events. Knights can be new people who enter a community, organization, or field of knowledge, introducing new ideas and energies, as well as changes and challenges. Because Knights represent mobility, they represent people who have reached the stage of life when they can go after the things they want, even if they have to go out of the way to do so. They are thus able to start fulfilling desires that they may have only dreamed of in the Page state.

With the Queen cards, there is an emphasis on what they can do for you (or for other people) as an expression of their style of nurturing. This assumes our cultural roles for women, who have traditionally been defined by their relationships to other people, but nurturing is nevertheless an important function for many women (and men) as a way for them to give blessing. One of the most important ways that Queens give blessing is by giving you their undivided attention. To fully appreciate the gift of attention, think about how *seldom* in this busy world other people—especially influential people—actually do give you the full quality of their time and attention. Queens are also concerned with the development of their inner lives, their social connections, and their ability to create an environment that reflects their values. They usually stand for mature women and mothers or mother figures, but under some circumstances, Queens can represent other people who are in positions of power and responsibility. Also, the Queens can be seen to represent sub-personalities of the Empress card, and as the third card in their respective court groups, they reveal different aspects of the Empress' creative nature.

The Kings have mastered the qualities of their suit in a way that enables them to wield real worldly power. As such, they are concerned with social, political, and economic order and organization, and are likely to be influential in corporations, government, and other institutions. Sometimes they may not represent an individual person, but an institution—especially when you are dealing with an institutional authority. However, in many readings, especially those of younger people, Kings are likely to represent fathers or people who act as father figures. As individuals, they tend to be ambitious, but capable of great self-control. They think in broad, general terms and are willing to sublimate some of their personal interests (even when this means controlling some of the expressive qualities of their suit) out of concern for the common good. Kings usually represent mature men, but under some circumstances they can represent other people who are in positions of power or responsibility. Also, the Kings can be seen to represent sub-personalities of the Emperor card, and as the fourth card in their respective court groups, they reveal different ways that the Emperor establishes order and stability.

Different Tarot systems have also attributed physical traits to the court cards, such as color of hair, eyes, and skin. I have seldom made use of these interpretations, preferring to deduce the identity of a card or choose a significator based on an individual's personality or walk of life. Also, I'm uncomfortable about the potentially prejudicial implications of associating character with coloring. However, if you find it necessary to choose or interpret court cards based on appearance (perhaps if your subject's personality and interests are unknown), Eden Gray (the author of a Tarot manual that has been in use since the sixties) offers the following system: Wands stand for blonde, blue-eyed people; Cups for people with light brown hair and hazel eyes; Swords for dark-haired, brown-eyed people; and Pentacles for people with black hair and brown eyes.[1]

Bear in mind that when you are reading about the most positive qualities of court cards, you are reading about idealized types—they are stereotypical personalities. Many of the people you know may display some, but not all, of the positive qualities of a court card personality, and they may have weaknesses as well. Also, few people are pure types. For example, a certain woman may have a natural preference for Queen of Cups–type behavior, but she may also have alternate personalities that would be represented by other cards, as well as other roles that she must fulfill, depending on the nature of her work and her relations with other people.

If you read about the court cards in older books, you may encounter some attitudes about hierarchies, which are levels of importance within these cards. Some interpreters feel that the court cards represent different levels of development, maturity, and accomplishment, with the Page representing youth and inexperience, the Knight demonstrating his knowledge in worldly ways, the Queen in positions of responsibility that allow her to express different styles of nurturing, and the King as having worldly power because he has best mastered the qualities of the suit. While these can be helpful distinctions for general purposes, I disagree with interpretations that describe the Queens as being on a lower level, less mature, less evolved, or less important than the Kings. Like everything else, the history of the Tarot has been influenced by cultural prejudice (that is, through time, different people have had different reactions to its images, based on their cultural conditioning), so you have to approach it intelligently, questioning stereotypes as you try to figure out what the images mean to you personally. In my own practice, I make use of most of the more traditional interpretations of King and Queen qualities, but I don't view one as being better or higher than the other. Also, I acknowledge that many women can possess the so-called "kingly" qualities, while many men have the caring, creative traits that we associate with the Queens. Thus, the appearance of a Queen may reveal that a person has taken on a nurturing role, while the appearance of a King may indicate that the situation requires the person to be a leader and assert power over others, regardless of what the person's sex may be.

Because your personal likes, dislikes, and opinions can influence your perception of other people, they can influence the court cards that come up in your readings. For example, as Sasha Fenton has pointed out in her book *Super Tarot,* a woman who is competing with another woman for the love of a man may see her rival as a coldhearted bitch, which is a type that could be indicated by the negative expression of the Queen of Swords, even though this might not otherwise be the case.[2]

And this leads to a discussion of the reversed cards. Some traditional systems of Tarot interpret reversed court cards as denoting people who display the most negative potential attributes of their personality types—if they are not described as downright evil. However, although reversed court cards do sometimes represent mean, weak, deceitful, untrustworthy, out-of-control, or otherwise unpleasant people (after all, these kinds of people do exist), I find that in my own experience they are most likely to represent individuals whose circumstances have placed them in roles that they aren't totally adapted to or comfortable with; therefore, they don't consistently exhibit the best qualities of the card, but they don't embody the worst potentials of the reversed card as described by traditional Tarot readers, either. Reversed cards may also signal that a person is acting out a role unconsciously. And, of course, reversed court cards may denote people whose personalities are experienced as negative by you. This is especially true if they are people who impose limitations on you, are working against what you believe to be your interests, or are standing in your way. Therefore, be sure to give a reversed court card interpretation much thought, look for clues in the surrounding cards, and weigh the factors against your own knowledge and intuition before you jump to any conclusions about whether you're dealing with a good or a bad person.

Occasionally, it may be difficult to determine whether the court cards that come up in a reading denote your own role and personality, or someone else's. Therefore, it is necessary to consider the question, context, and the card's position in a layout. For example, if you are asking a question about your personal development, the court cards are likely to represent aspects of your Self. On the other hand, if you are asking about the outside circumstances that you have to deal with, the court cards may well represent other people who have some influence or power over you. If the court card is card seven in a Celtic Cross Spread (see chapter 2), which is a position that stands for the role you are playing, then obviously the card is about you, while a card that occupies position eight, your environmental influences, is likely to represent someone near you. Other cases may be more ambiguous, so you would have to evaluate the court card in light of your intuition, feelings, and other knowledge, then watch to see who shows up displaying the court card's personality, while also observing how this personality may be active in your own life. These things are interrelated, for we often unconsciously attract people into our lives who mirror our own personality traits—including unconscious ones.

The pages that follow describe the sixteen court card personalities and a selection of situations to which they may apply.

The Hare

Seer of Wands

THE PAGE OF WANDS

The Page of Wands represents an enthusiastic person who is learning to express the active, creative, outgoing qualities of the Fire element. This is an alert and inquisitive person who gets excited about new trends and ideas, though she may lack concentration, and may jump from one thought or activity to another. This card often depicts a boy who grasps a long, straight wooden staff that has some leaves branching out of it. When you draw the Page of Wands in a reading, it may signify that you or another person are displaying this personality style, or it may apply to some of the conditions listed below.

Children

When the Page of Wands applies to a child, he is probably bright and energetic, but also impatient, and may get into trouble due to his impulsiveness. He is likely to be a sociable child, and one of his most notable qualities is his ability to communicate. He may chatter incessantly, and his continuous questions can get to be annoying. In his enthusiasm to talk, he may not listen. He is very open and may inadvertently blurt out embarrassing things, or other things that have not been well thought out. He likes to dramatize things, and may try on a lot of different "faces" as part of his ego development. When Page cards are reversed, they may denote children whose circumstances prevent them from expressing their personalities. Among other things, a reversed Page of Wands may represent a child who needs more freedom to express his natural curiosity, exuberance, and desire to communicate.

Communications

When Page cards don't pertain to people or personalities, they may represent letters, calls, news, conversations, and other types of communications. Therefore, if you have been hoping for some good news, this card is very promising. The news may take the form of a special announcement. (Depending on its position, this card could also indicate that you'll be the person making an announcement.) Generally, the active, social nature of the Page of Wands card could indicate a very busy period of time with all sorts of news and messages coming in, bringing greetings from friends as well as invitations to become involved in different activities. This card's association with new experiences could also indicate a job offer or another opportunity to take your life in a new direction. When this card is reversed, it can denote delayed communications or miscommunications. To deal with such a situation, it is important to make sure that all of your own communications are clear and timely, to act fast and not allow any paperwork to lie around, and to avoid go-betweens by handling things personally, if you can. When you send something out, it is a good idea to follow it up aggressively by making calls or writing additional letters to ensure that your message got through.

New Experiences

The Page of Wands may indicate a situation in which you are dealing with new ideas and ways of doing things. This is often the case for people who are getting into a new job (or working for the first time), because the work world expects things from you that are entirely different from what you learned or experienced at home or at school, and you may have to adapt to it quickly if you want to be successful. (To a lesser extent, this also applies to the transition from high school to college.) However, because the Wands cards' personalities like to seek out entertainment, you may also become involved, as a learner, in a project, sport, or activity just for fun. When the Page of Wands is reversed, it may indicate starting new projects or activities without having the interest or commitment necessary to carry them through. Alternatively, the reversed card may denote frustrations in your ability to get out into the world and experience new things.

Inner Child

When the Pages don't represent actual children, they may reveal that a person's "inner child" is active in the situation in question. When we are showing off, having adventures with friends, engaging in sports or other recreational activities, or doing other things to satisfy our curiosity or our need to blow off steam in a positive way, we are acting out the Page of Wands state. However, the negative aspects of this state can include irresponsibility, gossip, impatience, throwing tantrums, and attention-seeking behavior such as over-dramatizing problems.

Relationships

Because Pages can signify new experiences, the appearance of the Page of Wands can be good news for questions about romance or friendship. It can denote friends who share the same interests and are fun to be with. A romance could blossom, possibly with someone who comes from your circle of friends. However, like all Pages, this card would point to the relationship's early stages of development, so it would be too early to expect commitment. If this card is reversed, it could indicate that a friend or lover is somewhat immature and self-centered.

Testimony

Eden Gray, who wrote one of the most influential Tarot manuals of the sixties, said, "If this card appears next to a card representing a man, there will be favorable testimony concerning him."[3] In other words, this card may indicate that people are or will be speaking well of you. This bodes well for the loyalty of friends, the success of job reviews and references, and so on. If reversed, peoples' opinions may be more ambivalent.

THE KNIGHT OF WANDS

The Knight of Wands is often depicted ready for action upon a rearing horse. This card represents the sort of person who expresses the ardent, assertive, creative qualities of the Fire element. The Knight of Wands goes after whatever she wants, and is characterized by her energy and initiative. This is a person who gets excited about her own ideas and is very enterprising, which means that whenever she sees an opportunity to try something or to invent something new, she will figure out what needs to be done, round up the materials or helpers that she needs, then do it. She pursues the things that interest her, and seldom bothers to get anyone's permission or worries about what other people think. She seeks out entertainment, and may well be active in sports. Because of her resourcefulness and love of freedom, she is highly self-reliant. She is also competitive and likes to show off. When the Knight of Wands personality is expressed negatively, she may have a temper, be argumentative, start fights, and take risks. When you draw this card in a reading, it may signify that you or another person are displaying the Knight of Wands personality style, or it may apply to some of the following conditions, depending upon the nature of your question and the people and situations involved.

Empowered Action

In a reading, the Knight of Wands may indicate dealing with a matter in question by going after your desires—confidently and enthusiastically. This card may especially denote situations in which you demonstrate your "potency" by going on sensation-seeking adventures of

all sorts, being a skillful and passionate lover, showing off your sense of style, expressing yourself through creative work, expanding your social network, and exercising leadership skills. When a Knight card is reversed, it may indicate that you are not using your powers in the most effective or acceptable manner, perhaps due to a loss of direction and purpose. Knights of Wands types are likely to misuse their powers when they give over to selfishness, rage, bullying, mindless rebellion, and violence.

Graphic Symbolism

Pictorial details within the cards can sometimes take on special meanings. Because many Tarot artists portray the Knights on horseback, galloping off in one direction or another, you might examine your layout to see whether the Knight of Wands is facing a neighboring card. It is possible that the other card, or a symbolic object within that card, emphasizes a desire toward which the Knight is heading. For example, notice whether the Knight is heading into the past (left) or toward the future (right). Reversed cards may also take on similar graphic significance.

Involvement

A Knight often represents a person who gets you involved in a new endeavor or area of life, though the appearance of a Knight card may also denote the *act* of getting involved. The Knight of Wands may indicate involvement in a new club, activity, or enterprise. For many young people, this could pertain to sports, dance, drama, creative projects, service clubs, social clubs, and outdoor adventure groups—among many other possibilities. Because the Knight of Wands personality enjoys having a number of different things going on at once, you may find yourself drawn into more than one activity or project, or moving from one to another. When this card is reversed, it may warn of problems with scattering your energies.

Military

Because of the action orientation and mobility of the Knights, along with their military symbolism and place in a command hierarchy, these cards may denote people in the military. Knight of Wands types may especially be attracted to the army and marines because of their desire to see action. When this card is reversed, it could denote a number of things, including discharge or part-time duty, as with the ROTC, the reserves, or the National Guard.

Movement

Knight cards can denote moving into a new house or job, going on a journey, or other types of moves and changes. The Knight of Wands may especially apply to trips for business or entertainment, often to the city. The decision to go on such a trip may be sudden and spontaneous, and you may be accompanied by friends. When this card is reversed, it may point to frustrations in your desire to make a move of some sort, but implies that you will eventually gain more mobility.

Note: This card may also pertain to the means by which you get around in life. In some circumstances, it could refer to your car, or your getting a new car, as we live in a society where self-determination is often dependent upon mobility.

Romance

The Knights often predict love entering your life. In the case of the fiery Knight of Wands, this may point to a very passionate and impulsive affair, perhaps based on love at first sight. This Knight certainly represents sexual energy and attraction. When this card refers to your lover, his style and flair adds excitement to your relationship, and he is likely to be very demonstrative. You may meet such a person through your extended network of friends. When this card is reversed, it may indicate the cooling-off of an affair, or other impediments to a couple's being together.

Time Element

This card may point to sudden and unexpected events. Reversed, it may indicate an unstable condition—sudden actions are possible but unpredictable.

THE QUEEN OF WANDS

The Queen of Wands is usually pictured surrounded by symbols that reflect her warmth, strength, independence, and love of pleasure, such as sunflowers, lions, and cats. She is the Queen who most looks and acts like a movie star: regal, dynamic, glamorous, and commanding. As an idealized personality type, she is warm, energetic, sincere, and has a sparkling personality. She is likely to be intelligent, competitive, and ambitious. She speaks her mind, and, of course, has a wide range of knowledge and opinions on philosophy, politics, and everything else. It seems that she is always busy because she pursues so many different interests. She also has an artistic flair, and acts on her creative urges, which shows in her personal style, home decor, and type of work. She creates a lively environment around her, filled with activity and interesting people. Although others find it hard to keep up with her, they are attracted to the energy, capability, and self-assuredness that give her such charisma. When Queen of Wands energy is expressed negatively (which could be indicated by a reversed card), she may be self-centered, impatient, and easy to anger, lashing out at those around her when they don't work hard enough at keeping her flattered. Such temperament can undermine much of the good she is capable of accomplishing.

As with all Wands types, the Queen has a need to assert herself and to take her energy out into the world, so she is likely to be career-minded. She is especially attracted to positions that enable her to exert her personal influence and ability to inspire, such as those in education, religion, politics, communications media, advertising, and popular culture. Whatever she does, she is willing to step in and take charge. She tolerates no limits on her capacity for achievement, and, therefore, may start her own business. She may be a community activist who starts projects and brings people together for social activities, fundraisers, and other causes. Because she's so capable, she rises high in any organization.

In a Tarot reading, the appearance of a Queen card may act as a significator for your mother or another authority figure, or it may apply to yourself, if you are in a position of responsibility—especially responsibility for other people. The Queen of Wands may also apply to some of the issues listed below.

Parenting Style

As a parent, the Queen of Wands is a dominant presence in the home. She is openly affectionate and very proud of her children, who admire her because of her enthusiasm and love of fun. They can count on her personal involvement in their extracurricular activities. She also makes them feel special by praising their accomplishments, throwing parties, and taking them along on numerous adventures. However, because she pursues so many of her own interests, her children may sometimes feel neglected (this may be indicated by a reversed card). Because she can become impatient with children's needs and demands, she encourages them to take care of themselves at an early age.

Parenting Issues

When the negative aspects of a particular parenting style are intensified, we may develop psychological issues that affect our relationships, even after we are out on our own. Because of the Queen of Wands–type's competitive nature, she wants children that she can show off, and may be very critical if they are slow or unattractive. At the same time, she may imagine that her children are in competition with her. In either case, this can lead to fighting and estrangement. When the Queen of Wands card is reversed, it may represent a woman who wishes that she could have been somebody, but was never able to develop her talents. Consequently, she may push her children into things for which they have no enthusiasm, in an attempt to live vicariously through them. It is important for Queen of Wands types and their children to develop mutual respect for each other's separate talents and interests.

Romance

In a reading for a man, when the Queen of Wands doesn't represent a mother or authority figure, she may denote his female love interest, who is likely to be a woman with a very passionate nature. She is sexually aware, acts on her feelings, and pursues her desires. If this card is reversed, it may indicate problems with the woman in question, perhaps because she seeks attention from many admirers.

Seeking Help

A Queen often represents a person who is willing to help you in some way. In the case of the Queen of Wands, she is a person who makes things happen by bringing the right people, ideas, and things together. If she recognizes talent, enterprise, and accomplishment in you, she will give you encouragement, introduce you to important people, and use her influence to get you some good breaks. If this card is reversed, it may indicate that this busy, influential woman is difficult to approach. If you are very polite and can convince her that helping you will promote her own interests, you will be more likely to get her attention.

Success

This card traditionally predicts success. Because of the Queen's emphasis on creative inspiration (being both a Wands card and card number Three in the Wands court), success is especially likely to come from creative pursuits. If this card is reversed, you may need to better develop your creativity, as well as the will to carry it out.

Social Issues

Because the Queen of Wands may denote situations in which a woman is asserting her independence, making life choices, speaking her mind, expressing her creativity, and pursuing career advancement, it may also signal times when you are being forced to deal with larger social issues, as most human societies have tried to limit female self-determination. The Queen of Wands, in particular, has characterized the sort of "uppity women" who were historically targeted for criticism and punishment because their freedom of thought, action, and expression was seen as a threat to "the natural order." Although modern society is no longer openly dedicated to keeping whole classes of individuals "in their place," vestiges of these attitudes may still be encountered. Thus, the Queen of Wands calls you to examine your own attitudes toward women's rights to fulfill their potentials. The reversed card may denote the presence of instilled attitudes or social circumstances that prevent some women from earning the opportunities or recognition they deserve.

THE KING OF WANDS

King of Wands types are the world's natural leaders, pioneers, explorers, entrepreneurs, and promoters. They may use their inspired enthusiasm to make a difference in major areas of public influence, such as education, religion, politics, writing, communications media, advertising, entertainment, and popular culture. They enjoy being in the public eye, taking risks, and using their power to implement new and experimental ideas that bring about social changes. However, King of Wands energies can be used negatively when people believe that those of special birth or abilities are entitled to rule over others. Conquest and colonialism are among the historical abuses of this type.

As an idealized personality type, the King of Wands radiates great mental and physical vitality. Because of his energetic presence and charisma, he is very attractive and may achieve some fame. He is self-confident, optimistic, and devoted to self-betterment. Although he may have some false starts or setbacks in his career, he can always start over, confident that he will eventually be a winner. Because he wants to manage life on his own terms, he often prefers to run his own business. But though he values his personal freedom, he can be very domineering in his relationships with other people. His potential weaknesses are his egotism, temper, and his tendency to fall in love with his own ideas (conditions that may be indicated by a reversed card, or the presence of negative cards). The less "evolved" type, in his haste to act on his ideas, may not care about the feelings, needs, or input of other people, and he drives them as hard as he drives himself. Consequently, other people may either love him for his warmth and charm, or hate him for his arrogance.

In a Tarot reading, a King card may often act as a significator for your father or another authority figure, or it may apply to yourself, if you are in a position of mastery and authority. The King of Wands may also apply to some of the following issues.

Parenting Style

Some of the old Tarot readers saw the King of Wands as a good catch for marriage and family, perhaps because this personality type is openly affectionate and proud of his children. He wants them to enjoy life. Because of his active nature, he will take his family on many adventures, and energetically encourage and promote their interests. However, he may also pursue activities independently of family members: if they share his enthusiasm and can keep up with him, that's great, but if not, he can be quite content to go off on his own. A reversed card may denote a period when the King of Wands is withdrawing his light and warmth from his family circle. Eventually, out of sight is out of mind as far as he is concerned.

Parenting Issues

In our efforts to get along with parents, we often suppress fundamental aspects of ourselves. Because the more negative King of Wands type has a need to dominate any space that he is in, he may discourage his children from development in certain areas. For example, if the King of Wands is a thinking person, he may need to be the head thinker, and other family members' independent thoughts may be discounted. Similarly, if he is a feeling person, then perhaps no one else in the family is allowed to express feelings. When this problem is intensified (something that may be indicated by the cards with which this one is associated), children may develop the sort of negative identities that make them feel like nonentities. Consequently, when this King is reversed or surrounded by negative cards, it may indicate that the need to reclaim your personal power, to cultivate your own thinking or feeling nature, or to revive your interests or talents is influencing the matter in question. You may need to seek out people among whom you feel safe to experiment with personal expression.

Romance

When the King of Wands doesn't represent a father or an authority figure, he may denote a male love interest who is magnetic, virile, and adventurous. The reversed card may indicate a man who is unwilling to commit, perhaps because he is self-absorbed or wants to have multiple affairs.

Seeking Help

In Tarot readings, a King often represents a person (or institution) who can help you in some way. If the King of Wands represents someone who is friendly to you, he will make things happen for you. Because he has a generous spirit, is on the lookout for new talent, and doesn't mind taking risks, he may help you with a project of enterprise. The reversed card indicates that this man may be difficult to reach because he has so many projects of his own.

Success

If you have consulted the Tarot about whether or not a certain situation will go your way, this card shows you in a position of great strength (unless it is in a position or context that denotes a rival). If this card is reversed, it may indicate that to ensure success, you need to model more kingly energy and magnanimity. If you can learn to embody King of Wands' "presence," people will go out of their way to do favors for you, because it is a human instinct to seek approval from "the King."

THE PAGE OF CUPS

The Page of Cups represents an individual who is learning to experience and express the empathic, emotional, and imaginative qualities of the Water element. This card often depicts a boy who stands gazing into a large goblet. Page of Cups–type people are apt to be compassionate, kind-hearted, receptive, and intuitive, though they may also be impractical and illogical, with a tendency to be dependent and easily confused. They enjoy their home lives and have strong emotional ties to their families, especially their mothers. Other people are often impressed by Page of Cups–types' openness and sincerity. However, such people can also be chameleonlike in their eagerness to please, repressing their own needs in order to meet the desires of other people. When you draw the Page of Cups in a reading, it may signify that you or another person are displaying this personality style, or it may apply to some of the conditions listed below.

THE SALMON

SEER OF CUPS

Children

The Page of Cups card relates to children in a number of ways. For one thing, due to the Cups cards' association with fertility, this card may denote a pregnancy. As a child personality, the Page of Cups can be the idealized sort of affectionate, trusting, lovable child—dreamy, with unworldly charm. She can be a child of many moods who is bubbly one moment and sulky the next. Her feelings are easily hurt, so she needs a lot of emotional reassurance. However, she is responsive to the feelings of others, and will try to cheer them up and go to great lengths to make others happy. This

child is affected by her surroundings, so if there are fights and conflicts in her environment, they will affect her profoundly, manifesting in depression, attempts to escape reality, and low self-esteem. When Page cards are reversed, they may denote children whose circumstances inhibit the ideal unfolding of their personalities. Among other things, the reversed Page of Cups may indicate a child who needs to be treated with greater sensitivity.

Communications

Because Pages can represent message carriers and communications, the Page of Cups may denote emotionally charged letters, calls, and conversations. Perhaps someone will reveal his feelings for you. You may also express your personal, emotional needs to someone else, and this could turn out to be a very intimate interchange. When surrounded by cards of relationship, it could denote declarations of love or even a marriage proposal. More commonly, though, the Page of Cups represents pleasant social messages such as congratulations, thank-yous, invitations, and so on, as well as general news and calls from friends and family. When reversed, this card may denote emotionally muddled or ambiguous communications. Perhaps the communicator is indecisive or is repressing some strong emotions. If the Page of Cups card refers to you, you may want to put off some important communications until you are able to get your feelings sorted out.

Emotional Learning and New Experiences

This card may denote new learning that involves experiencing a range of emotions and the need to manage your moods. This implies that your life situations are or will be emotionally intense, though, unless surrounded by negative cards, the Page of Cups usually indicates that they will be positive and rewarding, bringing about emotional and spiritual growth. When this card is reversed, it may denote situations for which you have to detach from your own feelings and set them aside in order to respect and protect other peoples' feelings. Whether this is a good or bad thing depends on the situation. Dysfunctional families often force their members to repress their feelings, but, on the other hand, there are situations in which this is the right thing for an individual to do. Sometimes we have to control our emotions and do things that we don't feel like doing for the sake of a greater good.

Inner Child

The inner child is an unconscious facet of the personality that becomes activated at special times, like when we are having fun or when old childhood security issues come up. When the Page of Cups comes up for someone who isn't a child and doesn't have children to be concerned about, it may denote issues involving the inner child. When we are daydreaming and spinning fantasies, maybe even getting a bit silly and giggly as we discuss romantic dreams with our friends, we are indulging aspects of the inner child that relate to the Page of Cups. On the other hand, when we feel emotionally needy, exasperating our friends and lovers with our clinginess and desire for constant reassurance, we may be reliving childhood fears of abandonment. Reversed Page cards may denote an inner child that is active on a deeper, more unconscious level.

Love

The Page of Cups may represent a young person who is experiencing love for the first time, or a person of any age who is just opening to feelings and relationships. This card may therefore be an omen of love and romance. Reversed, this card may indicate a person who finds it difficult to express her love for another. It is important that new love be given a chance to develop in a "safe space" where everyone's feelings are protected.

Premonitions

Related to the Page's role as a message bearer and the Cups cards' connection with the psychic realm, this card may denote some form of premonition or intuitive knowledge. If you've had some hunches about a matter in question, this card would urge you to investigate what they are trying to tell you. The reversed card could indicate that you are acting against your instincts, that you are not paying attention to your intuitive knowledge.

Spirituality

The Page of Cups also represents a spiritual seeker. You may find yourself exploring a new religion or the deeper mystical traditions behind your family's religion. You may also experience interesting dreams, imaginative fantasies, psychic occurrences, and mystical philosophies. (The fact that you are reading a book on Tarot indicates that this is already happening for you.) The reversed card may denote frustrations with trying to find spiritual teachers and an ideal space for expressing and satisfying the needs of your soul. If this is the case, have faith that you will eventually link up with the spiritual philosophy and community that is right for you.

THE KNIGHT OF CUPS

The Knight of Cups card portrays a person who is moving toward his desires, related to the romantic, poetic, spiritual qualities of the Water element. This is a person for whom it is important to demonstrate his loyalty to loved ones, use intuition and creative imagination in his life and work, and look for deeper meanings in the events of daily life. When this card is expressed negatively (surrounded by negative cards), the Knight of Cups' faithfulness to his friends and lovers may be based on how they satisfy him emotionally; this kind of person moves on when he feels a need for new emotional sensations. When you draw this card in a reading, it may signify that you or another person are displaying the Knight of Cups' personality style, or it may apply to some of the conditions listed below.

Empowered Action

The Knight of Cups represents a stage in life when you have better developed the emotional and spiritual qualities of the Page, and your ability to utilize them in your relationships gives you a sense of empowerment. The Knight of Cups may especially denote situations in which you can be generous, sensitive, and caring. Some of the more specific ways that you might express Knight of Cups' energy could include becoming more involved in your family life, doing things to prove that you care about people, animals, and the environment, and exploring New Age and other metaphysical philosophies, among other things. When a Knight card is reversed, it may indicate that you are not managing

305

your energies effectively. A reversed Knight of Cups may denote a person who is emotionally reactionary. This means that he takes things personally, and believes that anyone who doesn't share his feelings must be a bad person. Negative Knight of Cups types may also be so absorbed by their own feelings that they don't think about other peoples' feelings, or about doing right by other people, and may react with what is called "narcissistic rage" when someone says "no" to them. (Narcissism is a negative type of self-love.)

Graphic Symbolism

Sometimes a Tarot card can have special meanings that relate to picture elements within the card. You might examine your layout to see whether the Knight of Cups is facing a neighboring card, as the other card, or a symbolic object within that card, may give clues to a relationship toward which the Knight is drawn. For example, note whether the Knight is heading into the past (left) or toward the future (right). Reversed cards may also have special graphic significance for the same reasons.

Involvement

Knights often represent active involvement in the life experiences associated with their suits, so the Knight of Cups may point to involvement in different types of close-knit social groups, child care and family maintenance activities, activities connected with your family's ethnic and cultural heritage, social causes, and religious groups or psychic study groups, among other things. A reversed card may denote a lesser degree of involvement, perhaps due to emotional conflicts.

Military

Knights may denote a military person or involvement in military service. For many young people, this is one of the major transformative experiences that our culture offers. Although sensitive Cups-type people aren't ordinarily attracted to highly disciplined, hierarchical organizations, some may join the military as an expression of patriotic love of homeland, or because they feel that the discipline can help them develop greater determination and maturity. Because the Cups have an affinity for water, this card could denote the navy, the Coast Guard, or the marines. The Knight of Cups could stand for medics and others in nonfighting positions. When this card is reversed, it could denote a number of things, including discharge or a part-time duty; for example, the ROTC, the reserves, or the National Guard.

Movement

The Knights can denote mobility and different types of moves, such as moving into a new house or job, traveling, or other changes. The Knight of Cups may indicate many things, including a change of residence, a honeymoon, or trips involving children and relatives, possibly to give emotional support or to celebrate family events. It could also indicate travel by water. When this card is reversed, it may point to frustrations in your desire to make a move of some sort, but implies that you will eventually gain more mobility.

Romance

The Knight of Cups is a card that traditionally predicts love entering your life. (This is its most common interpretation.) You may meet this new love through your circle of friends and family. As a lover, the Knight depicts the sensitive, idealistic sort who may be a bit shy, but who can be very devoted and self-sacrificing. This type of person makes a sensitive lover who enjoys cuddling and closeness. Although Knights are more apt to denote the start of romantic relationships, the Knight of Cups could represent a person who is marriage and family-minded. This person is looking for a soulmate, and appreciates spiritual qualities in a partner. Indeed, the Knight of Cups may represent a "fated" relationship. When the Knight of Cups is reversed, it could mean that someone you know is secretly in love with you, but is afraid to approach you for fear of rejection. Alternatively, it may denote some emotional distancing within an existing relationship.

THE QUEEN OF CUPS

The Queen of Cups is often portrayed as an enthroned woman whose connection with the instinctual life is represented by waters that lap at her feet, and with which she seems to merge. The idealized Queen of Cups–type is a charming, compassionate, imaginative person who experiences an empathic bond with the people and things in her life. She brings out the good in people, and they respond almost magically to her deep quality of sincerity. She also has a strong devotion to the spiritual life, and she is willing to make sacrifices for higher causes. When the Queen of Cups card is reversed, it may represent a person whose emotional needs are overwhelming. She may be depressed, brood over old wrongs, and use guilt to manipulate. Also, her infatuation with ideals can make her dreamy and unable to skillfully handle real-life demands.

Queen of Cups–type people like work where they can express their emotional, creative, and spiritual natures, so some of them may be writers, poets, actors, and artists. Because they are oriented to the needs of others, some may be counselors, ministers, missionaries, teachers, doctors, nurses, and people who work with animals. Because of their love of children, they may also be full-time mothers or go into professions that work with children. Whatever they do, they create a harmonious environment and strive to comfort the people around them. Because Queen of Cups–types are very sensitive to stresses, they should find time to retreat from work and community life when they require solitude and other regenerative activities.

In a Tarot reading, this card may be a significator for your mother or another authority figure, or for yourself, if you are in a position of responsibility—especially responsibility for other people. The Queen of Cups may also apply to some of the following issues.

Parenting Style

The Queen of Cups–type parent has been idealized in many sentimental songs, poems, and stories because of her sweetness, patience, and unconditional love. She is very affectionate and loves babies. She is sensitive to her children's feelings, gives them her full attention, and works hard to meet their needs. She is blind to her children's faults and will stick up for them, even when they do wrong. She values family ties, cultivating deep and continuing relationships with her children, grandchildren, parents, and extended family. She may also create a "family of choice" by bringing other people into her home. Sometimes her children may have difficulty responding to her need for closeness, especially if they are embarrassed about showing affection. When Queen of Cups mothering is negatively expressed, there may be a sort of role reversal, and her children must constantly listen to all of her problems and reassure her of their love. It is important for parents to realize that their children should not have to carry a parent's emotional burdens.

Parenting Issues

When the Queen of Cups card is reversed or in association with negative cards, it may warn of emotional weaknesses that can manifest in a number of ways, such as depression, addiction, attachment to abusers, a martyr complex, and so on. The parent's problems can taint the emotional atmosphere of the home, and she may even allow danger to come into the home (as would be the case with women or men who expose their children to conflict or abuse by sheltering individuals with serious personality problems). It is very distressing for children to be in an environment in which there can be no tranquility or security; however, a Queen of Cups–type person may possibly be swayed by emotional appeals if her children are able to convince her how badly the unstable home situation makes them feel. (I believe children in dysfunctional households often don't speak their feelings because self-repression becomes a habit.)

Pregnancy

Due to this card's association with fertility, it may denote pregnancy and mother-hood. If reversed, it may indicate that a woman is potentially fertile, but not emotionally prepared for motherhood.

Romance

This card may denote a female love interest who seeks fulfillment in relationships, and is openly romantic, sensitive, and caring. She is very approachable and responsive, and a relationship with the Queen of Cups will have a meaningful spiritual dimension. When this card is reversed, it may indicate that she is emotionally confused and undecided.

Seeking Help

This card may denote a friendly, understanding woman who is willing to help you. She is someone to whom to turn if you need to pour out your emotions, as she is a good listener, and she can validate your own feelings and intuitions about a situation in question. When reversed, this woman may be too wrapped up in her own emotional problems to be of much help to anyone else.

Soul Life

The Queen of Cups card represents inner world mastery and harmony, as the waters that surround her symbolize this ability to open yourself to a flow of spiritual and creative inspiration that nourishes your soul. (In her book *Women who Run with the Wolves,* Clarissa Pinkola Estes comments on the symbolism of water and the need to make a time and place for creative expression to flow, pointing out, "If one prepares a special psychic place, the being, the creative force, the soul source, will hear of it, sense its way to it, and inhabit that place.")[4] When this card is reversed, it may warn that the circumstances in question are cutting you off from your spiritual source.

Social Issues

Our culture is in the process of reevaluating the values that the Queen of Cups represents. Because feeling qualities were long considered weak-minded, feminine, and inferior, even feminists came to reject them. However, many women (as well as men) are now reclaiming the desire to nurture relationships, create extended families of friends, be an active part of a community, promote beauty and harmony, and include the creatures of nature in their moral universe. Indeed, the idea of creating relationship has become a major paradigm (a socially influential idea). This idea, traditionally a goal of the "heroine's quest," has now become part of the "hero's quest" as well, and is reflected in some unexpected aspects of pop culture. At the same time, some people believe that our society overemphasizes feelings and feeling values, and that we need more tough-minded policies. Thus, the presence of the Queen of Cups may indicate that larger social forces are pressing you to decide if or how you wish to express these feeling qualities, and what you consider to be their proper role.

THE KING OF CUPS

Some Tarot artists portray the King of Cups as sitting enthroned with his back to the ocean; this implies that he is connected to his intuitive and feeling nature, but has turned his attention to worldly affairs. This card depicts a socially responsible personality type who uses his position in the larger world to promote harmony and understanding. He is aware that spiritual and emotional needs are as important to people as their basic survival needs. Consequently, he may be involved in religion, psychology, social work, and other counseling professions, or he may be in medical professional or support positions, or in other healing or caregiving roles. Because art feeds the spirit, he may also be in a creative profession. If in other jobs, he brings sensitivity into whatever he does, respecting peoples' feelings and accommodating their needs. However, Cups types aren't often the most successful people in a competitive, modern society (unless they have the ambitious, secondary personalities of other King types).

As an archetypal personality, the King of Cups is a person who feels deeply, but manages his emotions because the well-being of others is his priority. He tends to be a well-connected person with strong family ties and friendships; because he's often very popular, it may be difficult to find him alone. He appreciates art and beauty, and his personal refinement makes him attractive to others. A reversed King of Cups may denote a person who is in a position of responsibility, but who has not cultivated emotional strength and a sense of commitment. Alternatively, a reversed King may point to an individual of another personality type who is trying to adopt King of Cups–type qualities, perhaps in the hope of improving his relationships.

In a Tarot reading, a King card may often act as a significator for your father or another authority figure, or it may apply to yourself, if you are in a position of responsibility and authority. The King of Cups may also apply to some of the following issues.

Parenting Style

The King of Cups–type person has reached such a level of maturity that he is willing to put aside personal pleasures (such as going on fishing trips or hanging out with friends) to give his family his full attention. He helps to create a comfortable home, and may even work out of home. Because the King of Cups–type person enjoys being in a committed relationship, he may marry and have children at an early age. It is important to him to teach his loved ones how to trust their feelings and follow their desires, albeit sensibly, without getting hurt. His children appreciate his affection, generosity, and willingness to spend time with them and listen to their problems. However, despite the King of Cups' role as the "nice guy father," there are some problems associated with his parenting style: he finds it difficult to be firm and wants to be his kids' best buddy, so he may not enforce discipline when needed. Some children regret this because there are times when they feel weak, and they *want* him to assert his strength and set reasonable boundaries for behavior. When the King of Cups is reversed, it may indicate a father who is not emotionally available to his children, perhaps because he is too wrapped up in his own emotional needs, or too busy taking care of other people.

Parenting Issues

We often act out issues that we have with our parents. Therefore, the appearance of the King of Cups may indicate that certain conscious or unconscious issues are influencing the matter in question. This may especially be the case with reversed cards, as they can indicate a father who is or was absent, emotionally distant, or otherwise uninvolved with his children, so now those children grieve the loss of affection, trust, and togetherness. The result may be emotional neediness or an inability to show affection themselves, so it is important for such people to learn to show warmth—and to extend it to their parents, too. When the King of Cups is associated with cards of strife and sorrow, it may sometimes denote a depressed, alcoholic, addicted, or abusive parent. On the positive side, people with emotionally deprived childhoods are often motivated to develop loving and nurturing King of Cups qualities out of a desire to provide a better life for their own children.

Romance

When a King doesn't represent a position of authority, a father, or an authority figure, he can represent a male love interest who is kind and sensitive. Because of the Cups cards' association with love and relationships, this card may especially be a predictor of eventual marriage. A reversed card may denote a potential lover who is unsuitable for various reasons, possibly because he wants to stay a bachelor or is already married.

Seeking Help

The King of Cups represents a generous and friendly man, so if you are seeking assistance from an individual or institution, this card may indicate that he or they will be helpful and cooperative. If reversed, it can mean that the individuals from whom you seek aid may be well meaning, but lack the power to make a difference.

Success

The King of Cups predicts success in any activity associated with the Cups suit, such as the creative arts, counseling, caregiving, religious service, and so on. If this card is reversed, it may indicate that you're getting there, but need to achieve greater mastery and probably also more self-discipline.

THE PAGE OF SWORDS

The Page of Swords represents a person who is learning to express the qualities of the mentally oriented Air element. This card often depicts a boy holding up a sword; he may be swinging this sword in a careless manner. The Page of Swords may be a bright, inventive, observant individual who is very curious about how the world works. She may be curious about people, and enjoys getting into long discussions with them, often asking probing questions. Because she is good at recognizing peoples' weaknesses, she also has the ability to manipulate. She is attracted to power, and is good at figuring out who has it and who doesn't. This Page can also be changeable, trying out different studies, hobbies, and career-training plans. When you draw the Page of Swords in a reading, it may signify that you or another person is displaying this personality style, or it may apply to some of the conditions listed below.

THE ADDER

SEER OF SWORDS

Children

A Page often signifies a child who figures in your life. This type of child can be fun to be with because he can share interests and carry on intelligent conversations with older people. However, this is also a child who is trying to learn peoples' expectations, and he may be testing people to see what he can get away with. The Page of Swords–type child is very concerned with justice, and is quick to spot inequality, unfairness, and hypocrisy. When Page cards are reversed, they may denote children whose circumstances prevent them from fully expressing their talents, so among other things, a reversed Page of Swords may indicate a child

whose intellectual gifts need more encouragement. The reversed card may also denote personality problems: when expressing negative traits, Page of Swords–type children can be viewed as brats because they can be sneaky, spiteful, and insensitive to other peoples' feelings.

Communications

When Page cards don't seem to refer to people, they often refer to communications such as calls, letters, and other types of news and information. The Page of Swords may denote a number of different types of communications, including those involving political issues, scientific information, legal notices, and other informative and analytical matters. Consistent with the Page's interest in observing people, this card can sometimes represent gossip, which may be very funny if you are not the person to whom it pertains. The Page of Swords traditionally also represents communications that can be disturbing or critical in nature. For young people, this may come in the form of disappointing grades or critical comments from parents, teachers, employers, and other authority figures. Although negative feedback is always painful, you may appreciate it later, when you can look back in a more objective frame of mind. Reversed Pages can represent miscommunications. In this case, communications may include contradictory information or hidden meanings, so it is important to ask a lot of questions to detect deception and avoid misunderstanding, and also to avoid overreacting to the "tone" of other peoples' comments.

Note: If the Page of Swords represents you, you may have to be the bearer of news or messages. If bad news is involved, you might want to think about how you can deliver it as sensitively as possible, and avoid gossip.

Inner Child

When the Page of Swords card does not apply to a child that you know, it may apply to your "inner child of the past," a subconscious personality that is imprinted on your psyche. This inner child is an unconscious motivator that is activated in situations in which you are freely enjoying yourself, or, alternatively, when you feel insecure and powerless. In its positive expression, the Page of Swords may denote the inner child state that enjoys playing games and encourages our natural curiosity and desire to learn. On the other hand, childhood trauma and the need to survive in difficult situations may have formed a suspicious inner child who encourages you to lie, cheat, and spy. When this card is reversed, the inner child self may be operating on a deeper, unconscious level.

New Experiences

The Pages are all learners, so the Page of Swords may denote an opportunity to participate in activities that will stimulate your mind and offer new ways of seeing things. This may indicate entry into college or another program of study. The reversed card may represent a person whose desire for intellectual experiences is somewhat frustrated; if this is true for you, you may have to go farther to find stimulating friends, or become a self-taught person.

Spying

Many interpreters associate the Page of Swords with spying, so depending on the question and the context, this card could signal that someone is closely watching you, or it could warn of a situation in which you will need to be suspicious and keep an eye on the actions and intentions of other people. If this card is reversed, it may indicate that it is necessary to be careful about what you say, because the people around you may be nosy and insensitive about keeping secrets. However, under such conditions it is still important to be reasonable so you don't allow yourself to become so suspicious that you damage your friendships.

Trickery

Trickery is another one of this card's traditional associations, and if it is accompanied by various negative cards, this game playing could be destructive, which is one of the reasons it is necessary to help children develop a sense of empathy, and to show them how con games actually hurt people. The reversed card may indicate a person whose manipulations are more unconscious.

GAWAIN

SEEKER OF SWORDS

THE KNIGHT OF SWORDS

The Knight of Swords card often portrays a young man charging into battle. This card may represent a person who is demonstrating his skill and potency through the sharp, intellectually competitive, but also idealistic qualities of the Air element. Such a person searches for all kinds of challenges, and may go running to the site of conflict. Even though the Knight of Swords–type person may see himself as a crusader with very humanitarian goals, when this card is negatively expressed, he can be developmentally unbalanced, devaluing human relationships and the types of social courtesies that are necessary to make other people feel comfortable. When you draw this card in a reading, it may signify that you or another person are displaying the Knight of Swords personality style, or it may apply to some of the following conditions.

Empowered Action

The Knight of Swords may denote situations in which you demonstrate your energy, intelligence, sense of humor, original thinking, critical observation, and ability to communicate. For many young people today, a sense of empowerment is achieved through computer skills and other high tech and futuristic interests. If this card is accompanied by negative cards, it may warn that Knight of Swords energy is being used dysfunctionally, which is something that can be expressed in a number of ways. For example, some Swords types think they're winning the game when they're putting a minimum effort into their work or relationships, coasting on their brilliance and charm; however, their professors and

318

employers aren't fooled for long, and they also alienate good and loving people. Other types misuse Swords energy when they view the world through a political lens and use their skill with words to demonize everyone who doesn't agree with them, or to discount anything that doesn't serve their agenda. The reversed card may indicate a person who has some intellectual aptitude but feels uncomfortable about developing her talents—in other words, an underachiever.

Fights

This card can sometimes denote quarrels and other painful conflicts (especially if it is associated with negative cards), possibly because the individuals involved are reacting to rumors or jumping to conclusions. The reversed card may warn of seething resentments. In either case, it is important to handle the situation in question as diplomatically as possible.

Graphic Symbolism

Sometimes you can discover special meanings within the graphic details of a Tarot card, so you might examine your layout to see whether the Knight of Wands is facing a neighboring card. It is possible that the other card, or a symbolic object within that card, emphasizes a goal or desire toward which the Knight is heading. For example, notice whether the Knight is heading into the past (left) or toward the future (right). Reversed cards may also take on graphic significance in depicting the Knight facing a different direction.

Involvement

A Knight card often represents active involvement in interests related to the suit, and the Knight of Swords may denote becoming involved in a new activity, club, or enterprise, such as those that have to do with music, computers, gaming, martial arts, social activism, and scholastic efforts and organizations—among many other possibilities. A reversed card may represent a more limited level of involvement. When surrounded by negative cards, the Knight of Swords could warn of someone who could drag you into fights and other types of problems.

Military

The Knight of Swords may indicate a military person or enlistment in military service—something that has concerned a number of young people in every generation. Knight of Swords–type people may identify with the warrior archetype (as ferociously depicted in the Rider-Waite-Smith illustration of this card), though, with their mental orientation, they may also be attracted by the opportunity for higher education and officer training. They may especially be found in military intelligence (espionage) and engineering, and the Swords' affinities with the element of Air also suggests the air force and other things that pertain to flying.

Movement

Because the Knights are often portrayed as on the move, they can denote mobility and different types of moves; the Knight of Swords may especially relate to moves or trips taken for legal or educational reasons; it may also denote travel by air. This card may pertain to the means by which you get around in life; in some circumstances, it could refer to your car, or to getting a new car.

Romance

The Knights often stand for love affairs, related to the idea of "the knight in shining armor" who comes rushing in to sweep you off your feet. The Knight of Swords may represent a very "mental" relationship with someone whom you find intellectually stimulating. This person is probably an idealist as well as a good talker. In fact, such a romance may come about as a result of meeting someone who shares your interest in a special cause. When this card is reversed, it may denote a relationship that has problems taking off because it is too platonic, or because there are unrealistic fantasies involved.

THE QUEEN OF SWORDS

QUEEN OF SWORDS

MORGAUSE

The Queen of Swords is often portrayed as a stern-faced woman with a raised sword, though some artists work in butterfly designs to remind us that she can have a lighter, airy nature. She is known for her analytical mind and her love of intellectual challenges. Outside influences do not affect her, as she is completely independent and self-assured. She is concerned with social justice, and she may have ideals about how things can be better, even if she approaches problems with a tough-minded pragmatism (that is, looking for the most efficient way to deal with things "as they are" in the "real" world). She makes decisions based on the common good, though what she thinks is good for other people may not be what they would choose for themselves. Some people may view the Queen of Swords–type person as coldhearted because she doesn't react to tragedies or express her emotions the way they think a person—especially a woman—ought to. It is a mistake to judge her this way, because some people feel very deeply, though they don't display their emotions outwardly. The Queen of Swords' sterner traits may be the result of personal sorrows that have forced her to become tough. When this card is reversed, it may denote a person with an embittered, hypercritical, cynical outlook, whose negativity creates an oppressive environment around her. She may be uncooperative and create obstacles for others, perhaps as a result of being too preoccupied with power.[5]

SIBYL OF SWORDS

The Queen of Swords tends to represent aggressively intellectual or career-focused individuals. Because of their penetrating insight into complex legal, technical, or theoretical matters, they may

REGINA DI SPADE   QUEEN OF SWORDS
REINE D'EPEES   REINA DE ESPADAS

KÖNIGIN DER SCHWERTER   ZWAARDEN KONINGIN

become attorneys, judges, engineers, programmers, scientists, physicians, and academics. Their interest in studying the mind may lead them into psychology, neurology, sociology, and criminology. Because they also have excellent communication skills, they may be journalists, educators, and spokespeople for corporations, organizations, and causes. They are often skilled in music and languages. Queen of Swords–type people prefer careers that rely on their expertise as opposed to working with other people, and in whatever they do, they will insist on attention to rules, facts, and details.

In a Tarot reading, this card may be a significator for your mother or another authority figure, or for yourself, if you are in a position of responsibility. The Queen of Swords may also apply to some of the following issues.

Getting Tough

Many Tarot readers have a negative reaction to this card, focusing on the Queen's vindictive traits. However, although most of us want people to like us, there are times when we have to do things that will make us appear mean to other people. Consequently, you may have to go into "Queen of Swords mode" when you are in a position of enforcing discipline or judging somebody else's performance, or when you have to stand up for what's right, or for your own rights. The reversed card may indicate that you aren't asserting your power, perhaps out of fear of offending others. (Find a Queen of Swords–type mentor to give you moral support.)

Parenting Style

As a parent, the Queen of Swords person is especially concerned with her children's development and educational needs. She may take a scientific approach, studying child-rearing theories and exposing her children to an assortment of experiences; she programs their schedules with stimulating activities such as music lessons, trips to museums, and so on. However, this type of parent may not easily relate to or value what are often considered to be "soft," feminine qualities, so she may find it difficult to be affectionate and nurturing. Because small children's demands can make it impossible for a parent to have a moment alone with her thoughts, this might encourage an introverted or thinking type of parent to lose her temper (a condition that may be indicated if the card is reversed or among negative cards). In recognition of how important cuddling and other expressions of love are to a child's development, such parents can benefit by seeking out good Earth Mother role models.

Parenting Issues

A negative aspect of the Queen of Swords personality (something that may be indicated by reverse or adverse cards) is her ability to cut people down, to wound with words. This can be a problem with an individual who is very "linear" minded, which means that she does not understand other peoples' emotional reactions, creative expressions, or attraction to spiritually intuitive ideals. As a parent, such a person may put down a child's ideas or dreams with cutting remarks. Jungian analyst Sibylle Birkhäuser-Oeri describes this personality as an archetype in fairy tales when she says, "She represents a highly destructive tendency of the mother principle and of the female principle in general, which often leads a woman to cut off her own instinctive channels as well as those of others [by] . . . cutting into natural life with the destructive knife of intellect."[6] (Of course, some fathers and other males do this, too!) When you meet with this kind of negativity, it's important to speak out and let people know when they hurt you, because they are usually quite unaware. You can also learn to identify this problem in interactions with friends, and speak up for yourself and for other people.

Romance

When they don't represent mothers or authority figures, Queens sometimes signify female love interests. The Queen of Swords is the least relationship-oriented of the Queens, but this card may denote a relationship in which there is a strong intellectual attraction, or the partners are concerned with advancing each other's careers. When this card is reversed, it may warn of power struggles within a relationship. It also has a traditional association with widows and widowhood.

Seeking Help

Although she may not have much warmth, the Queen of Swords is the best mentor for critiquing your work, giving you a professional opinion, and encouraging your education. She will help you focus on essentials. A reversed card indicates that you will have to be persistent, respectful, and concise in your requests if you want to approach her.

Social Issues

The Queen of Swords represents intelligence and authority, yet, as a woman, she also represents a group of people to whom real power and education was historically denied. As such, she may also represent minorities or other people whose intelligence and authority is or has been under attack. Fortunately, as society becomes more fair-minded, authority is increasingly based on merit (rather than heritage or the possession of a Y chromosome), and larger numbers of people are willing to respect competent individuals, regardless of race, sex, or other aspects. A practical model of equality is also found in families that allocate tasks and decisions according to what each partner does best. (An example might be a home where the man is a better cook and the woman is a better money manager.) Despite this, there are still people who believe that family relationships should be based on gender hierarchies, and who resent having to submit to any female (or "other") authority, no matter how great her knowledge. Consequently, the Queen of Swords card may indicate that these issues are involved in the matter in question, and you may have to examine your own attitude toward authority, as well as your right to be respected for your personal strengths.

THE KING OF SWORDS

MORDRED

The King of Swords card often depicts a serious-minded man whose drawn sword shows that he is ready for action—yet he remains on his throne as he considers all of the possibilities. King of Swords–type people make a difference in the world through their love of knowledge and order. Whether as lawmakers (such as lawyers, judges, and legislators) or law enforcers (police, detectives, military people, and bureaucrats), or as diplomats, counselors, and activists, they manage social conflict. They also promote order and culture by probing the laws of nature, whether as scientists, engineers, or inventors, or as writers, educators, and philosophers. However, the systems that they design and impose can sometimes fail to accommodate human individuals' often unique needs, circumstances, or motivations.

SAGE OF SWORDS

As an idealized personality type, the King of Swords is analytical and sets logic as his highest value; he organizes his life according to a clearly articulated and highly individual philosophy. His perception of how the world works through chains of cause and effect enables him to make long-term plans for success. However, although he may have truly humanitarian ideals, his emotional detachment and insistence on doing things in a scientific manner may cause other people to misjudge him as uncaring. Because the King of Swords card emphasizes rationality and objectivity as its key qualities, the reversed card may denote someone whose thinking is so detached that he lacks empathy. On the other end, it may also point to someone who prides himself on logic, yet whose judgements are influenced by his feelings, his ethnic and class attitudes, or his upbringing, for example.

RE DI SPADE / ROI D'EPEES / KING OF SWORDS / REY DE ESPADAS
KONIG DER SCHWERTER / ZWAARDEN KONING

(Indeed, an important topic in modern academic discussions is whether real objectivity exists, and whether thinking is ever truly separate from feeling.) When a person sets up his own beliefs as the definition of what is logical, he treats people who act or think differently as illogical, and, therefore, inferior.

In a Tarot reading, a King card may often act as a significator for your father or another authority figure, or it may apply to yourself, if you are in a position of mastery and authority. The King of Swords may also apply to some of the following issues.

Parenting Style

Although he may love his children deeply, the King of Swords type finds it easier to relate to them when they are old enough to carry on a conversation and to share some of his interests. He is apt to be involved in his children's education, and tracks their personal and intellectual development. He is willing to make many sacrifices so they can attain a higher education. Although he tends to be a disciplinarian, his children appreciate his fair-mindedness. However, they may regret not having a closer bond, or a parent who is more sensitive to their emotional and psychological concerns. The reversed King of Swords may denote the type of parent who, especially in the earlier years, does not often interact with his children, preferring to leave their care to others.

Parenting Issues

Do you find yourself carrying on extended debates with your parents' voices inside your head? If so, you may have internalized issues with a judgmental parent. One of the things the King of Swords most hopes to encourage in his loved ones is their ability to think and act independently, yet his controlling behavior can keep them dependent and afraid to assert their autonomy. When the King of Swords parenting style is expressed negatively, children may feel that everything they do is being viewed as foolish or not good enough. Some may react through open rebellion, while others may feel they always have to justify themselves with such internal dialogues, even when they are older and the parent is long out of the picture. (The latter may especially be indicated by reversed cards, which often portray unconscious influences.)

Judgement and Discipline

Because the King of Swords is depicted as one who sits in judgement, many Tarot writers see this card as indicating possible involvement with the legal system or another institutional authority involving obedience to rules, discipline, arbitration, and enforcement. If the surrounding cards are friendly, the King of Swords may be someone who will be on your side, such as a lawyer, counselor, or doctor. If this card is reversed, it could indicate that you might have to deal with authorities who may not be sympathetic. For the best results, be respectful and truthful, and tell your story in a concise and straightforward manner. The King of Swords has no tolerance for nonsense.

Romance

When a King doesn't represent a position of authority, a father, or an authority figure, he can represent a male love interest. The King of Swords is not the most romantic type because he is not very playful or affectionate; however, he can appeal to women who are attracted to power, or who need intellectual stimulation in a relationship. When this card is reversed, it may warn of the kind of emotional distance that can be a problem for King of Swords types.

Seeking Help

In Tarot readings, a King often represents a person who can help you in some way. Because the King of Swords is known for his knowledge and insight, he is a person to go to when you need an objective opinion—especially if you need someone to arbitrate a dispute or solve a problem. People seeking advice from this King must be willing to listen, even if what he says is not to their liking or hurts their feelings.

PAGE OF SHIELDS

THE BADGER

SEER OF PENTACLES

FANTE DI DENARI KNAVE OF PENTACLES
VALET DE DENIERS SOTA DE OROS

BUBE DER MÜNZEN MUNTEN SCHILDKNAAP

THE PAGE
OF PENTACLES

The Page of Pentacles represents a person who is
studying the cautious, practical, productive qualities of
the Earth element. This card often depicts a boy who
holds a pentacle or another disk or sphere high in the
air, examining it intently. The sort of person that this
card signifies is apt to be very loyal to her friends and
family, and is usually willing to help out. The Page of
Pentacles–type person is detail-oriented, which is good
for her studies, but she can also be single-focused. To
grow, she needs to broaden her vision of the world and
her place in it. When you draw the Page of Pentacles
in a reading, it may signify that you or another person
are displaying this personality style, or it may apply to
some of the conditions listed below.

Children

When the Page of Pentacles refers to a child, he often
demonstrates a sense of good judgement, so people
start entrusting this conscientious, serious-minded
youth with increasing responsibilities at an early age.
He carries out tasks, routines, and chores without com-
plaining, but it is important to him to receive specific
instructions on how to proceed; he doesn't like to go
forward without permission. He is an "unaffected"
child, which means that he is unlikely to go along with
fads and fashions, though in other situations he may
prefer to flow with the mainstream. He may worry
about security, and he doesn't like to see his environment disrupted. When Page cards are reversed, they
may denote children whose circumstances prevent
them from fully expressing their needs. Among other

things, a reversed Page of Pentacles may indicate a child who would like more opportunities to explore the world around him.

Communications

When Page cards don't seem to refer to you or people you know, they may often represent communications such as letters, calls, papers, and other forms of news and information. The Page of Pentacles may represent bureaucratic paperwork, business correspondence, or communications that transmit practical information. Because the Pentacles relate to money and finances, you could receive notice of a scholarship or other forms of money granted to you. This card could additionally relate to communications regarding hobbies, collections, and other absorbing interests. A reversed Page of Pentacles may indicate delayed communications or notices of delays and obstacles. It may be that a matter in question needs more time for study or development.

When the Page of Pentacles is also the communicator, she may have some problems articulating her words. However, when you want to trust her with a secret, she has the ability to keep silent.

Health

Since Pentacles have a lot to do with the needs of the body, the Page of Pentacles may denote a period in your life when you become preoccupied with your health—possibly for the first time, if health is not something you have ever had to worry about. It could indicate becoming a student-practitioner of a special health regimen, such as exercise, diet, herbalism, vitamin therapy, and so on. When this card is reversed, it may indicate a need to pay more attention to your body, because problems may be in an early stage of development.

Inner Child

We may be satisfying the inner child state that the Page of Pentacles represents when we take special pleasure in our material things, to the extent that even time is suspended as we admire and play around with these possessions. Taking great pleasure in stimulating the senses (for example, enjoying good food) also brings out this child. When surrounded by negative cards, the Page of Pentacles may denote an inner child whose unsatisfied security needs cause him to overeat or to hang on to material things; because our things are always *there* for us, they won't walk out and leave us; they also preserve our memories. When this card is reversed, the inner child may be active on a deeper, more unconscious level.

Learning

This is a person who is learning by doing. He may be someone who is in an educational program that involves vocational or on-the-job training. He can be a very diligent student, for though he may not have the quick comprehension of others, he compensates by putting in longer hours of study and greater attention to quality and accuracy. He wants to learn all about the world, though he may pursue his studies in a quiet, introverted manner. He is proud of his accumulation of knowledge, and enjoys demonstrating his competence. When reversed, this card may indicate that obstacles to educational goals may require you to be more of a self-taught person, or to go out of your way to get the instruction you need.

New Experiences

Pages often predict that you will open to new experiences, and when the Page of Pentacles comes up, these experiences may come in the form of a new job or a new line of work. They could also involve taking up a rewarding craft or hobby, or getting into nature study. When this card is reversed, it may indicate that it will take some effort on your part to make these experiences happen.

Relationships

If you are concerned about romance or other types of relationships, the Page of Pentacles may indicate that there is the potential for a relationship to grow, but it must not be hurried. This relationship may also awaken you to the experience of your body and senses. When this card is reversed, the growth of the relationship is problematic (perhaps due to unconscious security issues), so all the more patience is required.

THE KNIGHT OF PENTACLES

The Knight of Pentacles is often depicted as an armored knight on horseback who gazes beyond the pentacle that he holds before him; perhaps he is planning for the future. This card represents the type of person who is trying to prove his competence and worth by embodying the materially resourceful qualities of the Earth element. He is even-tempered and emotionally steady, and he prides himself on his common sense. However, he tends to be indecisive, taking his time to weigh all of his options. When this card is negatively expressed, this Knight can get bogged down in the details of projects and in other aspects of his daily life. When you draw this card in a reading, it may signify that you or another person are displaying the Knight of Pentacles personality style, or it may apply to some of the following conditions, depending upon the nature of your question and the people and situations involved.

Empowered Action

Knights represent the developmental stage when you get to use your real-world skills and have more personal freedom. The Knight of Pentacles may especially denote situations in which you can demonstrate your self-reliance by being organized, holding down a job and other positions of responsibility, gaining recognition for your skills, earning and managing your money, shopping and displaying your nice things, helping others, and living up to your personal values. When a Knight is reversed, it may indicate that your

energies are too narrowly focused. With Knight of Pentacles types, this may be expressed as insistence on trivial details and rigid attitudes.

Graphic symbolism

Sometimes picture elements within a Tarot card can have special meanings. You might examine your layout to see whether the Knight of Pentacles is facing a neighboring card, because that other card, or a symbolic object within that card, may emphasize a goal toward which the Knight is heading. There may also be significance in whether the Knight is heading into the past (left) or toward the future (right). Reversed cards may also take on graphic significance in depicting the Knight facing a different direction.

Involvement

A Knight often represents a person who gets you involved in a new endeavor or area of life, though the appearance of a Knight card may also denote the *act* of getting involved. For many young people, the Knight of Pentacles may indicate involvement in the work world, or in arts and crafts, health care, and different types of organizations such as service clubs, scholastic societies, and nature study groups—among many other possibilities. A reversed card could indicate that circumstances prevent your full involvement.

Jobs and Job Hunting

Because Knight of Pentacles–type individuals are diligent and conscientious, people in power are always handing them responsibilities and offering them work. In a reading, this card may, therefore, point to a successful job hunt or assured advancement in a future career. If this card is reversed, it tends to indicate that there is a good job out there waiting for you, but you need to become more focused about what you want to do, and put more effort into the job hunt. You might also want to make sure that all of the details in your applications, resumés, and other paperwork are in order.

Military

Knights may denote a military person, or the act of joining the military. Although military service is not for everybody, it is one of the major cultural institutions through which a number of young people receive training, experience, and an introduction to a wider world. Pentacles-type people may join the service because of conservative values or the opportunity to get solid job skills. Because of the Pentacles' earth connection, this card may especially indicate the army, the infantry, bureaucratic positions and paperwork, logistics, construction units, and other aspects of the military that involve services and supplies. When this card is reversed, it could denote a number of things, including discharge or a part-time duty, such as the ROTC, the reserves, or the National Guard.

Money

This card could denote money coming into your life; reversed, it might also indicate money, but perhaps not as soon as you might be expecting.

Movement

The Knight of Pentacles may denote moves or travels, possibly involving a job, money, health, or shopping; these trips are likely to be well planned in advance. This card could also point to a move to the country. When this card is reversed, it may denote frustrations in your desire to make a move of some sort, but implies that you will eventually gain more mobility.

Romance

The Knight cards often denote love about to enter your life. If the Knight of Pentacles represents a prospective lover, she is apt to be a serious-minded person who enjoys the idea of an old-fashioned courtship, is very natural in expressions of love, and is looking for someone with whom she can feel comfortable. A relationship with such a person may have a very physical emphasis, because the Pentacles types enjoy the things of the senses. However, this relationship is likely to develop slowly; it may come about as a result of meeting someone at school or work. If this card is reversed, it may indicate that there is a mutual attraction involving a person of this description, but there are obstacles to the development of a relationship.

Igraine

Sibyl of Pentacles

THE QUEEN
OF PENTACLES

The Queen of Pentacles is often portrayed in a lush garden, among animals and other symbols that reveal her attunement with the life force of the earth. As an idealized personality type, the Queen of Pentacles is an affectionate person who appreciates the physical aspects of existence. She can be cautious, responsible, sensible, well organized, and prepared for the future. She is good at taking care of things and finding practical solutions to problems. When Queen of Pentacles types are overwhelmed by the demands of a fast-paced world, they can lose connection with their special Earth energies, which can cause them to become fatigued, pessimistic, and overly materialistic. They may also cut themselves off from spiritual and emotional values and experiences (a condition that may be indicated by a reversed card).

Two common expressions of the Queen of Pentacles personality type are the Earth Mother and the practical businesswoman; one cultivates an organic garden and devotes herself to macramé projects, while the other cultivates social status and builds her portfolio. Whether at home or in the office, the Queen of Pentacles is good at looking after peoples' physical needs, and she is attracted to jobs in which her business sense, attention to detail, and nurturing qualities will be valued. She may be a small businesswoman, perhaps one who comanages a "mom and pop" enterprise. Queen of Pentacles types may also be found in jobs that involve maintenance, caretaking, and domestic concerns, such as nursing, childcare, and food service. Because they enjoy working with their hands, especially with the things of nature, they may be craftspeople who make things that are beautiful but functional.

334

They may also be scientists who study nature, or engineers who look for practical solutions to needs. Because of their interests in the earth, they may even go into real estate, horticulture, and animal care. Although these are highly capable women, they are apt to be underappreciated, and may not be rewarded commensurate with their service.

In a Tarot reading, this card may be a significator for your mother or another authority figure, or for yourself, if you are in a position of responsibility—especially responsibility for other people. The Queen of Pentacles may also apply to some of the following issues.

Parenting Style

The Queen of Pentacles parent may identify with the image of the "old fashioned" mother who has a gift for cooking, gardening, and the ability to manage a large household. She is eager to provide her children with all possible comforts, though she also tries to ground them in practical reality. Her type is often at the center of a multigenerational family, looking after aging parents as well as children and grandchildren. However, she may be overworked, perhaps from trying too hard to live up to traditional ideals, and she may resent it when other family members are unwilling to work as hard as she does. A reversed Queen of Pentacles may sometimes indicate the negative mothering styles to which a type can be prone. A particular problem with the Queen of Pentacles type could be an overemphasis on social conformity and "practical" things to the extent that she doesn't nourish her family's personal and creative growth needs. When her own world is too narrow, she doesn't encourage their spirits to soar.

Parenting Issues

A common frustration within relationships is a parent's inability to see her older children as more than the small, helpless tots they once were—even when they are adults or have demonstrated competence and maturity. A reversed Queen of Pentacles may indicate that this is an issue affecting the matter in question, especially if you have a parent who is hypercritical or who tries to micromanage everything you do. It is important for a parent to make the attitude shift necessary to see a person as she really is, because to truly *see* someone is a form of validation. It is also a form of blessing, because in a magical sense, to see someone makes that person real, while not to see that person makes her invisible. Of course, it is also important for children to learn to see their parents as real people, with their own hopes, dreams, and sorrows.

Pregnancy

Because of this card's emphasis on fertility, the Queen of Pentacles can signify pregnancy and motherhood. If reversed, it may indicate that a woman is potentially fertile, but the time is not yet right for motherhood.

Prosperity

The Queen of Pentacles is traditionally a card of abundance, predicting material wealth, security, and a gracious lifestyle. Reversed, it may denote the ability to live reasonably well on limited means, though it can also warn of the need to work harder to provide for the future, and to avoid the selfish behaviors that accompany "poverty thinking." (Sometimes people who are really well off, as well as those who are deprived, will behave greedily and shabbily because the fear of scarcity has become ingrained.)

Romance

When reading for a man, if the Queen of Pentacles does not represent a mother, authority figure, or position of responsibility, she may represent a female love interest who is sensual and fond of luxury, but also practical and mature; she probably has some motherly qualities. When this card is reversed, the relationship may be troubled by issues pertaining to self-sufficiency or fear of physical closeness.

Seeking Help

The Queen of Pentacles is a woman who can help you financially, or with other forms of material aid. When this card is reversed, she may help you only if you offer something in return, such as your labor or services.

Social Issues

Because the Pentacles, as the Earth suit, have a lot to do with labor and human maintenance needs, the Queen of Pentacles can signify responsibility for managing a home and some of the other low-paid or no-paid jobs that have traditionally been considered "women's work." In the past, women were restricted to a very narrow range of work, and this was looked down upon because women did it. Society, not appreciating the importance of this work to human comfort and survival, viewed women's work as something that anyone could do, and viewed women as imbeciles because that's the only kind of work that they would do (that is, that they were allowed to do). Although an extensive body of labor history and research now confirms how essential all varieties of women's work have been to both home and national economies, there are still people who express this denigrating attitude. (A reversed Queen of Pentacles may especially signify her devaluation.) Consequently, when you draw the Queen of Pentacles, the situation in question may involve larger social attitudes concerning the value of work. It may be that you have to question your own attitude as you reconsider your feelings about your mother, or as you make important life choices, such as what kind of career you want, or whether to choose between home and career. When you make the choice that you believe is right for you, you may find yourself fighting for recognition of the value of what you do—whatever that may be.

King of Shields

UTHER

SAGE OF PENTACLES

RE DI DENARI   KING OF PENTACLES
ROI DE DENIERS   REY DE OROS

KÖNIG DER MÜNZEN   MUNTEN KONING

THE KING
OF PENTACLES

The King of Pentacles is often portrayed in a lush garden, surrounded by symbols of earthly wealth. This card stands for the type of person who has achieved material world mastery. Such individuals are the builders and maintainers of societies, who create order and set efficient social and economic systems in place. They are concerned with the control of material resources, and are often found in fields like banking and money management, fundraising, manufacturing, retail, real estate, agriculture and food production, and businesses and bureaucracies of all sorts. Through their financial support of the arts, sciences, and other innovative endeavors, they also contribute to culture. King of Pentacles types promote the social values that they identify with, but when this tendency is expressed negatively, they may fail to recognize injustice, discrimination, and the ways in which certain cultural institutions can repress individuals' needs for self-expression.

As an idealized personality type, the King of Pentacles tends to be a patient, dependable, and goal-oriented person who plans for the future and prepares for emergencies. Although a fear of poverty and hardship may be a recurring theme in his life, his attitude is one of cautious optimism. As a materialist, he knows the value of things and insists on quality. However, in his celebration of earthly goods and earthy ways, the King of Pentacles may display some contradictions—perhaps surrounding himself with expensive things and other cultural refinements, yet remaining plain and casual in personal style. A reversed King of Pentacles traditionally denotes a person who has access to wealth and power, but is either wasteful or greedy. Alternatively, a reversed card may point to a person of another type who is trying to adopt King of Pentacles qualities, perhaps in the hope of better managing his business affairs.

In a Tarot reading, the King card may often act as a significator for your father or another authority figure, or it may apply to yourself, if you are in a position of mastery and authority. The King of Pentacles may also apply to some of the following issues.

Parenting Style

The King of Pentacles father expects obedience, and tries to instill respect for authority, and for traditional values. He wants to ensure security and stability, and is proud of his role as a provider. He teaches his children that self-esteem must ultimately come from the self-management that results in confidence and accomplishment. A Pentacles type who is very physical may be a strong presence in his home and do many things with his children, whether it be roughhousing, camping, or working on various hobby projects together. He also enjoys giving his children practical advice and showing them how to succeed in the real world. He can be quietly supportive when family members run into problems. When his fathering style becomes exaggerated (something that may be indicated by surrounding cards), he can run to two opposite extremes. On the one hand, he may shower his family with expensive things, with the result that they could turn out spoiled and superficial. On the other hand, he may be very stingy, believing that his children will only grow wise through hardship. When the King of Pentacles is reversed, it may indicate a father who is not physically or emotionally available to his children, perhaps because he is too busy.

Parenting Issues

We often replay issues that we have with our parents as inner dialogues, lasting resentments, or other behaviors that interfere with the enjoyment of life. Parents who embodied negative King of Pentacles styles may imprint a child in a number of ways. People who must constantly convince themselves of their own worth may have had parents who believed in withholding affection until their children could accomplish a certain standard of achievement or perfection, thus depriving them during the years that they most needed to build their self-esteem and confidence. Also, the parent who withheld financial aid when he could easily have afforded it may be bitterly resented by the child who could not afford to go to college or start a business, and therefore cannot develop his potentials to the extent that he might otherwise have done. Ironically, parents who are stingy with money and affection often believe that they are instilling attitudes that will assure their children's future security, when they may actually be doing the opposite.

Romance

When the King of Pentacles doesn't represent a father or an authority figure, he can represent a male love interest who wants a traditional marriage, and is reliable, generous, and possibly quite sensual. He may be a somewhat older man. A reversed card may denote impediments to such a relationship, perhaps because the man in question is too preoccupied with business.

Seeking Help

The more enlightened King of Pentacles types have a desire to help others, so if you are seeking financial assistance from an individual or institution, this card would indicate that he or they will help you. If this card is reversed, it may indicate that help is available, but to receive it, you must prove yourself. Remember that the King of Pentacles only puts money into things that are likely to pay off, and he must be convinced that you have already demonstrated some common sense and reliability. He is also apt to put conditions and delays on his offered aid.

Success

The King of Pentacles predicts success in any activity associated with the Pentacles suit, such as those dealing with finances, material goods, and business organizations. This card is also a predictor of financial growth and prosperity (possibly through a family firm or inheritance). If this card is reversed, it may indicate that to enjoy a measure of success, you must work your way through a number of obstacles.

APPENDIX A
SIGNIFICATOR CARDS

Some traditional layouts, such as the Celtic Cross, may include the use of a significator card, which is a card specially selected from the deck to represent the querent, whether that be you or someone for whom you are reading. Significators can also be used to represent groups, institutions, or organizations. Also, when cards come up that can be recognized as standing for people we know, we may also refer to these as their significators.

When selecting a significator card to represent you or another person, you can use the list of cards suggested in this appendix, or any other card that you feel is best descriptive. Most people have a number of different character traits, so more than one card may apply. Use your intuition to decide which is most fitting in the context of your question and present circumstances. This list provides the most common significator uses for cards, but the card interpretation sections (especially for the court cards) may suggest additional associations, including personality types linked to reversed cards or more negative aspects of the cards.

By the way, even though we all have good and bad characteristics, it's customary to pick a positive, upright image that highlights your subject's better qualities. Even if your own view of a person is somewhat negative, focusing on the person's better qualities will also have a magical effect of calling out those qualities. Also, in choosing a significator for yourself, in some cases you might wish to choose a card that represents the ideal you—the person you would like to become.

The Fool: A young person or child, an innocent or inexperienced person, a foolish person, an adventurer or traveler, an individual who is about to set out on an adventure.

The Magician: On one end of the spectrum (represented by older decks), a person who is developing her potential, on the other end (as portrayed in more modern decks), a person who has achieved a high level of mastery. Also, an idealized man, a scientist, a technical wizard, an artist.

The High Priestess: A person who is exploring his inner world, an intuitive person, an idealized woman or dream woman, an individual who holds a secret, a psychic, a wise woman, a scholar or researcher.

The Empress: An influential woman who has the power to help you—possibly also a mother or mother figure, a pregnant woman, a female political figure, a boss or employer, a creative woman.

The Emperor: An influential man who has the power to help you—possibly also a father or a father figure, a male political figure, a captain of industry, a boss or employer. Also, the government, a corporation, the military.

The Hierophant: A teacher or mentor, a religious leader, someone concerned with ceremony or hierarchy, a keeper of traditions. Also, a religious or educational institution.

The Lovers: A couple—this card usually pertains to romance, but it can apply to other close relationships, such as friends, siblings, and the like. In older versions, which show a man trying to choose between two women, it can represent someone who must make a decision.

The Chariot: A person who works in transportation, a visitor, or people in the military.

Strength: A person with great inner strength, a forceful person, a courageous person, an athlete.

The Hermit: A seeker of knowledge, an elderly person, a person looking into the past, a guide, a counselor, a loner.

Justice: A person who must weigh a decision, someone involved in law or law enforcement, an arbitrator. Also, the legal system or a law enforcement agency.

The Hanged Man: A person who feels that his life isn't going anywhere, a person who has retreated from everyday life to spend time on meditation and reflection, someone who is making a sacrifice, a prisoner, a patient in a hospital.

Temperance: A healer, a manager, a self-disciplined person, a resourceful person, a conservationist, an artist, a protective spirit.

The Devil: A very destructive person. The human figures sometimes pictured can represent people who are their own worst enemies.

The Star: Someone who offers unexpected help, a protective spirit, an inspiring person (a "muse"), a deeply spiritual or inspired person, an artist, an entertainer.

The Moon: Sometimes used to signify animals (especially dogs) and wildlife.

The Sun: A child or children (depending upon whether it's a version that pictures one or two children), a person celebrating a birthday, a celebrity, a person with a sunny personality.

Judgement: People who have undergone major transformations, or people who are being judged.

The World: A self-actualized and fulfilled person, a happy person, a dancer, a naturalist, a world traveler.

Two of Wands: A business partnership or a creative partnership. Also, a person having to make a choice between two opportunities.

Three of Wands: A person involved in commerce; it can also stand for a corporation.

Four of Wands: A wedding party or people gathered for a ceremonial occasion, or people buying or building a house or starting a household.

Five of Wands: A sports team or other group of competitors.

Six of Wands: A victorious person, a person who is managing her business very well.

Seven of Wands: A person engaged in a struggle, a lone visionary, an outsider, a person holding his own against opposition.

Nine of Wands: A defensive person, a person handling multiple activities. Also, military personnel.

Ten of Wands: A laborer, a heavily burdened or overworked person. Also, a labor union.

Page of Wands: A youth who is communicative, active, outgoing, enterprising, and adventurous. Someone who takes employment at an early age. Also, a messenger.

Knight of Wands: A person who is involved or who involves others in new projects, directions, and adventures. It can also signify the appearance of someone who is very attractive and romantic.

Queen of Wands: a businesswoman or entrepreneur, an inspiring leader, a "take-charge" type of woman, a woman involved in lots of activities and projects, a woman who is very independent and passionate.

King of Wands: A businessman or entrepreneur, an inspiring leader, a "take-charge" type of man, a man involved in lots of activities and projects.

Two of Cups: A couple of friends, lovers, or partners.

Three of Cups: A trio or other group of close friends. It can also signify brothers, sisters, and cousins who are close. Also, party people, popular people.

Four of Cups: A contemplative person, a person who is dissatisfied with things as they are.

Five of Cups: A person suffering from burnout, a regretful or embittered person, a person who has experienced major changes in her emotional situation.

Six of Cups: Children, childhood friends, people from the past.

Seven of Cups: A daydreamer, an imaginative person.

Eight of Cups: A person who is evaluating his emotional life, possibly a person who is leaving a situation—at least emotionally.

Nine of Cups: A person who has many blessings, a generous host, a person who enjoys luxury, a person who overindulges.

Ten of Cups: A family or a circle of longtime friends, or a very close-knit community of choice.

Page of Cups: A youth who is sensitive, imaginative, and affectionate; an emotionally dependent person.

Knight of Cups: An attractive, romantic, idealistic person. Also, a lover, a person who brings love into your life.

Queen of Cups: A woman with strong feelings, empathy, dreams, visions, and religious ideals. Also, an attractive woman, an idealized woman, a caretaker, a social worker.

King of Cups: A man who is affectionate, sensitive, religious, and idealistic. Also, an idealized father, a member of the clergy, a social worker, a counselor, a nice guy.

Two of Swords: Someone who is mediating a dispute.

Four of Swords: A person recuperating from an illness, a person on a retreat.

Five of Swords: Someone who has the upper hand in a situation, someone who is victorious over others.

Six of Swords: A group of travelers.

Seven of Swords: A clever person, a person who is getting away with something, a thief.

Eight of Swords: Someone who feels trapped by circumstances, a prisoner.

Nine of Swords: A person with many worries and anxieties.

Ten of Swords: A victim, a person suffering from an illness.

Page of Swords: A precocious youth, a young person who is studying power relationships.

Knight of Swords: A person who is intellectual, assertive, and brave; a person who is involved in or gets others involved in conflicts or causes.

Queen of Swords: A woman who is intelligent, perceptive, and analytical. Also, a woman who has the power to fight on your behalf, a lawyer, a military woman, a professor. In some traditions, a widow or an adversary.

King of Swords: A man who is intelligent, perceptive, and analytical. Also, a man who has the power to fight on your behalf, a military man, a lawyer, a professor. Sometimes an adversary.

Two of Pentacles: A person who must juggle many duties and obligations.

Three of Pentacles: An artist or craftsperson. Also, a small group of artisans or productive people.

Four of Pentacles: A home owner, a wealthy person, a miser. Also, a bank or financial institution.

Five of Pentacles: People coping with illness or hardship, the homeless.

Six of Pentacles: A philanthropist, a person who is spending money. Also, a service club or charitable institution.

Seven of Pentacles: A farmer, an investor, a planner.

Eight of Pentacles: A worker, a craftsperson, a clerical person. Also, a labor union.

Nine of Pentacles: A self-sufficient person, a person who is able to work out of her home, a pet owner.

Ten of Pentacles: A family, a dynasty, people with inherited wealth.

Page of Pentacles: A youth who is serious and conscientious, a student.

Knight of Pentacles: A person who is reliable, hard-working, sensible, and cautious. Also, a manager.

Queen of Pentacles: A woman who is gracious, socially conscious, practical, cautious, and financially secure. Sometimes a matriarch, a property owner, a patron of the arts, or a businesswoman.

King of Pentacles: A man who is responsible for others, practical, cautious, a good money manager, a patriarch, a property owner, a patron of the arts, or a businessman.

APPENDIX B
THE USE OF COLOR

An understanding of color symbolism can be helpful to your study, interpretation, and meditation on different Tarot cards. Through the years, Tarot artists have used color to make a philosophical statement. (For example, in the old *Tarot of Marseilles* deck, the Temperance angel wears a red- and blue-colored dress and mixes fluid in red and blue goblets to show her ability to unite opposing forces.) The modern decks' use of color can be more varied or more subtle, but still carries profound meanings. When new artists choose different colors for their card designs, they shift the emphasis but allow us to see new aspects of these cards. Color symbolism can also be important if you are choosing a cloth or container to keep your cards in, or if you want to use candles or other accessories in Tarot spells (see chapter 5 for other uses of the Tarot). Following is a list of color correspondences that is based on the combined traditions of Tarot symbolism, dream imagery, folklore, and psychology. (This list is taken from my book *Playful Magic*.)

Black: Total concentration, impenetrability, protection, immovability, firm and somber resolve, absence of light.

Black and White (Combined): The Cabalistic colors of knowledge— black representing understanding because it absorbs all light, and white representing the quintessence of divine light.

Blue: Depth of emotion, peace, serenity, relaxation, honesty, fidelity, truth, kindness.

Blue, Dark: Understanding, introspection, concentration, patience. Dark blue is the contractive (inward directed) aspect of intellect. This is the ceremonial color of philosophy faculties in American colleges.

Blue, Light: Peace in the home, sincerity, loyalty, empathy, devotion, gentility, delicate charm, gracefulness.

Blue, Green: Emotional soothing, healing and nourishment, the healing power of art, mystical unity with nature, regeneration, intuitive vision.

Blue-Violet (Indigo): spiritual reflection, meditation, intuition, going deep within.

Brown: Pride in simple ways, love of simple pleasures found in living close to the earth, the earth powers, strength rooted in the earth, stability, supportiveness, the security and emotional riches of home and hearth.

Gold: Personal pride and self-confidence, radiance, charisma, attractiveness, expansiveness, creative activity and success, initiative, leadership, power and authority, prosperity, luck.

Green: Living nature, the freedom of wilderness, youth, growth, fertility, resilience, adaptation, regeneration, bodily healing, the ceremonial color of medical faculties in American colleges, opportunity, prosperity, money, financial security, comfort, the Druidic color of knowledge.

Orange: Warmth, high energy, vitality, focused energy, self-motivation, free expression, boldness, action directed by intellect, unity of mind and body (combining thought, will, and action), persuasion, endurance. This is the ceremonial color assigned to engineering faculties in American colleges.

Orange-Red: Assertiveness, activity, competitiveness, enthusiasm, wildness, force of will.

Mauve: Qualities of pink, but more retiring; desire for subtlety, dignity.

Peach: Warmth and softness, social harmony (it makes people feel safe and assured and enables people to connect well with each other). Peach takes the softness of pink, but adds the enthusiasm and energy of orange.

Pink, Rose: Affection, loving and nurturing, warm feelings, feeling good, well-being, pride in femininity, pleasure in self. Everything looks better in the glow of pink or peach. Pink is the ceremonial color assigned to music faculties in American colleges.

Purple, Violet: Altered states of consciousness, spirituality, psychism, inspiration, dynamic creativity (combines intuition with action), love of drama, dignity, focused power, authority, high stations in life, nobility, generosity, appreciation of variety and tolerance for differences. This is the color worn by law faculties in American colleges.

Red: Energy, vital force, enthusiasm, activity, impulse, anger, immediate action, human love, desire, passion, sexuality, eroticism, conception, childbearing and childbirth.

Red, Dark (Maroon and Deeper Shades): Sensitivity combined with the active and sensual qualities of red; a craving for the riches of life. This color brings love of power, wealth, and position to the intense drive of red.

Red Violet: Ambition, noble actions; adds more passion to the spiritual and mystical nature.

Silver: Subtle lunar energies, ethereal beauty, romantic feelings, mysterious charm, mystique, purity of understanding, the receptive aspects of creativity. Association with clarity and purity pertains to integrity, honesty, self-worth, and idealism.

White: Purification, purity of intentions, innocence of spirit, psychic energy, spiritual strength, purified emotions and absence of negative feeling, unity and harmony (because white is the result of all the colors in the spectrum combined).

Yellow: Brightness, happiness, cheer, hopefulness, expectations, intellect, alertness, wit, wisdom, science, confidence, spontaneity, enjoyment of action, communication, questing for alternative experience. The active (outward directed) aspect of intelligence.

Yellow-Green: The calming and centered qualities of green, but more emphasis on intellect and activity; cool, but with the confidence and love of challenges of yellow.

APPENDIX C
READING FOR ADVICE

Although Tarot cards are most commonly used to gain information about the past, present, or future, the cards can also provide us with different types of advice. You may often have to deal with a situation in which you already know what is going to happen, but you may be wondering what to do about it. Also, if you do a regular (divinatory) reading that predicts a disappointing outcome, you may want to know what you can do to prevent it, or at least how to make things better.

While advice can sometimes emerge from the reading itself (for example, if you get warnings of danger, it is obvious that you should be more cautious), there is also a special method for asking the Tarot to suggest courses of action. This method, which I have developed and described at length in my last book, *Tarot: Your Everyday Guide,* involves a different way of phrasing your questions, as well as a somewhat different mode of interpreting the cards. While there isn't sufficient space to reproduce all of that information in the card chapters of this book, the technique can be quite simply explained.

Basically, when you are ready to pose your question and shuffle your cards, remind yourself that you are not asking for predictions, so instead of asking the cards something like, "What is going to happen?" ask questions like, "What can I do about such-and-such a situation?" or "How can I improve my relationship with my parents?" or "Please suggest ways that I can get that special guy to notice me" or "What can I do to get the most out of this day?" and so on. Then, you can lay out the cards in any manner you choose. You can pull a single card and let that represent the best course of action, or you can do a Three-Card Spread by interpreting the central card as the focal one, and the flanking cards as giving additional suggestions or ways to apply the central card's advice.

When you interpret your cards, you do not use their traditional divinatory meanings (except when the conventional meanings also imply certain courses of action). Instead, you study the images in the cards and then think about how you could imitate them or act them out, relative to the situation in question. Consider how the cards' images may suggest behaviors you can model, attitudes you can take, courses of action, and circumstances that you can set up. Also, think about other aspects of the cards, including their incidental graphic elements and symbols, elemental associations, and numerical significance in order to gain additional suggestions. For example:

- The Five of Wands may be in favor of joining a competition.

- The Ace of Cups may suggest extending your hand to help other people, perhaps to offer physical or emotional nutrition.

- The Three of Cups may suggest staging a party or celebration, or just enjoying good times with friends.
- The Two of Swords may indicate that you should not take sides in a dispute, or possibly that you could act as a go-between during a conflict.
- The Eight of Swords may apply to situations in which you should do something that ties you down so you can accomplish a task or avoid a temptation.
- The Four of Pentacles may suggest holding on to your money.
- The Five of Pentacles may suggest that you voluntarily undergo some hardships.
- Because the Hermit (in most versions) holds his lamp to the left, this card could suggest looking to the past.
- The Devil may be advising you, "No more Mr. Nice Guy." You may have to get tough with someone who deserves it, even if in her eyes, you will be a devil for doing so.
- The Sun may suggest changing your attitude to think more positively.

I could go on, but the above examples demonstrate the general principles. You will be able to think of many other potential courses of action as you study the cards you draw. However, you do not have to do everything that the cards suggest. In fact, you do not have to do anything that the cards suggest. If you don't like the advice, or if you think of something better, the act of performing the reading will at least have stimulated trains of thought that enable you to think of a range of choices.

Notice that when you give advice readings, there are no positive or negative cards. In this context, a card that might normally predict something bad is neutral, because it merely suggests different things that you can do.

Do bear in mind that with advice readings, as with everything else, you have to stick to your own high principles. Go with the most ethical course of action that you can discern from the cards, and do nothing that would unnecessarily harm anyone or cause you to dishonor your necessary obligations. Also, while the Tarot can offer some guidelines for action, you should use your own knowledge, intuition, and good judgement in making any final decisions.

NOTES

Introduction

1. See Michael Talbot, *The Holographic Universe* (New York: HarperPerennial-Harper-Collins, 1991).

Chapter One: A Closer Look at the Cards

1. See Stuart Kaplan, *Tarot Classic* (New York: Grosset & Dunlap, 1972), 16. Note that some writers have identified these cards with those of the Gringonneur deck that was mentioned in an old French document—though it is not known whether the Gringonneur cards were actually Tarot cards.

2. For more information on the triumphs, see Gordon Kipling's *Enter the King: Theatre, Liturgy, and Ritual in the Medieval Civic Triumph* (Oxford: Clarendon, 1998), and Robert Payne's *The Roman Triumph* (London: Abelard-Schuman, 1962).

3. See Stuart Kaplan's *Encyclopedia of Tarot,* vol. 1 (Stamford, Conn.: U.S. Games Systems, Inc., 1978), 35.

4. See Robert Payne's *The Roman Triumph* (London: Abelard-Schuman, 1962), 237.

5. See Terry Donovan Smith's "Popular Culture and the Visual Messages of the Lord Mayor's Procession." (*The Cultures of Celebration.* Ray B. Browne and Michael T. Marsden, editors. Bowling Green, Ohio: Bowling Green University Popular Press, 1994), 75–92.

6. Kaplan, *Tarot Classic,* 32.

7. See Angeles Arrien, *Tarot Handbook* (Sonoma, Calif.: Arcus, 1987), 16.

Chapter Two: Ready to Read

1. See Signe E. Echols, Robert Mueller, and Sandra A. Thompson, *Spiritual Tarot: Seventy-Eight Paths to Personal Development* (New York: Avon, 1996), 20–22.

2. See Mary K. Greer, *Tarot for Your Self: A Workbook for Personal Transformation* (North Hollywood, Calif.: Newcastle, 1984), 28–35.

3. Kaplan, *Tarot Classic,* 172–74.

4. See Arthur Edward Waite, *The Pictorial Key to the Tarot* (New York: Rudolf Steiner Publications, 1971), 299.

5. Kaplan, *Encyclopedia of Tarot,* 337.

Chapter Three: Pointers on Reading and Interpretation

1. See Vicki Noble, *Motherpeace: A Way to the Goddess through Myth, Art, and Tarot* (San Francisco: Harper & Row, 1983), 176.

2. See Barbara Walker, *Secrets of the Tarot* (San Francisco: Harper, 1984), 149–50.

3. For a discussion of this matter on card numbers Eight and Eleven, see Mary K. Greer, *Tarot Constellations: Patterns of Personal Destiny* (North Hollywood: Newcastle, 1987), 195–99.

4. Ibid., 199.

5. See Eden Gray, *The Tarot Revealed* (N.Y.: Bell, 1969), 49.

6. See Sasha Fenton, *Supertarot: New Techniques for Improving Your Tarot Reading* (London: Thorsons-HarperCollins, 1991), 132.

7. See Trish MacGregor and Phyllis Vega, *Power Tarot* (New York: Simon and Schuster, 1998), 26.

8. See Anthony Louis, *Tarot Plain and Simple* (St. Paul, Minn.: Llewellyn Publications, 1996), 298.

9. See Laura G. Clarson, *Tarot Unveiled: The Method to Its Magic* (Stamford, Conn.: U.S. Games Systems Inc., 1988), 134.

Chapter Five: Other Uses for the Tarot

1. See Bernie Siegel, *Love, Medicine, and Miracles* (New York: Harper & Row, 1986), 155–56.

2. See Jeanne Achterberg, *Imagery and Healing: Shamanism and Modern Medicine* (Boulder, Colo.: Shambhala, 1985), 134.

3. See Silver RavenWolf, *Teen Witch* (St. Paul, Minn.: Llewellyn Publications, 1999).

4. See Dorothy Morrison, *Everyday Magic* (St. Paul, Minn.: Llewellyn Publications, 1998).

5. See Janina Renée, *Tarot Spells* (St. Paul, Minn.: Llewellyn Publications, 1989).

Chapter Six: The Major Arcana

1. See Federico García Lorca, "Ballad of the Little Square," *Selected Poems of Federico García Lorca.* Edited by Francisco García Lorca. (New York: New Directions, 1955), 11.

2. See Jean Bolen, *Ring of Power: The Abandoned Child, the Authoritarian Father, and the Disempowered Feminine—A Jungian Understanding of Wagner's Ring Cycle* (San Francisco: Harper, 1992), 28.

3. See Clarissa Pinkola Estes, *Women who Run with the Wolves: Myths and Stories of the Wild Woman Archetype* (New York: Ballantine, 1992), 181.

4. See Robert Moore and Douglas Gillette, *King/Warrior/Magician/Lover: Rediscovering the Archetypes of the Mature Masculine* (New York: HarperCollins, 1990), 62–63.

5. See Robert Bly, *Iron John: A Book About Men* (Reading, Mass.: Addison-Wesley, 1990), 110.

6. Moore and Gillette, 61.

7. See Merriam Webster's Collegiate Dictionary, 10th edition (Springfield, Mass.: Merriam-Webster, Inc., 1993), 852.

8. For more information on the treatment of both men and women in patriarchal societies, as well as the relationships of different archetypes to patriarchy, see Jean Bolen's books *Gods in Everyman* and *Ring of Power,* and Jennifer Barker Woolger and Roger J. Woolger's *The Goddess Within.*

9. Moore and Gillette, xvii.

10. The Shelley quotation is from "Defense of Poetry, Part First." Internet file, 11 October 2000, www.library.utoronto.ca/utel/rp/criticism/shell_il.html. Source: The Bodleian Shelley Manuscripts: A Facsimile Edition, XX, Michael O'Neill, editor. (New York and London: Garland, 1994).

11. See Rachel Pollack, *Seventy Eight Degrees of Wisdom* (London: Thorsons-HarperCollins, 1997), 59.

12. See Echols, Mueller, and Thompson, 58.

13. See Mary Pipher, *Reviving Ophelia: Saving the Selves of Adolescent Girls* (New York: Putnam, 1994).

14. For a discussion of the numbering of Strength and Justice, see Greer, *Tarot Constellations,* 195–99.

15. See Fred Gettings, *The Book of Tarot* (London: Triune Books, 1973), 57.

16. In some of the more ancient zodiacs, the sign of Scorpio was pictured as an eagle rather than a scorpion.

17. Waite, 108–111.

18. "Jeder ist sein Glückes Schmied" is roughly pronounced, "Yay-dur ist zain (rhymes with "sign") Glook-ess Schmeed."

19. Gettings, 55.

20. Eden Gray, 88.

21. Ibid., 90.

22. See Robert Jay Lifton, *The Broken Connection: On Death and the Continuity of Life* (New York: Simon and Schuster, 1979), 53, 47.

23. See Jennifer Barker Woolger and Roger J. Woolger, *The Goddess Within: A Guide to the Eternal Myths that Shape Women's Lives* (London: Rider, 1990), 233.

24. Estes, 365.

25. See William Pollack, *Real Boys: Rescuing Our Sons from the Myths of Boyhood* (New York: Random House, 1998).

26. Estes, 366.

27. Heinrich Böll is quoted by Lifton, 8.

28. Merriam Webster's, 1213.

29. See Richard Mott Gummere, *Seneca the Philosopher and His Modern Message* (New York: Cooper Square, 1963), 65.

30. Merriam Webster's, 1212.

31. See Grimaud, B. P., *Tarot of Marseilles* (Paris, 1969), 21.

32. Greer, *Tarot for Your Self,* 168.

33. Estes, 46.

34. Rachel Pollack, 118.

35. Gettings, 89.

36. See Marcus Bach, *The Wonderful Magic of Living* (Marina Del Ray: DeVorss, 1970), 29.

37. See Karen Hamaker-Zondag, *Tarot as a Way of Life: A Jungian Approach to the Tarot* (York Beach, Maine: Weiser, 1997), 170.

38. Chögyam Trungpa Rinpoche is quoted by Pema Chödrön in "Not Preferring Samsara or Nirvana," excerpt from *The Wisdom of No Escape,* 1991, rept. in *Ordinary Magic: Everyday Life as Spiritual Path,* John Welwood, editor. (Boston: Shambhala, 1992), 44–45.

39. MacGregor and Vega, 75; also Clarson, 121.

40. See Amber Jayanti, *Living the Tarot* (St. Paul, Minn.: Llewellyn Publications, 1993), 311–312.

41. Lifton has said that transformation "depends not just on acceptance of a new 'reality' . . . but also on the inner construction of psychic forms, altered or new, that help one through the changed self-world relationships," 188.

42. Luisa Teish, audiotaped speech from *The Fabric of the Future: Women Visionaries Illuminate the Path to Tomorrow.* From the book edited by M. J. Ryan (Berkeley, Calif.: Conari Press, 1998), audiotape by Dove Audio, 1998.

43. See Gary Snyder, *Earth Household: Technical Notes & Queries to Fellow Dharma Revolutionaries*, 1957 (New York: New Directions-Laughlin, 1969), 116.

Chapter Seven: The Wands

1. Eden Gray, 13.

2. See Gail Fairfield, *Choice Centered Tarot* (Smithville, Ind.: Ramp Creek, 1984), 51.

3. See Jon Katz, *Geeks: How Two Boys Rode the Internet Out of Idaho* (N.Y.: Villard, 2000), i.

4. Ibid, xxx.

5. Waite, 182.

6. See Henry David Thoreau, *Walden; or Life in the Woods.* 1854 (New York: Dover, 1995), 59–60.

Chapter Eight: The Cups

1. The Cups suit and the element of Water have been linked to what the psychologist Carl Jung described as the "feeling" function, and as such, are often seen as the opposite of the Swords, which are commonly associated with the "thinking" function (though some systems relate Earth and Pentacles to thinking). However, while concepts like the four suits of the Tarot, or the four elements, or even Jung's four functions of consciousness provide convenient ways of classifying reality, in real life, things aren't that neatly divided. Some theorists now assert that feeling and thinking can't be totally separated, because one always colors the other. Studies of other cultures have contributed to this understanding. For example, anthropologist Unni Wikan relates that among the Balinese people, "thought, will, and desire [are] inextricably linked, truly one concept"; they are "aspects of one process," which Wikan translates as "feeling-thinking." She translates the Balinese concern with self-management as "bringing the feeling-thought" (see her book *Managing Turbulent Hearts: A Balinese Formula for Living* [Chicago: University of Chicago Press, 1990], 95, 29). I mention this not to confuse you—because we can certainly detect and discuss differences in our modes of thinking and feeling—but merely to keep things in perspective in order to avoid dogmatic notions. This is important because the debate between feeling and thinking is currently reaching extremes, as people on one end of the political spectrum seem to privilege individual's feelings above everything else in the world, while reactionaries on the other end are damning all feeling values (as well as the so-called feminine values with which they are interrelated). But to get back to the Tarot: remember that issues brought up by the Swords cards will also be influenced by feelings, while even the unconscious responses represented by the Cups cards have been conditioned by thinking processes.

2. Estes, 299.

3. Different mythological traditions held that there were different numbers of graces with different names, but the aforementioned three are the ones that are best known.

4. See Patricia Monaghan, 136.

5. See Alexander Murray, *Who's Who in Mythology* (New York: Wings, 1988), 175.

6. Eden Gray, 29, Waite, 220.

7. See Angeles Arrien, *The Tarot Handbook* (Sonoma, Calif.: Arcus, 1987), 167.

8. Waite, 218.

9. See Chic Cicero and Sandra Tabatha Cicero, *The New Golden Dawn Ritual Tarot* (St. Paul, Minn.: Llewellyn Publications, 1996), 97.

10. Eden Gray, 31.

11. Waite, 212.

12. See Jean Shinoda Bolen, *Goddesses in Every Woman* (New York: Harper & Row, 1984), 229, 230.

13. See Ellen Cannon Reed and Martin Cannon, *The Witches Tarot Deck* (St. Paul, Minn.: Llewellyn Publications, 1996).

14. See Vicki Noble and Jonathan Tenney, *The Motherpeace Tarot Playbook* (Berkeley, Calif.: Wingbow Press, 1986), 59.

15. Louis, 90.

16. See John Bradshaw, *Homecoming: Reclaiming and Championing Your Inner Child* (New York: Bantam, 1990), 209.

17. Estes, 166, 172.

18. Waite, 206.

19. See Virginia Satir, *Peoplemaking* (Palo Alto, Calif.: Science and Behavior Books, 1972), 12.

Chapter Nine: The Swords

1. Moore and Gillette, 79–86.

2. Waite, 252.

3. Lifton, 194.

4. Echols, Mueller, and Thompson, 148.

5. See P. Scott Hollander, *Tarot for Beginners* (St. Paul, Minn.: Llewellyn Publications, 1996), 180.

6. See Brian Brown, editor. *The Wisdom of the Chinese* (New York: Brentano's, 1920), 25.

7. Rachel Pollack, 221.

8. See Mary K. Greer, "The 7 of Swords." *Tarot Newsletter* (Spring 1998), 8.

9. Fairfield, 59.

10. Fenton, 167.

11. See Ernest Hemingway, *A Farewell to Arms*. 1929 (New York: Charles Scribner's Sons, 1957), 258.

12. The Terry Gorski quotation is from John Bradshaw, 200.

Chapter Ten: The Pentacles

1. See William G. Gray, *Magical Ritual Methods* (Cheltenham, Glos.: Helios, 1969), 83.

2. Greer, *Tarot for Your Self,* 225.

3. See J. E. Circlot, *A Dictionary of Symbols,* Jack Sage, trans. (New York: Philosophical Library, 1962), 223.

4. Satir, 4.

Chapter Eleven: The Court Cards

1. Eden Gray, 21–24, 37–40, 53–56, 69–72.

2. Fenton, 52.

3. Eden Gray, 21.

4. Estes, 299.

5. In her book *Ring of Power,* Jungian analyst Jean Shinoda Bolen gives us some insight into the ways that people raised in authoritarian homes can turn to the quest for power, pointing out, "When we find that we are not loved or are loved only for what we do or what we own, power in some form becomes the substitute . . ." (10).

6. See Sybille Birkhäuser-Oeri, *The Mother: Archetypal Image in Fairy Tales,* Michael Mitchell, trans. (Toronto: Inner City Books, 1988), 142–43. Oeri is especially concerned with this archetype as it acts not through a person's own mother, but through that person's shadow and/or "animus," causing that person to undercut her own development. Thus, negative Swords traits may also be influences within ourselves, not just something experienced in other people.

GLOSSARY

Following is a list of some terms that you may encounter in this book. This is not a comprehensive explanation of each term, but is intended to aid an understanding of the way they are used in this book. Many of these terms are more thoroughly explained in the introduction, or in other chapters.

Affirmations

Affirmations are statements that many people recite as a means of reprogramming their attitudes. The mind responds best to positive statements phrased in the present tense; for example, "I enjoy exercising" instead of "I will stop hating exercise." You can create affirmations based on Tarot images that portray certain ideals that you want to bring into your life.

Allegories

The Tarot illustrations are allegorical, that is, they use symbolic images to convey certain poetic, philosophical, psychological, and religious concepts. These concepts are often portrayed in human form (for example, Strength is portrayed as a woman subduing a lion). From ancient times up through the Middle Ages and the Renaissance, people from all walks of life were comfortable with allegorical thinking; in some cases, they treated thoughts as real things.

Arcana

Arcana is a plural term (the singular form is Arcanum) that refers to collections of secret wisdom. The Major Arcana consists of the twenty-two cards that form the spiritual and philosophical core of the Tarot. The cards of the Minor Arcana resemble those of a regular pack of playing cards, having four suits and a set of court cards; they are more concerned with the affairs of everyday life.

Archetypes and Archetypal Images

Archetypes are regarded as patterns within the mind that correspond to important human instincts and experiences. The Tarot is a collection of archetypal images; for example, the Hermit is an image designed to portray the archetype of the search for wisdom, the Empress is an archetype of loving nurturance, and so on. Archetypes such as Love, Wisdom, Justice, and the like, tend to be almost universal, appearing in different cultures in recognizable—though culturally relevant—forms. Archetypes are especially significant to us when they operate through our personalities. For example, the High Priestess card relates to the facet of your personality that yearns to explore the mysteries of the universe, while the Emperor corresponds to the part of you that wants to build stable foundations and create order around you. In other words, you have a "priestess within" and a "king within," as well as a wise elder, a fool, a magician, and many other characters inside of you that correspond to the main Tarot cards. Of course, some of these archetypes may be more active than others, or active at different phases of your life.

Associations

Thinking about the pictures and meanings of the Tarot cards can trigger certain trains of thought, enabling you to relate them to your own experiences as well as other things such as other common human experiences, popular sayings, scenes from movies, song lyrics, and so on. These associations aid a further understanding of the cards' meanings.

Cabala, The
(also Cabbala, Caballah; sometimes spelled with a *K* or *Q*)

The Cabala is a Jewish mystical system (though not a part of mainstream Judaism) whose written documents appeared in the Middle Ages, but may have roots in the mystical schools that flourished in the earlier centuries of the current era (A.D.). Many scholars of the Tarot believe that the cards originated with or were influenced by cabalistic philosophy (for example, there are twenty-two Tarot cards in the Major Arcana and twenty-two letters in the Hebrew alphabet), so a number of modern systems are dedicated to finding Cabalistic correspondences.

Collective Unconscious

The great Swiss psychologist C. G. Jung noticed that certain dreams, myths, symbols, archetypes, and fantasies recurred throughout time, in numerous individuals and in widely distant societies. This led him to speculate that humanity shares a collective unconscious that serves as a great reservoir of information and experience, which different cultural groups as well as individuals can tap into for knowledge, images, and ideas.

Context

This word, which refers to the setting in which something exists, as well as the factors that influence it, is used in two different ways: (1) when reading a card, it is necessary to consider the context of the card, such as whether it is accompanied by very positive or negative cards, as these will bring out different shades of meaning; and (2) it is necessary to consider the personal context, that is, the lifestyle, personality, and other conditions of the person for whom you are reading, in order to determine which areas of this person's life a particular card is most likely to apply to. (For example, a card that denotes competition may indicate pleasure for one type of person and stress for another type of person.)

Correspondences

Practitioners of the Tarot have found that the cards have a number of correspondences, which are symbolic relationships to a network of other natural and symbolic objects. For example, the Minor Arcana Pentacles typically correspond with the element of Earth, Cups with Water, and so on. Other correspondences include connections between the cards and the planets, signs of the zodiac, letters of the Hebrew alphabet, colors, musical notes, and more. An exploration of a card's correspondences can enable you to appreciate more of its nuances and levels of meaning; however, the chapters in this book don't make much use of correspondences (other than the Minor Arcana elemental associations) because they can vary with different decks and systems.

Crowley Thoth Tarot Deck

Also called the Thoth deck, this is a deck designed by the artist Lady Frieda Harris, under the guidance of Aleister Crowley. Because Crowley and Harris brought in some new images for some of the Major Arcana, plus labels for the Minor Arcana cards, I sometimes refer to this deck when it enlarges our understanding of a particular card.

Deep Mind

This is a term that I sometimes use to describe the unconscious, and it also implies the place where the personal unconscious connects with the collective unconscious.

Destiny

In this book, I occasionally use the term "destiny," but as different people use this word in different ways, I want to make it clear that I am not referring to a destiny or fate that is narrowly laid out or unchangeable. I believe that people can take their lives in any direction they choose by taking different actions and making different choices. However, because we are the individuals that we are, with specific likes and dislikes, and specific things that motivate and inspire us, we tend to key into certain things that lead us in certain directions. Furthermore, I also believe that we have spirits or souls that develop through many lifetimes, including lives spent in spirit realms, and that our souls have a guiding principle that sets certain general goals for us, which is why we gravitate toward certain things. When we are able to follow paths that enable us to use our talents and make us feel that our lives are meaningful, then we have linked up with a good destiny. However, this destiny may be general rather than specific. For example, because you are attracted to a certain type of work, you are likely destined to live in a city, but it may not make any difference whether that city is London, Chicago, Austin, or Sacramento (unless some other factors are involved, such as family or industry ties). *See* Life Path.

Divination

Divination is a categorical term for practices such as Tarot reading, rune casting, astrology, I Ching, tea leaf reading, and others; these techniques are designed to gain information about the future and other types of hidden knowledge. (Many practitioners prefer to use this term instead of "fortunetelling.") Ancient people believed that to "divine" the future is to try to understand the workings of divine forces—an act that puts you in harmony with the universe.

Elements

Some ancient philosophers speculated that everything in the material world is composed of the elements of Fire, Earth, Air, and Water, and that, furthermore, these elements also have certain mystical qualities that go beyond the physical world realities that we can see and touch. In this book I capitalize these terms when referring to the elements to show that Air, for example, is understood as being more than just the air we breathe, but the whole complex of philosophical and psychological ideas associated with elemental Air. Although modern science no longer uses the Four Elements Theory, many mystical and philosophical systems find it provides useful, inspirational, and psychologically meaningful ways of organizing human experience and insights. In the Tarot, Cups generally relate to the qualities of elemental Water, Pentacles to Earth, Wands to Fire, and Swords to Air—although some systems associate Swords with Fire and Wands with Air.

Esoterica

This term refers to very specialized (metaphysical) knowledge, known only to a small group of people.

Individuation

This is a process that includes making sense of your world, discovering the things that have genuine meaning for you, learning to express yourself and develop your personal gifts, understanding and improving your relationships with others, making a place for yourself in the world, appreciating your place in the larger cosmos, facing your shadow nature, and exploring your spiritual life. This process is a lifelong adventure.

Layout or Spread

Tarot cards are usually set out on a table in patterns called layouts or spreads. The spread you use is decided in advance by the reader, and each card position in the spread usually has an assigned meaning (such as for past, present, or future events).

Life Path

In various places in this book, I mention ways that the Tarot may reveal things about a person's "life path." This concept is similar to my definition of "destiny" (see above).

Marseilles Deck

The *Tarot of Marseille* is a French deck that is representative of a family of decks that were popular through the last five centuries, and versions of which are still around, though probably less popular than modern decks that provide pictorial illustrations (as opposed to simple arrangements of Wands, Swords, and so on) for the Minor Arcana. Because some of its Major Arcana illustrations can also be contrasted with those of modern decks, I sometimes refer to this deck when it enhances our understanding of a particular card.

Meditation

This term actually refers to two different practices. In Eastern traditions, it involves stilling the mind in order to achieve altered states of consciousness. In the Western (European) traditions, it involves focusing on a specific topic and thinking about it in great depth.

Metaphysics

In a broad, general sense, this is the study of things that are outside of ordinary reality. As such, it deals with things that are considered psychic and supernatural, but there is much more to it, such as questions about the origins of being and the nature of reality.

Mystery School

This refers to a group of people who work together on the study and development of a particular metaphysical philosophy.

New Age

This is a blanket term applied to a number of movements and interests that emerged in the latter decades of the twentieth century (but many of which have roots in far older traditions). The main thrust of New Age beliefs and practices is that there is a spiritual order behind ordinary reality, and that we can improve ourselves by connecting with this spiritual dimension of existence. New Age interests include the study of ancient cultures and religions, mystical and psychic practices, spiritually uplifting art and music, holistic approaches to health, respect for cultural diversity and the rights of individuals, and relationship with the environment.

Pentacles and Pentagrams

In many modern decks, the suit of Pentacles, portrayed as round disks inscribed with pentagrams (five-pointed stars), corresponds to the suit of Coins or Disks in the older decks, and is associated with elemental Earth. In magical practice, a pentacle is a platelike object, usually circular, and is used both to represent Earth, and as a base upon which to set certain ritual objects. Although some dictionaries don't distinguish between pentacles and pentagrams, a pentagram is the five-pointed star that is often etched onto the pentacle. In different philosophical systems, the pentagram has represented the perfectibility of humanity, and the four elements combined with the fifth element of spirit (among other things).

Pip Cards
This is another term for the cards belonging to the Minor Arcana.

Querent
The querent or questioner is the person for whom a reading is being done. When reading for oneself, querent and reader are the same.

Relational Self, The
Because a given person can have an assortment of identities as a result of being different things to different people, and because she can identify with other people, psychology has come to recognize the "relational Self." Because of the large number of life roles and personality types portrayed by the Tarot, the cards can reveal things about this sense of selfhood that shifts in response to different social contexts and expands to include other beings.

Reversed Card
A card is considered reversed when its image is laid out upside down. This is from the perspective of the reader, not the querent, unless they are sitting side by side. (A reader's choice whether or not to use reversed cards will determine how they are shuffled.)

Rider-Waite-Smith Deck
This deck, which is also known as the Rider deck (after the company that first printed it), the Rider-Waite deck, or just the Waite deck, was designed by the Jamaican artist Pamela Coleman Smith under the direction of Arthur Edward Waite. It came out in 1910, and was novel in presenting more artistic renditions of the Major Arcana (in contrast to the older decks, which were often somewhat crude and simple), as well as full-picture illustrations for the Minor Arcana. The interpretations in this book use the Rider-Waite-Smith deck as their main reference because it is possibly the most popular of all decks, and most newer decks make use of its basic images.

Serendipity
When things work out for you, often in ways that involve strange luck, coincidences, and unusual turns of events.

Shadow
Different Tarot cards and Tarot positions can reveal shadow material, which includes personality traits, emotions, and experiences that we have never recognized, or that we have repressed (forced out of our conscious minds), usually because they were socially unacceptable. There are many instincts and urges that need to be repressed so we can live our lives as reasonable people. However, if we can become aware of this shadow material and gain greater understanding, repressed contents will cause fewer problems when we let our

guard down, and we will be less likely to blame our own shadow traits on other people. Positive traits can also be included in the shadow, as some families and societies discourage their members from showing kindness, self-assertiveness, creative talent, leadership ability, and so on. Also, some chapters in this book touch upon ways in which certain cards deal with society's shadow.

Significator
This is a card that is chosen to represent the person who is the subject of a reading (often the questioner).

Subconscious
This term generally refers to short-term memories, older memories that have been reactivated, impulses, intuitive responses to environmental cues, and other mental activities that are operating not too far below your level of conscious awareness, that is, just below the "threshold" of consciousness—and that is how the term is used in this book. However the word "subconscious" is sometimes used interchangeably with the word "unconscious," used in a larger sense to mean everything that exists within your mind, but to which you cannot easily gain access. *See* Unconscious.

Subject
I use this term to denote a person for whom a reading is being done, as well as images within certain cards that seem to denote that person.

Trump
This is a term that refers to the twenty-two cards of the Major Arcana, and comes from the Italian word for "triumph."

Unconscious
The use of the word "unconscious" can be confusing because different schools of psychology have different preferences in usage, and sometimes this term is also used interchangeably with the word "subconscious." In this book, however, the word "unconscious" is used two ways: (1) it can describe instincts, urges, memories, and motives that you are unaware of, as in "Cups cards can reveal that unconscious motivations are influencing the matter in question"; and (2) used as a noun, it can refer to *the* unconscious, which can be likened to a place where your memories and experiences are stored and processed, and from which you can gain ideas and inspirations. For example, "The Cups also bring up issues from the unconscious."

This latter usage, the comparison of the unconscious to a place, is also used in two senses: (1) when considering issues of interest to an individual, it usually means the *personal* unconscious, which contains the memories and experiences of the person in question, and produces her emotions, dreams, fantasies, and other types of responses;

and (2) sometimes this book speaks of the unconscious in a generic sense, as when discussing how the symbolism of the Tarot corresponds to images within the unconscious.

Also, the "unconscious" is distinguished from the "collective unconscious" and the "subconscious," which are also described in this glossary.

Visualization

Visualization is the practice of concentrating on mental images, trying to perceive them as real as possible, in order to achieve a goal. Various clinical experiments have shown that the mind responds to vividly held images as if they were real. For example, when some athletes concentrate on images of themselves improving their games, there is a notable increase in their performance.

Witches Tarot Deck

This newer deck was designed by Ellen Cannon Reed and Martin Reed in 1989, and incorporates a combination of Neopagan and Cabalistic symbolism. Because it provides new picture images for the Minor Arcana, I sometimes refer to it in the interpretive sections.

BIBLIOGRAPHY

Achterberg, Jeanne. *Imagery and Healing: Shamanism and Modern Medicine.* Boulder, Colo.: Shambhala, 1985.

Arrien, Angeles. *The Tarot Handbook.* Sonoma, Calif.: Arcus, 1987.

Bach, Marcus. *The Wonderful Magic of Living.* Marina Del Ray: DeVorss, 1970.

Birkhäuser-Oeri, Sybille. *The Mother: Archetypal Image in Fairy Tales.* Translated by Michael Mitchell. Toronto: Inner City Books, 1988.

Bly, Robert. *Iron John: A Book About Men.* Reading, Mass.: Addison-Wesley, 1990.

Bolen, Jean Shinoda. *Goddesses in Everywoman: A New Psychology of Women.* New York: Harper & Row, 1984.

———. *Gods in Everyman: A New Psychology of Men's Lives and Loves.* New York: Harper & Row-Perennial, 1989.

———. *Ring of Power: The Abandoned Child, the Authoritarian Father, and the Disempowered Feminine—A Jungian Understanding of Wagner's Ring Cycle.* San Francisco: Harper, 1992.

Bradshaw, John. *Homecoming: Reclaiming and Championing Your Inner Child.* New York: Bantam, 1990.

Brown, Brian, ed. *The Wisdom of the Chinese.* New York: Brentano's, 1920.

Cicero, Chic, and Sandra Tabatha Cicero. *The New Golden Dawn Ritual Tarot.* St. Paul, Minn.: Llewellyn Publications, 1996.

———. *The New Golden Dawn Ritual Tarot: Keys to Rituals, Symbolism, Magic and Divination.* St. Paul, Minn.: Llewellyn Publications, 1996.

Circlot, J. E. *A Dictionary of Symbols.* Translated by Jack Sage. New York: Philosophical Library, 1962.

Clarson, Laura G. *Tarot Unveiled: The Method to It's Magic.* Stamford, Conn.: U.S. Games Systems, Inc., 1988.

Chödrön, Pema. "Not Preferring Samsara or Nirvana." Excerpt from *The Wisdom of No Escape,* 1991. Reprinted in *Ordinary Magic: Everyday Life as Spiritual Path.* Edited by John Welwood. Boston: Shambhala, 1992.

Circlot, J. E. *A Dictionary of Symbols.* Translated by Jack Sage. New York: Philosophical Library, 1962.

Echols, Signe E., Robert Mueller, and Sandra A. Thompson. *Spiritual Tarot: Seventy-Eight Paths to Personal Development.* New York: Avon, 1996.

Estes, Clarissa Pinkola. *Women who Run with the Wolves: Myths and Stories of the Wild Woman Archetype.* New York: Ballantine, 1992.

Fairfield, Gail. *Choice Centered Tarot.* Smithville, Ind.: Ramp Creek, 1984.

Fenton, Sasha. *Supertarot: New Techniques for Improving Your Tarot Reading.* London: Thorsons-HarperCollins, 1991.

Ficino, Marsilio.*The Book of Life* (Liber De Vita, or De Vita Triplici). Translated by Charles Boer. Dallas: Spring Publications, 1980.

Franklin, Anna. *The Sacred Circle Tarot: A Celtic Pagan Journey.* Illustrated by Paul Mason. St. Paul, Minn.: Llewellyn Publications, 1998.

Gettings, Fred. *The Book of Tarot.* London: Triune Books, 1973.

Gray, Eden. *The Tarot Revealed.* New York: Bell, 1969.

Gray, William G. *Magical Ritual Methods.* Cheltenham, Glos.: Helios, 1969.

Greer, Mary K. *Tarot Constellations: Patterns of Personal Destiny.* North Hollywood: Newcastle, 1987.

———. *Tarot for Your Self: A Workbook for Personal Transformation.* North Hollywood, Calif.: Newcastle, 1984.

———. "The 7 of Swords." *Tarot Newsletter* (Spring 1998): 8–9.

Grimaud, B. P. *Tarot of Marseilles.* Paris: 1969.

Gummere, Richard Mott. *Seneca the Philosopher and His Modern Message.* New York: Cooper Square, 1963.

Hamaker-Zondag, Karen. *Tarot as a Way of Life: A Jungian Approach to the Tarot.* York Beach, Maine: Weiser, 1997.

Hemingway, Ernest. *A Farewell to Arms.* New York: Charles Scribner's Sons, 1957.

Hollander, P. Scott. *Tarot for Beginners.* St. Paul, Minn.: Llewellyn Publications, 1996.

Jayanti, Amber. *Living the Tarot: Applying an Ancient Oracle to the Challenges of Modern Life.* St. Paul, Minn.: Llewellyn Publications, 1993.

Kaplan, Stuart R. *The Encyclopedia of Tarot.* Vol. 1. Stamford, Conn.: U.S. Games Systems, Inc., 1978.

———. *Tarot Classic.* N.Y.: Grosset & Dunlap, 1972.

Katz, Jon. *Geeks: How Two Lost Boys Rode the Internet Out of Idaho.* New York: Villard, 2000.

Kipling, Gordon. *Enter the King: Theatre, Liturgy, and Ritual in the Medieval Civic Triumph.* Oxford: Clarendon, 1998.

Lifton, Robert Jay. *The Broken Connection: On Death and the Continuity of Life.* New York: Simon and Schuster, 1979.

Lorca, Federico García. "Ballad of the Little Square." *Selected Poems of Federico Garcia Lorca.* Edited by Francisco García Lorca. New York: New Directions, 1955.

Louis, Anthony. *Tarot Plain and Simple.* St. Paul, Minn.: Llewellyn Publications, 1996.

MacGregor, Trish, and Phyllis Vega. *Power Tarot.* New York: Simon and Schuster, 1998.

Merriam Webster's Collegiate Dictionary, 10th edition. Springfield, Mass.: Merriam-Webster, Inc., 1993.

Monaghan, Patricia. *The Book of Goddesses and Heroines.* St. Paul, Minn.: Llewellyn Publications, 1990.

Moore, Robert, and Douglas Gillette. *King/Warrior/Magician/Lover: Rediscovering the Archetypes of the Mature Masculine.* New York: HarperCollins, 1990.

Morrison, Dorothy. *Everyday Magic: Spells and Rituals for Modern Living.* St. Paul, Minn.: Llewellyn Publications, 1998.

Murray, Alexander S. *Who's Who in Mythology.* New York: Wings, 1988.

Noble, Vicki. *Motherpeace: A Way to the Goddess Through Myth, Art, and Tarot.* San Francisco: Harper & Row, 1983.

Noble, Vicki, and Jonathan Tenney. *The Motherpeace Tarot Playbook: Astrology and the Motherpeace Cards.* Berkeley, Calif.: Wingbow Press, 1986.

Payne, Robert. *The Roman Triumph.* London: Abelard-Schuman, 1962.

Pipher, Mary. *Reviving Ophelia: Saving the Selves of Adolescent Girls.* New York: Putnam, 1994.

Pollack, Rachel. *Seventy Eight Degrees of Wisdom.* London: Thorsons-HarperCollins, 1997.

Pollack, William. *Real Boys: Rescuing Our Sons from the Myths of Boyhood.* New York: Random House, 1998.

RavenWolf, Silver. *Teen Witch.* St. Paul, Minn.: Llewellyn Publications, 1999.

Ratey, John J., and Catherine Johnson. *Shadow Syndromes: Recognizing and Coping with the Hidden Psychological Disorders that Can Influence Your Behavior and Silently Determine the Course of Your Life.* New York: Pantheon, 1997.

Reed, Ellen Cannon, and Martin Cannon. *The Witches Tarot Deck.* St. Paul, Minn.: Llewellyn Publications, 1996.

Renée, Janina. *Playful Magic.* St. Paul, Minn.: Llewellyn Publications, 1994.

———. *Tarot Spells.* St. Paul, Minn.: Llewellyn Publications, 1989.

———. *Tarot: Your Everyday Guide.* St. Paul, Minn.: Llewellyn Publications, 2000.

Satir, Virginia. *Peoplemaking.* Palo Alto, Calif.: Science and Behavior Books, 1972.

Shelley, Percy Bysshe. "Defense of Poetry, Part First." Internet file, 11 October 2000. www.library.utoronto.ca/utel/rp/criticism/shell_il.html. Source: The Bodleian Shelley Manuscripts: A Facsimile Edition, XX. Edited by Michael O'Neill. New York and London: Garland, 1994.

Siegel, Bernie. *Love, Medicine, and Miracles*. New York: Harper & Row, 1986.

Smith, Terry Donovan. "Popular Culture and the Visual Messages of the Lord Mayor's Procession." *The Cultures of Celebration*. Edited by Ray B. Browne and Michael T. Marsden. Bowling Green, Ohio: Bowling Green University Popular Press, 1994.

Snyder, Gary. *Earth Household: Technical Notes & Queries to Fellow Dharma Revolutionaries*. New York: New Directions-Laughlin, 1969.

Talbot, Michael. *The Holographic Universe*. New York: HarperPerennial-HarperCollins, 1991.

Teish, Luisa. Audiotaped speech. "The Fabric of the Future: Women Visionaries Illuminate the Path to Tomorrow." From the book edited by M. J. Ryan, Berkeley, Calif.: Conari Press, 1998. Audiotape by Dove Audio, 1998.

Thoreau, Henry David. *Walden; or Life in the Woods*. 1854. New York: Dover, 1995.

Waite, Arthur Edward. Circa 1910. *The Pictorial Key to the Tarot*. New York: Rudolf Steiner Publications, 1971.

Walker, Barbara. *Secrets of the Tarot*. San Francisco: Harper, 1984.

Wikan, Unni. *Managing Turbulent Hearts: A Balinese Formula for Living*. Chicago: University of Chicago Press, 1990.

Woolger, Jennifer Barker, and Roger J. Woolger. *The Goddess Within: A Guide to the Eternal Myths that Shape Women's Lives*. London: Rider, 1990.